I0815435

# A Way to Live Now

# A WAY TO LIVE NOW

# HOW JOURNALISM SHAPED *Ernest Hemingway*

JOHN FENSTERMAKER

LOUISIANA STATE UNIVERSITY PRESS • BATON ROUGE

Published by Louisiana State University Press
lsupress.org



Designer: Kaelin Chappell Broaddus
Typefaces: Miller Text Roman, text; Bodoni Poster, Gaulois, Futura, display

Portions of this book first appeared, in somewhat different form, in the following essays: "Ernest Hemingway in *Esquire:* Contextualizing Arnold Gingrich's Posthumous Portrait(s) of Man and Artist, 1961–73," in *Literature and Journalism: Inspirations, Intersections, and Inventions from Ben Franklin to Stephen Colbert,* ed. Mark Canada, 187–207 (New York: Palgrave Macmillan, 2013); (with Michael S. Reynolds and Keneth Kinnamon) "Hemingway in the 1930s: A Conversation," *Arkansas Review* 30, no. 2 (1999): 143–62; and "Why *Esquire*? The Multiple Voices of Hemingway's Complex Public Persona," in *Key West Hemingway: A Reassessment,* ed. Kirk Curnutt and Gail Sinclair, 206–19 (Gainesville: University Press of Florida, 2009).

Library of Congress Cataloging-in-Publication Data

Names: Fenstermaker, John, author.
Title: A way to live now : how journalism shaped Ernest Hemingway / John Fenstermaker.
Description: Baton Rouge : Louisiana State University Press, 2025. | Includes bibliographical references and index.
Identifiers: LCCN 2024033166 (print) | LCCN 2024033167 (ebook) | ISBN 978-0-8071-8257-4 (cloth) | ISBN 978-0-8071-8360-1 (pdf) | ISBN 978-0-8071-8359-5 (epub)
Subjects: LCSH: Hemingway, Ernest, 1899–1961—Criticism and interpretation. | LCGFT: Literary criticism.
Classification: LCC PS3515.E37 Z5899 2025 (print) | LCC PS3515.E37 (ebook) | DDC 813/.52—dc23/eng/20240821
LC record available at https://lccn.loc.gov/2024033166
LC ebook record available at https://lccn.loc.gov/2024033167

Hemingway wrote with simple genius. Had he not been able to write the way he did, his oversized life would have been an oversized joke. What he did with truth-telling was to show how complicated the simplicity of it was. In doing so, he changed the rules of writing. . . . If Hemingway had a credo, it would be "accuracy equals truth." In a certain way, he was always doing journalism.

—Roger Rosenblatt, *PBS NewsHour with Jim Lehrer,* July 21, 1999, on the one hundredth anniversary of Hemingway's birth

# CONTENTS

# A Way to Live Now

All good books are alike in that they are truer than if they had really happened and after you are finished reading one you will feel that all that happened to you and afterwards it all belongs to you: the good and the bad, the ecstasy, the remorse and sorrow, the people and the places and how the weather was. If you can get so that you can give that to people, then you are a writer.

—"Old Newsman Writes," *Esquire,* December 1934

# Introduction

In April 1965, Arnold Gingrich organized *Esquire*'s Seventh Literary Symposium at the University of North Carolina around the topic "The Novelist as Journalist." Norman Podhoretz's keynote assertion: "We may be looking in the wrong place for the achievements of the creative literary imagination when we look for them only where they were last seen—in novels and plays."

Gingrich, *Esquire* founding editor and publisher, understood and affirmed this serious focus on the novelist as journalist. He knew writers and writing. Over four decades, he would publish in *Esquire* sixteen writers who were or would become Nobel laureates, beginning with Ernest Hemingway in the magazine's premier issue, October 1933. He had recognized and appreciated in Hemingway's early professional writing an active imagination expressed in prose clear, masculine, authoritative, and timely—irrespective of subject.

In helping to launch *Esquire* in 1933, Hemingway initially agreed to be the principal contributor each month—a decision that was inordinately consequential. His career achievement and reputation in essay journalism centers in *Esquire.* He remained uniquely *present* in the magazine over four decades: publishing twenty-five essays from 1933 to 1936; then six short stories in the years 1936–39, including “The Snows of Kilimanjaro,” perhaps his finest; serving as the subject of printed interactions among editors, subscribers, and critics from 1933 to 1961; and appearing *posthumously* in its pages via reprintings, miscellanea, general reader commentary, and as the subject of serious discussion and debate, from a wide range of contemporary writers and scholars, over thirty-four issues, 1961–73.

• • •

Ernest Hemingway's journalism and his fiction must be understood as the offspring of a single creative intellect.

In both genres, hunting, fishing, and war may be his most familiar and enduring subjects. Regardless, Hemingway continually shapes, explores, memorializes, basic human aspirations and interactions. Subjects overlap; techniques repeat. The realist *Esquire* essay “On the Blue Water” (April 1936) offers a lesser, albeit exact, example of such literary interrelationships or parallels: in broad outline, including specific details, this earlier article remarkably anticipates Santiago's fictional experience in *The Old Man and the Sea* (1952).

Moreover, Hemingway's principal writing modes share techniques—such as allusion, ambiguity, irony, and paradox, including recurring images and tropes. Across genres, also, is the familiar, authoritative Hemingway first-person “voice”: the writer as critic, poet, prophet, and more informally, as hunting-fishing guide or bullfight aficionado. His texts continually prompt new ways of seeing and judging contemporary “man in motion,” perhaps most dramatically “man at war” or engaged with other contemporary violences. No less characteristically, a male figure—often the author himself—distills meaning from the ageless rhythms of the natural world, as in Santiago's relationship with *la mar.*

Hemingway's varied journalist voices, particularly throughout his twenty-five *Esquire* essays, describe explicit acts—sometimes stark, sometimes poetic—juxtaposing and memorializing personal reflections and judgments. Often fraught, not infrequently accusatory, his texts can and do take on both specific individuals and representative "types"—particularly among contemporary journalists and columnists: Heywood Broun, H. L. Mencken, Westbrook Pegler, William Saroyan, and others. Disparate voices continually urge him to write explicitly about the current economic times, to establish a public position regarding "revolutionary issues."

A broad, severe—albeit not atypical—personal attack on Hemingway, both man and writer, came from a major fellow professional, the literary critic Edmund Wilson. His criticism of a lack of social awareness in Hemingway's texts constituted a sharp "slap" centered in the author's personal appearance and lifestyle: "This *Esquire Man:* he, who with the sportsman's tan and outdoor grin . . . poses with a giant marlin . . . [exploiting] . . . in well-paying and trashy magazines . . . the Hemingway of loose disquisitions—arrogant, belligerent, and boastful—the worst-invented character . . . in the author's work" (*Atlantic Monthly,* July 1939). Although this criticism appeared late in the "hungry '30s," Hemingway had consistently opposed pressures to write as Wilson wished: "Don't let them suck you in to start writing about the proletariat, if you don't come from the proletariat, just to please the recently enlightened critics. . . . Write about what you know and write truly and tell them all where they can place it" ("Old Newsman Writes," *Esquire,* December 1934).

Not surprisingly, criticism such as Wilson's prompted other professionals to respond, often in the same vein—in *Esquire* and, more widely, across various print outlets, even broadcast venues. A uniquely personal Hemingway reaction to criticism of this sort, one slighting both author and work, appeared early in the *Esquire* years and notably in a *primary text:* an explanatory-self-defense monologue in *Green Hills of Africa.* This unusual volume—publisher Scribner perhaps eyeing a Depression-era Hemingway audience that was previously untapped—was initially serialized in *Scribner's Magazine,* May–November 1935.

The storyline narrative features real people, including Hemingway and his wife Pauline, on safari in Africa. Particularly apt because as a polymorphous text—not exactly journalism nor fiction nor biography—this narrative unfolds as an illustrated, semiautobiographical memoir. Hemingway's "Foreword" describes his literary experiment: "The writer has attempted to write an absolutely true book to see whether the shape of a country and the pattern of a month's action, if truly presented, compete with a work of art."

Within the volume's primary action, Hemingway expatiates judgmentally in his own voice, addressing contemporary literature and literary figures, describing the nature of literary art—all while simultaneously unpacking a teeming defense of his own subjects and vision. His feelings unspool pointedly and powerfully in a singular prose ars poetica, fulfilling friend Archibald MacLeish's famous dicta regarding literary essence: "A poem should be equal to: Not true. . . . A poem should not mean: But be." Away from threats of international conflagration and economic and political turbulence at home—all subjects of his recent *Esquire* essays—Hemingway pauses in *Green Hills* to pen a personal "brief," a manifesto of sorts stunningly expressed in a single sentence.

Reporter-journalist Hemingway produces here the fine writing of a literary artist—that is, not describing but shaping, imaging "something" new, "round and whole and solid" and "true"—anchoring matters both personal and literary:

> That something I cannot yet define completely but the feeling comes when you write well and truly of something and know impersonally you have written in that way and those who are paid to read it and report on it do not like the subject so they say it is all a fake, yet you know its value absolutely; or when you do something which people do not consider a serious occupation and yet you know, truly, that it is as important and has always been as important as all the things that are in fashion, and when, on the sea, you are alone with it and know that this Gulf Stream you are living with, knowing, learning about, and loving, has moved, as it moves, since before man, and that it has

gone by the shoreline of that long, beautiful, unhappy island since before Columbus sighted it and that the things you find out about it, and those that have always lived in it are permanent and of value because that stream will flow, as it has flowed, after the Indians, after the Spaniards, after the British, after the Americans and after all the Cubans and all the systems of governments, the richness, the poverty, the martyrdom, the sacrifice and the venality and the cruelty are all gone as the high-piled scow of garbage, bright-colored, white-flecked, ill-smelling, now tilted on its side, spills off its load into the blue water, turning it a pale green to a depth of four or five fathoms as the load spreads across the surface, the sinkable part going down and the flotsam of palm fronds, corks, bottles, and used electric light globes, seasoned with an occasional condom or a deep floating corset, the torn leaves of a student's exercise book, a well-inflated dog, the occasional rat, the no-longer-distinguished cat; all this well shepherded by the boats of the garbage pickers who pluck their prizes with long poles, as interested, as intelligent, and as accurate as historians; they have the viewpoint; the stream, with no visible flow, takes five loads of this a day when things are going well in La Habana and in ten miles along the coast it is as clear and blue and unimpressed as it was ever before the tug hauled out the scow; and the palm fronds of our victories, the worn light bulbs of our discoveries and the empty condoms of our great loves float with no significance against one single, lasting thing—the stream. (148–150)

Even when removed from its original 1935 context, Hemingway's monologue constitutes a purposeful, controlled apologia. In matter and method, it responds to the unidentified, albeit numerous, "ignorant" or "fake" critics of his lifestyle and writing—those who cannot understand why he writes of bullfights and safaris, even garbage scows, in the middle of a depression.

Fuller answers to these questions and other reader reservations unfold consistently—often directly and at length—across his *Esquire* essays.

## Hemingway Writes in *Esquire*, 1933–1939

Throughout his career, Hemingway differentiated between the timeliness of journalism and the timelessness of art. What was the attraction of *Esquire*? The early 1930s constituted a critical period in his personal life and career, principally shaped by negative published criticism of each. The launching of *Esquire* in 1933 offered a superb venue for crafting a continually unfolding (often literary) *apologia pro vita sua*—a dynamic Hemingway expressed in multiple voices.

Each Hemingway *Esquire* essay was informational. He spoke as magister—literally and figuratively, teacher: early, the Philadelphia Academy of Science funded personnel to investigate and report on his several articles speculating on varying characteristics among marlin species. Even so, his monthly "letters" soon ranged beyond a sportsman's expertise and adventures—beyond descriptions of Gulf Stream fishing and African big-game hunting.

In *Esquire,* Hemingway proved informed and astute. Beginning with his earlier wartime reporting from Paris for the *Toronto Star,* he had observed firsthand the developing political unrest in Europe. A decade later, he explained, argued over, judged, the "contemporary moment" in controversial, even iconoclastic voices. Expatiating in *Esquire* as an insider—teacher, sportsman, raconteur, literary artist, war veteran—he increasingly took up the social dimensions of an overlapping of politics and economics as Depression realities in America joined ever-broadening global conflicts and human suffering.

Hemingway fronted himself a hard worker, a journalist knowledgeable and concerned about the warmongering disarray of the contemporary moment. A sensitive intellect, but no stranger to pressing a point in strident prose, he shaped for himself in *Esquire* a first-person authoritative voice. He wrote of politics, propaganda, and war. Of the last, "*We must keep out of it*" ("A Paris Letter," February 1934).

Reprinted in the collection *American Points of View: 1934–1935*

(Cordell and Cordell) and judged by Erskine Caldwell, John Gould Fletcher, and Burton Rascoe, Hemingway's "Notes on the Next War" (September 1935) won first prize:

> —Caldwell: "Mr. Hemingway has dusted off the essay and made it as bright as modern fiction. What he has to say is important because he is able to share his knowledge with the reader. In style and in content it is definitely of 1935";
>
> —Fletcher: "Many of the recent writings of this author have been unimportant news briefs on unimportant facts. Here Hemingway discusses a phase of modern life that he understands and has experienced profoundly, and that is, at the same time, so important as to affect us all. Written with sober restraint and yet full of feeling for its subject, this essay is so important as to warrant a high place";
>
> —Rascoe: "It is unquestionably one of the most effective pieces of pacifist writing, in short form, that we have had. It is based upon experience, backed by observations by a man who has trained himself to observe, and written with the force of a man who knows how to write." (Quoted in Grimes, "Years with *Esquire*" 375)

Tracking ominous political signs in Spain and then graphically describing Mussolini's invasion of Ethiopia, Hemingway envisioned an/the imminent "next" war. A singular barometer touching the import and quality of such *Esquire* pieces is a letter sent to Hemingway by his Scribner fiction editor, Maxwell Perkins: "There isn't a living man who can write about war's horrors who [compares] with you. This goes for . . . the last five, or six, or seven, articles in *Esquire*. They ought to be published in a more permanent form" (January 1936).

Whether considered with or distinct from his creative texts and his specific on-scene war coverage of the 1930s, Hemingway's twenty-five essays and six short stories for *Esquire*, 1933–39, in volume, scope, and timeliness, constitute a unique writing achievement: a continuously unfolding "apologia"; a major body of work.

## Hemingway Is Written About in *Esquire*

Over forty years—but particularly 1933–58—editor Arnold Gingrich often took up and responded to reader reactions about Hemingway, "public man" and "*Esquire* author": from subscribers and, especially in the early years, in pointed screeds from contemporary journalists and critics; and from 1961 to 1973—in multivarious subscriber texts *and* professional critiques Gingrich explicitly commissioned. Collectively, these later responses, especially those by professionals, constitute the most extensive continually published assessments touching Hemingway, man and work, appearing in a single source over the first posthumous decade: sixty pieces in thirty-four *Esquire* issues.

And Gingrich himself? Unsurprisingly, in his personal columns —"Backstage with *Esquire*," "Editor's Notes," and "Publisher's Page"—he occasionally expressed himself in print on the magazine's principal personality. And as editor: "For the first two years, Hemingway was . . . *Esquire*'s most conscientious contributor. He [sent] copy from all over the world. . . . He more than once chartered planes . . . to make a deadline" (June 1937). In a singularly provocative observation, Gingrich deemed Hemingway's phrase *death in the afternoon* "the greatest four-word poem in the language." Acting in accord with his praising words, in the October 1970 issue, Gingrich celebrated the posthumous publication of Hemingway's *Islands in the Stream*, printing a thirty-four-thousand-word excerpt from the novel.

And more—at the end: For *Esquire*'s fortieth anniversary, October 1973, Gingrich reprinted the magazine's two "biggest" names in mid-1936 voices: Fitzgerald, "Pasting It Together," one of his three "Crack-Up" essays; Hemingway, "On the Blue Water" (prefiguring *The Old Man and the Sea*) and "The Snows of Kilimanjaro," arguably his finest story. Gingrich published sixteen Nobel laureates in *Esquire*. He devoted more space to Hemingway than to any other of these figures.

Hemingway's *Esquire* essays, both individually and collectively, stand out as a singular nonfiction achievement much as specific novels, *The Sun Also Rises, A Farewell to Arms,* and stories, "Hills Like White Elephants," "A Clean, Well-Lighted Place," stand out within his fiction canon. Fully assessing Hemingway as writer would include parallels, differences, and continuities across the complete works. Focus in this study centers specifically on Hemingway as *reporter-journalist,* as *periodical essayist,* and as *fiction writer,* more particularly on his major work in each category.

## General Overview

In the beginning was the word.

Ernest Hemingway published approximately fifteen thousand words in the Oak Park and River Forest High School newspaper, *The Trapeze,* 1916–17; apprenticed six months as a reporter for the *Kansas City Star,* 1917–18; and produced 191 articles for the *Toronto Star Weekly* and the *Toronto Daily Star,* 1920–24. Literary experiments in Paris, 1923–24, led to publication and acclaim for his early fiction in America: *In Our Time* (1925), *The Torrents of Spring* (1926), *The Sun Also Rises* (1926), *Men Without Women* (1927), *A Farewell to Arms* (1929).

For the *Toronto Star,* Hemingway experimented with a creative nonfiction journalism. He further refined that earlier mode in *Death in the Afternoon,* a history-apologia for the Spanish bullfight tradition (1932), and *Green Hills of Africa,* a nonfiction "novel"-memoir (1935). Such personal journalism—an admixture of history, biography, fact, and fiction—anchored Hemingway's twenty-five *Esquire* essays (1933–36). These texts ranged among big-game sport, travel, literature, and contemporary political-economic stresses—as did his six short stories for *Esquire* (1936–39).

In addition to the bullfight volume, the novel-memoir, and the *Esquire* canon, Hemingway's most productive decade yielded a significant variety of creative texts: *Winner Take Nothing* (stories,

1933); *To Have and Have Not* (novel, 1937); *The Fifth Column* (play, 1938; on Broadway, 1940); *For Whom the Bell Tolls* (novel, denied a Pulitzer nomination, 1940).

Despite the breadth of contemporary issues and settings of these creative works, Hemingway's writing with the broadest recurring threads in these years—reporting, essay journalism: in *New Masses,* two passionate political pieces: "Who Murdered the Vets," graphically detailing government (Civilian Conservation Corps) irresponsibility in the hurricane deaths at Matecumbe Key of more than four hundred World War I veterans building the Overseas Highway (1935); "Fascism is a Lie," an address to the American Writers' Congress (1937); and war coverage (1937–41) in Spain and China for *NANA, Ken,* and *PM*—in Spain, including his narrative text for the documentary film *The Spanish Earth* (1937); later, continuing war as subject and theme, an introduction to *Men at War* (anthology, 1942) and personalized war reporting with the Allies in England and France for *Collier's* (1944).

Wide-ranging magazines, newspapers, journals—for example, *Holiday, Life, Look, Sports Illustrated, Time, New York Times Book Review* (*NYTBR*), *Paris Review*—and news dailies (including regular *New York Post* interviews with Leonard Lyons and Earl Wilson) continually highlighted Hemingway in articles and photographic spreads. Additionally, this widely quoted and excerpted literary figure wrote blurbs, introductions, prefaces, forewords, reviews, public letters, even endorsements—Ballantine beer, 1951; Pan American Airways, 1956 (Bruccoli, *Mechanism of Fame*). On the most popular level, albeit from distinctly opposite poles, Hemingway appeared routinely in national "sports" magazines as "male" expert and exemplar—on both land and sea; simultaneously, in fiction "pulps," he strutted about as a grossly "outsized action hero" amid glossy hypermasculine, misogynistic illustrations.

Residing in Cuba after 1940, the ubiquitous Hemingway continually traveled and engaged contemporary issues. A staple "presence" in American news outlets, not least in newsreels, he shared space continuously with sports figures (Jack Dempsey, Babe Ruth,

Joe DiMaggio, Rocky Marciano, Gene Tunney) and film stars (Gary Cooper, Clark Gable, Spencer Tracy and Ingrid Bergman, Marlene Dietrich, Ava Gardner). (His Hollywood associations began as early as 1932, when Paramount paid eighty-five thousand dollars for screen rights to *A Farewell to Arms.*) Also, as earlier, Hemingway continued to be a primary subject for print journalists, newsmen, columnists, critics—some friendly over the years (Malcolm Cowley, A. E. Hotchner, George Plimpton, Lillian Ross, Earl Wilson); some not (Heywood Broun, H. L. Mencken, Westbrook Pegler, William Saroyan, Gilbert Seldes, Alexander Woollcott); some depending . . . (Edmund Wilson).

New Hemingway fiction in the 1950s appearing initially *in* magazines included: novels—*Across the River and into the Trees* (serialized, *Cosmopolitan,* 1950) and *The Old Man and the Sea* (published whole, with illustrations, in *Life,* September 1, 1952); and stories: *Atlantic* published the last original fiction—"Get a Seeing-Eyed Dog" and "A Man of the World," November 1957. In September 1960, *Life* serialized "The Dangerous Summer," contextualizing competitions between Spain's two greatest living matadors—appropriate subject matter for Hemingway's final journalism.

In these later years, universal coverage burgeoned following major awards acknowledging the breadth and distinction of Hemingway's literary career: for *The Old Man and the Sea,* a Pulitzer in 1953; for his overall writing career, the Nobel in 1954. (In Cuba, the highest civilian award: the Order of Carlos Manuel de Cespedes, 1954.)

And as already noted, *Esquire*'s fortieth anniversary issue featured the magazine's two most famous contributors in their mid-1936 voices: Fitzgerald, "Pasting It Together," one of his three autobiographical "Crack-Up" pieces; and Hemingway, "On the Blue Water"—which anticipates *The Old Man and the Sea*—and "The Snows of Kilimanjaro," Hemingway at his best.

Gingrich's own personal reflections, judgment, he recaptures from December 1966, he then referencing Hemingway's first posthumous publication, *A Moveable Feast.* Gingrich's title raises the central question one would expect from *Esquire*'s founding editor, reflecting on the magazine and American letters in the 1930s—"Scott, Ernest, and Whoever: When Fitzgerald and Hemingway both sat at the moveable feast, where was the head of the Table?" The answer proves complicated.

# 1

When a guy is hard up for copy it is a swell stall to run some personals so here is some of the same.

—**"Ring Lardner Returns,"** ***Trapeze,*** **May 4, 1917**

# Oak Park High School Journalist, 1913–1917

Ernest Miller Hemingway was born July 21, midway through the last year of the nineteenth century. Despite obvious transitioning to a new century and less obvious decaying of an old order, surely this day proved perfectly ordinary for most citizens of Oak Park, Illinois, a village ten miles southwest of Chicago.

For Hemingway, however, birth at this time and place proved remarkably good fortune. As Michael Reynolds has observed: "Born a year later than 1899, he would not have been old enough to drive Red Cross ambulances on the Italian front and would never have written *A Farewell to Arms.* Had he not returned to Chicago in the fall of 1920, he might never have met Sherwood Anderson, who directed him to Paris when young Hemingway was determined to return to Italy. Had he missed Paris, he would also have missed Gertrude Stein, Ezra Pound, and James Joyce, not to mention the summer of 1925, and we would not have *The Sun Also Rises* to read" ("Portrait of the Artist" 13).

To speak thus is not to ignore or to diminish Hemingway's fierce competitiveness, extraordinary ambition, and strict self-discipline—other influences furthering his achievements, including those both as journalist and storyteller. Nevertheless, the timing of his birth, the character of his family (including an inordinate pride in their English forebears), and the specific locales of his nurture—Oak Park and northern Michigan—fostered an ideal matrix: competitiveness, ambition, self-discipline, heritage, and formal education.

Moreover, while experiences immediately following the formative Oak Park years certainly modified his earliest beliefs, Hemingway never wholly abandoned the village or its enunciated ideals. They centered a broadening-as-maturing sensibility living through and absorbing extraordinary cultural, economic, and social changes, prompting an interesting, perhaps not altogether offhand, reflection in later life on why he avoided directly taking up his hometown in his writings: "I gave Oak Park a miss and never used it as a target. You wouldn't like to bomb your home town, would you?"

In Oak Park, as elsewhere across America in these years, evolving evangelical and utilitarian principles broadly affected everyday life from basic literacy and print to nuances underpinning middle-class capitalism. Such dramatic changes reshaped all manner of beliefs—in Hemingway's youth and young adulthood, not least those impacting social and legal reforms, particularly regarding class and gender roles and rights. Responding to these diverse and widespread complexities, Hemingway and other artist contemporaries of the post-Victorian, post-Progressive, postwar era developed original ways of "seeing," distilling new ideas into intellectual constructs that would shape the modern era.

### Oak Park: The Village

Amid the larger nation's social-intellectual ferment, Oak Park, with a population of thirty-five thousand by Hemingway's high school graduation, June 1917, overtly anchored its youth in a Protestantism stressing masculinity such as that conspicuously epitomized in outdoorsman patriot Theodore Roosevelt. More broadly, a midwestern value system yoking individualism and patriotism produced a middle-class paradigm exalting duty, love, home. Civil War veterans marched in full regalia on holidays. Town fathers (and mothers) supporting family and community pursued social reforms and opposed big government. Patriotic fervor arose in 1917 as the United States armed four million soldiers. Published estimates suggested that the village owed service in this "war to end all wars" from 300 men and women: 2,150 actually wore the uniform; 56 gave their "last full measure of devotion" (*Trapeze*).

Among the village's twenty churches, the major religious voice was First Congregational pastor William E. Barton, a Lincoln scholar whose published writings also included Civil War stories for children. Clara Barton, his renowned sister, founded the American Red Cross (1881), and his son Bruce Barton, an advertising executive, published *A Man Nobody Knows* (1925), heralding Jesus as "the founder of modern business." Pastor Barton promoted the Victorian "muscular Christian." Like Roosevelt, he exalted family and the "wholesome male." He routinely decried youthful excesses, believing that immorality centered in, was an unavoidable by-product of, dancing, swearing, smoking, drinking.

With family sacrosanct, propriety ruled. In October 1913, Hemingway's freshman year, a strident *Oak Leaves* newspaper editorial examined the "debauching taste" of popular music: "Ever since the group dance gave way to the waltz, the influence of the dissolute has been growing until now . . . everybody is 'doing it, doing it.'" By Hemingway's senior year, ordinances protected young people from "uncensored movies, boxing matches, information on venereal disease or birth control, all forms of gambling and prostitution, and any consumption of alcohol" (Reynolds, "High Culture and Low" 26).

In this Oak Park—later frequently delimited by Hemingway commentators as "broad lawns and narrow minds"—Ernest mastered *Pilgrim's Progress* at eleven. He joined the vested choir at thirteen, the Christian Endeavor Society at fourteen (with sister Marcelline reading the entire King James Bible), and the Plymouth League at sixteen. At seventeen, he recruited Christian speakers for the Boys High School Club and, for the all-male Hanna Club, successful businessmen emphasizing Focus, Dedication ("Work alone is noble"), Perseverance ("Each day is a stone in the building of character"), and Duty.

A simpler, "humane" centeredness—expressed in more imaginatively varied texts—characterized Ernest's and elder sister Marcelline's eagerly pursued daily reading. At home, and from bags of books transported to the family's Windemere cottage in Michigan, even preteen brother and sister read seriously and daily. Marcelline listed as at-home treasures sets of classics: Scott, Dickens, Thackeray, Stevenson, and Shakespeare. Individual favorites of both siblings included Stevenson, *The Suicide Club* and *Treasure Island,* Kipling, and, particularly, Horatio Alger. Thackeray, albeit more formidable than Dickens or Stevenson, slowed the pair only "a little," they reading *Vanity Fair* "cover to cover." "Grabbed" the minute they arrived in the mail were journals and periodicals, juvenile and adult: *The Youth's Companion, St. Nicholas Magazine, National Geographic, Ladies' Home Journal, Harper's, Atlantic Monthly, Good Housekeeping* (Sanford, *At the Hemingways* 133–34).

Despite conservatism and affluence, Oak Park's professionals, viewed collectively—businessmen and industrialists, doctors, lawyers, journalists and editors, scientists—were not politically reactionary. After religion, culture, broadly, predominated. The village embraced progressive ideas, particularly registered in extraordinary support for public education. The high school precollege curriculum emphasized English language studies: reading, discussing, memorizing, and reciting literary selections and continuous writing practice. School leaders also stressed extracurricular activities: physical (sports) and intellectual (clubs).

With culture a crucial enterprise, the village boasted an art center, opera house (the Warrington Opera Company importing drama and vaudeville from Chicago), a motion picture theater, two playhouses, a symphony orchestra, numerous church choirs, and the library and other facilities of the Scoville Institute (Lynn 16). Local faculty from the University of Chicago and national social leaders gave lectures—Booker T. Washington, Jane Addams, Clara Barton, William Jennings Bryan.

The club constituted a primary vehicle for adult education. Literary and historical subjects predominated. The Nineteenth Century Club included Mrs. Grace Hemingway and Mrs. Frank Lloyd Wright. (Wright spoke on "Life as Related to Art," May 1902.) Among "women's interests" clubs, topics ranged from childbearing to suffrage. The village's commitment to art and learning included current social issues such as immigration, child labor, unionization, capital punishment, prohibition, and female suffrage. By 1911, Oak Park women could vote in all local elections (Nagel, "Hemingways and Oak Park" 10).

## Parents

Albeit not wealthy, Hemingway's parents were respected Oak Park professionals: Clarence a man of science and medicine; Grace a talented vocalist and accomplished musician, teacher, choir director, and composer. Later in life, Grace achieved local distinction as a landscape artist.

Clarence Hemingway graduated from Oak Park High School in 1890. Receiving his medical education at Oberlin, he became senior obstetrician at the Oak Park hospital. As founder and president of the local chapter of the Agassiz club, he introduced young boys formally to nature. He taught camping and survival skills—for example, how to build a fire, whether bathed in sunshine or drenched in rain; prepare animals and fish for cooking (even rudimentary-skills mastery of taxidermy); wield an axe with other tools to establish a campsite and construct a shelter. In addition, an interest from childhood in American Indian cultures produced a continuous missionary commitment and financial support from adult Clarence.

A Civil War veteran and lifelong patriot, Clarence's father, Anson, was first general secretary of the Chicago YMCA. In his footsteps, paterfamilias Clarence believed that God spoke directly through Scripture. He opposed drinking, gambling (even card playing), dancing, and smoking. Possessed of a razor strop—to intimidate and for occasional use—he tolerated no hesitation to commands when directing his children.

Ernest's mother, Grace Hall, graduated from Oak Park High School in 1891. Her parents had emigrated from England in 1840, and she was a dedicated and vocal Anglophile. Her artistic mother, Caroline, sang professionally and played piano and melodeon. Her paintings decorated rooms throughout her home. Daughter Grace inherited both her artistic talent and predisposition. Studying in New York, she became a classically trained musician and, as contralto, prepared for an operatic career—an aspiration ending when stage lights hurt her eyes.

Having returned from New York to Oak Park, Grace married Clarence in 1896. Despite demands on her as a mother ultimately of six (albeit with sufficient hired domestic help), Grace enjoyed a successful "career" as a music (piano and violin) and voice teacher, not infrequently earning more than her ever-generous and readily available spouse. As early as 1895, at twenty-three, Grace publicly performed her own compositions, and two publishing companies later printed her works (Reynolds, "High Culture and Low" 28). She routinely exercised a prominent, sometimes formidable vocal role in the village's social life and artistic endeavors.

### Northern Michigan

In 1898, on Walloon Lake in the Petoskey region of northern Michigan, the Hemingways built a small summer cottage designed by Grace and named "Windemere" (after the Windermere of her British literary heritage—English Romantic "Lakes Poets" William Wordsworth, Samuel Taylor Coleridge, Robert Southey). In 1905, Clarence purchased Longfield farm, where, over the years, he and a tenant, and later Ernest and friends, harvested hay, vegetables, and fruit for sale or to bring back to Oak Park. Dr. Hemingway, licensed to practice medicine in Illinois and Michigan, often gratuitously attended to minor emergencies among campers, lumbermen, and local Indians. Among those whom young Ernest knew well, a number later appeared in his early short stories: Billy Tabeshaw, Prudence and Richard Boulton, Billy Gilbert, Simon Green.

Two quite different communities, Horton Bay and Petoskey, had developed in the immediate area. Tiny Horton Bay, four miles from Windemere, frequently offered teenaged Ernest shelter, particularly following disputes with, even disciplinary action by, his parents. Hemingway often took meals under the sympathetic watchful eye of Liz and Jim Dilworth at their Pinehurst restaurant. Later he moved into the Pinehurst Inn, and he would live briefly in Horton Bay, where, in 1921, he married Hadley Richardson.

• • •

By his late twenties, Ernest Hemingway had achieved international acclaim as a literary artist and, before thirty, celebrity status. Accolades lasted throughout and beyond his lifetime. Yet in the fall following his high school graduation, few locals would have envisioned that excellence and success. Among those who believed in him were Margaret Dixon and Fannie Biggs, his English teachers and principal writing mentors; after graduation, Biggs would recommend Ernest to two Chicago newspaper editors. And Sue Lowrey, a fellow student editor of the *Trapeze,* who drafted the caption for Ernest's picture in the yearbook, the *Senior Tabula,* stated, "None are to be found more clever than Ernie."

Ernest grew up among Oak Park achievers. They attended prestigious colleges, made respectable marriages, and, among the men, developed distinguished careers in law, medicine, commerce, and industry. Judged thus, his B average and decision not to attend college, his personal mannerisms (often seeming "boastful" or "conceited"), and his routinely "unkempt" dress neither promised nor even suggested personal or professional success.

Regardless, Ernest's solid academic average represented an accomplishment, having been attained while he participated in more extracurricular organizations and events than all but one or two others in the Class of '17. In part owing to this breadth of activity, Ernest became a "name." The high school *Trapeze* and the *Tabula* certified his prominence. During junior and senior years, between February 1916 and May 1917, these publications mention him or he appears in photographs in seventy-two separate items, exclusive of his own writing and reporting (Maziarka and Vogel 125–28).

Ernest's persona proved genuinely multifaceted, especially when including the delinquent who, in Michigan, illegally shot a blue heron, making him a felonious youth "on the run," evading authorities. At home, too, an "out of bounds" Ernest and several high school friends briefly designed a "newspaper" they named the *Jazz Journal,* producing a single copy. Fulfilling the title's sexual suggestiveness, it featured illustrations and off-color jokes, some referencing teachers. Principal McDaniel intercepted the paper, then moving among selected readers, and the authors certainly feared expulsion. Although the crisis finally evaporated without serious consequences—apparently through the intervention of Fannie Biggs—such acts surely disturbed his parents (who proffered no assistance to him) and, prospectively, Reverend Barton, and *Oak Leaves* editors worried about his youthful misbehaving. Regardless, for Ernest—that fellow "touting an astonishing argot of 'cusswords' and rich assortment of expletives" (Helmle 90), sometimes drinking, smoking, gambling, swearing, poaching, even being a briefly-in-flight game law fugitive—the imaginative improprieties of the *Jazz Journal* somehow fit finally under the broad umbrella of "forgivable youthful excesses."

Hemingway's high school summers also figured dramatically in his maturation and character development. His father remaining in Oak Park, Ernest—and shotgun—routinely hiked the Michigan woods. Experiencing tension between a naturalist-conservationist impulse and the passion to hunt—sometimes excessively, sometimes illegally (e.g., shooting the heron)—teenaged Ernest had not yet established equilibrium between these competing forces. When he was older, he would develop perspective and self-discipline, his interests growing intellectual as well as emotional. Reynolds pointedly observes: he "studied trout streams in several countries, Gulf Stream marlin, Spanish bulls, and African game. He studied the flight of birds, the bends of rivers, and the flow of country" ("High Culture and Low" 25). Moreover, the mature Ernest—"sportsman and natural historian"—would later re-create, flesh out, and memorialize these "studies" in enduring texts.

## Ernest Writes: Journalism

Senior year, beginning in November, Ernest consistently published *Trapeze* pieces—roughly five hundred to six hundred words in length—including four on November 24, 1916, and, again, on February 2, 1917. Except in rare, straight reporting, he often employed a virtually "Dickensian" ear to produce, for comedic or satiric purposes, his peers' vocabulary, speech rhythms, and principal doings and frettings. Further, these texts often embodied a singular, unmistakable likeness to Chicagoan Ring Lardner's barely literate journalist idiom. Typical is Ernest's pointedly open letter to sister Marcelline, "Ring Lardner Returns," written in the persona of a journal editor short of material (*Trapeze,* May 4, 1917):

> Dear Marce:—They tell me subscriptions and advertising has both fell off something immense since I writ one of these letters last and so as I ain't very busy I might as well try and put some of what Mussy calls good old JAZZ into the publication again.
>
> But do not think I am stuck on myself because that is not so as you must know, living right in the same house with me all these years. Is it not so, Marcelline? . . .
>
> Say, Marcelline, did you know that there is 5 pairs of brothers and sisters in school and invariabsolutely it is a strange coincidence that the sister is good looking and the brother is not? Schwabs, Shepherds, Condrons and Krafts and Hemingways. Is it not most peculiar

that except in one family the sister is an awful lot better looking than the brother? But we are too modest to say which family is the exception. Huh? Marce?

Now don't get sore and cut that out of the paper because you ain't got no proof I meant our family, and you know what "Blight" Wilcoxen says, "they can't can you if they ain't got nothing on you . . ."

When a guy is hard up for copy it is a swell stall to run some personals so here is some of the same;

*Pure Personals*

Miss Biggs gave a Senior Prom Friday night. Several couples attended the charming affair. A pleasant time was had by all who were present who united in expressing what a fine time they all had each and every one severally. . . .

The "Round Table Club" were entertained at "cards" by Mr. Frederick Stewart Wilcoxen Saturday night. The genial host loaned us car fare home. . . .

Mr. Lewis O. Clarahan, '15, returned from Illinois U. Saturday night and on Monday Mr. Clarahan demonstrated to us the overwhelming superiority of 4 aces over a full house. Mr. Clarahan refused to loan us car fare. . . .

Proctor S. Gilbert, '16, has decided to economize during the war and so during the duration of the awful conflict Mr. Gilbert will roll his own. As a further measure of economy Mr. Gilbert will borrow the makin's.

Well, Marce, I had better quit now but if you and Mr. Gehlman let this go thru you will be glad because think of the joy it may bring to some suffering heart.

"Lovingly?"
"Ernie"

Mixing "Lardner" style with school topics, Ernest achieves here a broad, albeit gentle, "dig" at village taboos (gambling and smoking) and at authority figures and school-sponsored events—Miss Biggs as the faculty advisor working with the prom committee; John Gehlmann, whose name is misspelled, as the faculty advisor to the *Trapeze.*

• • •

Oak Park boys lived surrounded by claims for the dominant "masculine" epitomized by the physically fit, self-reliant male in the "muscular Christianity" preached by Barton and, no less, in the concept of "manliness" sweeping the nation through the life and writing of Theodore Roosevelt—athlete, explorer, soldier, president, Great White Hunter. This dominant male hero figure for Ernest's generation became a literal "presence" in Oak Park as early as 1910—then on screen in newsreels, that year specifically in footage of the former president on safari. Ernest's six *Trapeze* articles on the Hanna Club, wherein successful area businessmen addressed all-boy audiences, reveal how late-Victorian and thoroughly Rooseveltian notions of hard work, perseverance, and duty permeated school activities and the culture generally and took hold of Ernest and his teen fellows at Oak Park and River Forest High School in the year before the United States entered the Great War.

Hanna Club presentations tracked this influence and the commitment to be moral, focused, diligent, hardworking. Regarding a lecture on "Business Careers of High School Boys," Ernest summarizes the "keynote": "'Every fellow should have will to labor and determination to win.' Other maxims—'Purpose is better than talent'; 'If your work is drudgery, quit the job'; 'Each day is a stone in the building of character'; 'Genius and success are 98 per cent perspiration and 2 per cent inspiration.' The conclusion: 'as soon as a fellow begins to be satisfied with his work he is on the down grade'" (February 17, 1916).

A month later, Reverend Gray, a former athlete and a "big gun" from Chicago, who "certainly had the range and the angle of fire," declaimed on the "Problems of Boyhood." Ernest's summary editorializings suggest an unmistakable captivation: "He spoke at the first of the ambitions of boyhood, how we all at an early age want to be a fireman, a groceryman, or a conductor. To illustrate this point he read a poem by Riley, about a little boy that wanted to be a grocery man. He spoke of his own 'joys' working his way through college, and then came to his big point, that the soul of no one man touches the soul of any other man. Mr. Gray said that initiative, not genius, is what is important in life, and that persistence is what makes men great. He backed these statements up with many convincing proofs, and his talk was appreciated and enjoyed by every fellow in the room" (March 9, 1916).

After graduation, Ernest became a cub reporter for the *Kansas City Star,* building on journalism skills developed for the *Trapeze* under the tutelage of Fannie Biggs. The following spring, he committed to the war effort, volunteering for ambulance duty with the American Red Cross in Italy. Such action owed much to ideas about "a man's responsibility" enunciated in Hanna and Boys High School Club presentations, in Barton's pulpit oratory, and—he was then in Kansas City—in the speeches of Billy Sunday.

## Ernest Writes: Fiction

Not as a journalist nor as a patriot did Ernest Hemingway achieve lasting renown—rather, as an imaginative writer. His creative writing in the *Tabula,* to a degree, suggests what he would do. On the whole, the fiction of this time, as writing, is technically more ambitious than the journalism. His three short stories share the ironic vision dominant in his creative *Trapeze* work and much of his later fiction. Unfolding without women, these tales deal with men facing sudden, unexpected violence. Interestingly, none suggests any obvious debt to or awareness of the scruples and tenets of Rev. William E. Barton or any Hanna Club speaker.

Each story reflects the interests of a seventeen-year-old Ernest. Two are set in the northern woods; the third draws upon his boxing knowledge and experience. Two feature an "insider" addressing a young listener he may be trying to "educate" or "initiate." Hemingway biographers have approved these brief fictions: Baker finds the narratives "tough-minded," "firmly plotted," and "original" (*Life* 27). Mellow asserts: "Hemingway, well before any traumatic experience in his life, had already begun to work toward the grammar of violence and death that marked his later work" (26). Focusing on technique, Marut notes a compact style established prior to any influence by the *Kansas City Star* and before any discussions with Sherwood Anderson, Gertrude Stein, or Ezra Pound, "the debt more properly belonging to Oak Park teachers Frank Platt, Fannie Biggs, and Margaret Dixon" (82).

In fact, English teachers Margaret Dixon and Frank Platt persuaded Ernest to submit "Judgment of Manitou" (677 words) to *Tabula,* the high school yearbook, in February 1916. Set in the Canadian woods, it features two trappers, Dick Haywood and his Cree Indian partner, Pierre. Initiating action, Pierre believes Haywood has stolen his money. Revenge ensues: Pierre sets a trap to immobilize Dick long enough for the minus-forty-two-degree weather and/or the timber wolves to complete his payback. After Dick leaves, Pierre discovers that a squirrel had carried off his wallet. Dashing "coatless and gloveless" five miles cross-country to rescue his partner, he arrives too late, discovering only a "shapeless something" earlier left by wolves, now being abandoned by two ravens. Stunned, Pierre blunders into a bear trap. Broken, remorseful, he turns his rifle on himself.

Tight plotting and a "Jack London" rendering of brutal winter weather embrace man and beast in the deep, snow-filled woods. Albeit absent significant character development, Ernest exploits his knowledge of Indian culture: Haywood, sensing something following him but discovering nothing, remembers "Kootzie-ootzie," the "little bad god of the Crees"; Pierre judges being ensnared in the bear trap a just fate, he accepting the "judgment of Manitou" (*Manitou,* Ojibway for "God").

"A Matter of Colour" (908 words) derives from Ernest's early boxing passion. It appears in April 1916, approximately when Grace declared her music room in the house off-limits to teenage pugilists. Continuing the influence of Lardner's sports pieces—and perhaps further exploiting "the unexpected reversal" as in O. Henry, another Hemingway favorite—the story demonstrates boxing world knowledge and idiom. A veteran insider narrates:

> "WHAT, you never heard the story about Joe Gan's first fight?" said old Bob Armstrong, as he tugged at one of his gloves.
>
> Well son, that kid I was just giving the lesson to reminded me of the Big Swede that gummed the best frame-up we ever almost pulled off.
>
> The yarn's a classic now; but I'll give it to you just as it happened.

The "frame-up" becomes necessary because Montana Dan Morgan cannot fight, having injured his right hand, his only serious weaponry. With "everything" bet on the fight, narrator-manager Bob Armstrong accepts a simple plan: "'Bob,' says Danny, 'I've got a scheme. You know the way the ring is out there at the Olympic? Up on the stage with that old cloth drop curtain in back? Well, in the first round, before they find out about this bad flipper of mine, I'll rush the smoke up against the curtain (you know Joe Gans was a "pusson of color") and you have somebody back there with a baseball bat and swat him on the head from behind the curtain.'"

The plan fails. The Swede hits the white man instead of the Black, because "I bane color blind!"

Achievement here lies in an idiomatic narrative voice that affects a credible character and makes concrete an unromanticized milieu: for example, "I'd gotten along pretty well with the bird, and we'd collected sundry shekels fighting dockwallopers and stevedores and preliminary boys out at the old Olympic club."

The longest story (983 words), "Sepi Jingan," published in November 1916, is Ernest's only *Tabula* fiction his senior year. Employing a worldly-wise narrator positioned between tale and auditor, this story represents a technical advance, clear in the opening action, when Billy Tabeshaw is introduced:

> "VELVET'S" like red hot pepper; "P. A." like cornsilk. Give me a package of "Peerless."
>
> Billy Tabeshaw, long, lean, copper-colored, hamfaced and Ojibway, spun a Canadian quarter onto the counter of the little northwoods country store and stood waiting for the clerk to get his change from the till under the notion counter.
>
> "Hey, you robber!" yelled the clerk. "Come back here!"
>
> We all had a glimpse of a big, wolfish-looking, husky dog vanishing through the door with a string of frankfurter sausages bobbing, snake-like, behind him.
>
> "Darn that blasted cur! Them sausages are on you, Bill."
>
> "Don't cuss the dog. I'll stand for the meat. What's it set me back?"
>
> "Just twenty-nine cents, Bill. There was three pounds of 'em at ten cents, but I et one of 'em myself."
>
> "Here's thirty cents. Go buy yourself a picture post-card."
>
> Bill's dusky face cracked across in a white-toothed grin.

Tabeshaw, an unpretentious character, tells his auditor "about Sepi Jingan." This violent tale concerns the tracking down and killing of Paul Black Bird, who murdered Billy's cousin, a game warden. Tabeshaw discovers the warden's body, and knowing that "there never was a white man yet could catch an Indian in the Indian's own country," he tracks Paul Black Bird with Sepi.

The ending finds Paul Black Bird, having gotten the upper hand, preparing to kill Billy with a pike pole. Taunting his nemesis, the murderer asks, "Where's your dog, dog man?" Even then, Sepi is crawling quietly toward him. The dog springs like a "shaggy thunderbolt" and kills the Indian in an instant: "With a side snap of his head, his long, wolf jaws caught the throat." Billy then places the body on the Pere Marquette railroad tracks; later everyone assumes that Paul Black Bird got drunk celebrating the Fourth of July and died having fallen asleep on the tracks. (One of several ironies in the story is that Paul Black Bird cannot get drunk.)

"Sepi Jingan," like "Judgment of Manitou," offers solid plotting; it is superior in the nuances of Tabeshaw's character. He stands forth not so much through idiom or Indian background but through knowledge uniquely his (knowing that Paul Black Bird cannot get drunk) and through his idiosyncratic interest in pipe tobacco (identifying by smell or otherwise commenting on seven brands and having as his "tag" line, "Me for 'Peerless'").

Tabeshaw is more fully conceived than Bob Armstrong, the speaker in "A Matter of Colour," in that the fight manager is wholly defined by details limited to the boxing world. Tabeshaw's knowledge about Paul Black Bird's drinking and about tobacco have nothing to do with his being an Indian, and his language, except for the "Me for 'Peerless'" tag, is identical to that of the other speaking character in his story: "I took Sepi, who was just a pup then, and we trailed him (that was two years ago). We trailed him to the Soo, lost the trail, picked it up at Garden River, in Ontario; followed him along the north shore to Michipicoten; and then he went up to Missainabie and 'way up to Moose Factory. We were always just behind him, but we never could catch up."

One may imagine Principal McDonald's raised eyebrow over the subjects in all three stories. Regardless, a "justice" consistent with Oak Park's Christian principles develops in each: Pierre, responsible for his friend's death, pays with his life; Bob Armstrong's scheme miscarries; Paul Black Bird, a murderer, forfeits his life.

As in Hemingway's later published fiction, however, moral and ethical ambiguities abound and remain without authorial comment or definitive answers: Pierre's paying with his life is "right," but he dies by suicide. The auditor offers no final remarks in "A Matter of Colour," and so we cannot know whether he shares the values of Armstrong, who implemented the failed scam. Similarly, the listener in "Sepi Jingan" does not respond to Tabeshaw, who uses the train to erase evidence about the killing of Paul Black

Bird, even when Billy asks his young companion at the end, "Funny, ain't it?"

• • •

The "Class Prophecy" (2,599 words) constitutes Ernest's final high school fictional narrative. Herein, the class "wit" excelled. He selected a familiar technique: develop a simple storyline and assign a future career nearly the opposite of each classmate's known plans or inconsistent with his or her personality type (e.g., scholar and later English professor Edward Wagenknecht is a baseball star). Ernest's narrative used as backdrop the war, which the United States had entered into just two months earlier:

> "GO over to that table and take the news as it comes from the front," said General Wilcoxen to me. I seated myself at the radio table in the headquarters and adjusted the phones to my ears. Clickety, click, click, click, click, click went the receivers.
>
> "Read it off to me as it comes in," said General Wilcoxen, and I read off the messages as rapidly as possible.
>
> "Dale Bumstead, great powder magnate, captured and held for ransom by the Germans. Shall we pay the $2,000,000 asked for his return?"
>
> "Don't ask foolish questions," snapped the general.
>
> "General Taylor, Major Swanson and Colonel Rawls have been recommended to command the new expeditionary force. Have you any choice which is the best?"
>
> "Say there is no choice," growled the commander-in-chief."

Within the larger narrative, smaller stories develop, at least one with darker tones. Marcelline Hemingway appears as a well-known veterinarian, a fitting profession for the daughter of Dr. Clarence Hemingway. But her sole act—an apparently premeditated "hit-and-run" accident that kills the victim—notably (inexplicably?) undercuts Marcelline.

In the same section, Carroll Dyrenforth, Ernest's only opponent in the election for Class Prophet, is found at menial work scrubbing the steps of an office building:

> We thanked Bud and barely got across the street in front of a speeding Ford driven by M. Hemingway, the noted lady veterinarian. As the car whizzed by us it struck an elderly lady who was crossing the street and hurled her senseless to the pavement. Hastening to her aid, we found it to be Jessie Brown! "Who done it?" she gasped. "Doc. Hemingway," Fred replied. "I knew she'd get me finally," wheezed Jessie, and passed away. We carried her lifeless body into the office building and really nearly tripped over Carroll, "I'll call a bellboy," and at her ring Gertrude Early, Edith Ebersold and Grace Dabbert appeared attired in their snappy livery and gently took the body upstairs.

The choice of Dyrenforth's drudge employment (certainly without "snappy livery") is also, as with the portrayal of Marcelline, at least unexpected.

The "Class Prophecy" is one of the few instances when teenaged Ernest writes about women, and, although he assigns nonprofessional jobs to others—motorcycle "copette," taxi driver, and, as here, bellboy—he typically imagines his female classmates more in accord with Oak Park expectations. Referring to the various careers for women in the "Prophecy," Reynolds's observes: "Oak Park expected more than menial positions for its daughters: Red Cross Nurse, high school teacher, actress, ballet dancer, opera singer, temperance leader, model, editor, and social worker." The role depicted most often for the young women in Ernest's narrative is that of the "wife of some prominent man. . . . [but those who work, generally] . . . take their place in humanitarian positions, public service, or in the arts" ("Portrait of the Artist" 15).

Alas for Carroll Dyrenforth and some few others. And for sister Marcelline!

The "Prophecy" appeared in the *Tabula,* and Ernest delivered it on Class Day. At the graduation ceremony, Marcelline, who had referred to "Prophet" Ernest in the *Trapeze* as "that bearded patriarch of wisdom," presented her commencement address on "The New Girlhood." Edward Wagenknecht, future English professor, gave the Valedictory, sensitive remarks in wartime on "Tomorrow."

• • •

Indefatigable, teenage Ernest would boat, box, camp, fish, hike, hunt, and, competitively for the high school, run, play football, swim, and play water basketball. He was track team manager. At church, he belonged to numerous organizations, including the vested choir. Among several guises—insider sports reporter, playful Ring Lardner wit-cum-"witling," and senior wise-guy—he reported news and features. With his own byline, he often played a role in his stories, his name recurring throughout the text. He published forty-five nonfiction pieces (twenty-nine his senior year) in the *Trapeze* (including in his role as sports editor and editor-in-chief for the "Class of '17" final edition); in *Tabula*, the yearbook, three short stories, four poems, and the "Class Prophecy."

Despite the particular success of "Ernest," self-consciously playful wit, it is difficult finally to see much of the future "Hemingway" in his approximately fifteen thousand words of *Trapeze* writing, even among the better Lardner imitations. Characteristics of the mature fiction do appear in the three *Tabula* stories—the Canadian and Michigan woods and specific techniques, subjects, and themes—but all of these earmarks will undergo extensive modification over the following eight to ten years.

Missing from the high school publications is the *personal* Ernest. Lewis Clarahan—Oak Park friend and Michigan woods fishing and camping companion—later remarked about Ernest's need, semi-regularly, to secret himself away in his Oak Park bedroom for serious writing and personal reflection. Clarahan recalled the diary Hemingway sometimes kept, where he recorded, in addition to ideas for stories, private thoughts and impressions. An example is an excerpt from March 21, 1915, which finds fifteen-year-old Ernest "taking stock." After itemizing his possessions, he continues:

> I desire to do pioneering or exploring work in the 3 last great frontiers—Africa, Southern Central South America or the country around and north of Hudson's Bay. I believe that the Science, English and to a certain extent the Latin that I am now studying in the High School will help me in this object. I intend to specialize in the sciences in college and to join some expedition when I leave college. I believe that any training that I get by hiking in the spring or farm work in the summer or any work in the woods which tends to develop resourcefulness and self-reliance is of inestimable value in the work I intend to pursue.
>
> I have no desire *absolutely* to be a millionaire or a rich man but I do intend to do something toward the scientific interests of the world. Ernest M. Hemingway. (Reynolds, *Young Hemingway* 29–30)

These sentences highlight Ernest Hemingway's Oak Park legacy. Certainly Clarence Hemingway, William E. Barton, the businessmen who spoke before the high school boys' clubs, indeed, Theodore Roosevelt himself, would applaud such reflections. Moreover, they suggest, and reflect, English writers and heroes, part of his own worldview and family heritage—the British influence so central to his mother's world: nineteenth-century Victorian adventurers, scientists, and writers like David Livingstone, Charles Darwin, Richard Burton, and, among authors, his mother's especial favorite, "aspirational" poet Robert Browning: "A man's reach should exceed his grasp / Or what's a heaven for?"

Ernest's boyhood experiences and accomplishments provided him rich and complex resources for the adult life to come. *Tabula* creative writer Hemingway publishes the "Class Prophecy," three stories, and four poems. *Trapeze* journalist Hemingway, both seriously and tongue-in-cheek, consistently stresses *expertise*, the elemental characteristic of his later authoritative texts and personas. Contained in these pieces and his diary reflections *is* the future Ernest Hemingway in his multiple guises: varying from inside reporter to the resourceful and self-reliant scientist who compiled new data on Gulf Stream marlin and other big-game fish; the historian-apologist who wrote extensively of the Spanish bullfight tradition; the natural historian–sportsman who became an expert on the habits of the wild game he hunted on several continents, including Africa; the linguist, who used his "little Latin" to help with the French, Italian, and Spanish necessitated by his travels; and the writer, who revolutionized the use of his native English, redefining the craft of fiction.

• • •

Ernest spent the summer following graduation in Michigan at Longfield Farm, working hard, consciously avoiding disputes with both parents, struggling with questions about his future—the issue most pressing, what to do next. Possibilities . . .

—stay in Michigan or travel to California and work near Grace's brother Leicester;

—go to college: on September 22, 1917, Clarence writes to Ernest, then closing down farmwork in Michigan, that six men from the Scribblers Club at Northwestern University have come to the house hoping to persuade him to enroll there;

—take a job with the *Chicago Tribune* or the *Examiner*, if Fannie Biggs's efforts with either newspaper prove fruitful: on September 27, 1917, Walter Howey Day, managing editor of the *Chicago Examiner*, writes that he has no position but encourages Ernest to come talk with him and bring a letter from Fannie Biggs; on September 29, 1917, E. S. Beck, managing editor of the *Chicago Tribune*, has no position, despite the war's drain on personnel, but "it would do no harm for him to call on Mr. Smith, the city editor, bringing a memorandum of this note with him"; or

—take a position as cub reporter with the *Kansas City Star* arranged through Clarence's brother Tyler.

By mid-October, the *Star* and Kansas City have won out.

Clarence, without Grace, sees his son off for Kansas City from Chicago's LaSalle Street train station. Ernest leaves hometown Oak Park after eighteen years on the last day of the World Series. Perhaps propitiously, his team, the Chicago White Sox, concludes the season by beating the New York Giants.

On this day, also, Ernest sees for the first time, and crosses, the "mighty Mississippi"—for him a veritable Rubicon.

• • •

On that October afternoon in 1917, one would have had to be truly prescient to forecast accurately Ernest Hemingway's future achievements. Even so, Fannie Biggs and Margaret Dixon, who had taught him much and watched him grow as a writer, and classmate Sue Lowrey, who like Biggs and Dixon had read both his imaginative writing and his journalism and, in her own case, had worked long hours with him on the *Trapeze,* could not be blamed for sensing his extraordinary potential. Today who can doubt that these publications satisfy and confirm Lowrey's yearbook assessment: "None are to be found more clever than Ernie."

# 2

# Youthful Professional

## REPORTER, WARTIME AMBULANCE DRIVER, ASPIRING AUTHOR

Through his Uncle Tyler's connections, a young "Ernest" accepted a position (sixty dollars a month) with the *Kansas City Star.* On October 17, 1917, a steadily maturing "Hemingway" took up writing as an adult profession: *reporter-journalist.*

His earliest assigned posts—police station, hospital, railroad terminal—presented a moral universe radically unlike Oak Park's. Through police contacts at each base, his reporting ranged from crime, accidents, and exposure to contagious diseases (also including moral corruption among hospital administrators) to developing information shaping impromptu interviews with notables at the railroad station. Among them were government officials, including President Wilson's vice president Thomas R. Marshall; sports "names" such as Jess Willard and Grover Cleveland Alexander; and various British and American military officers.

A wit, a quick study, a lively talker, this high-energy reporter often abandoned assigned posts, jumping into a squad car or ambulance either to pursue simple instinct or to follow up a specific suggestion—perhaps made only in passing—touching a newsworthy person or unfolding event. Unquestionably, too, young reporter

Hemingway savored exposure to the illicit and illegal. Extending his police station coverage toward the stockyards, the Missouri River, and the railway head, he probed regulars in the seamier pool halls, dance palaces, and eateries habituated by prostitutes and drug dealers and those seeking otherwise varied underworld experience. Briefly, he cultivated an interest in the argot of homosexual males around the rail yards, incorporating the formulation "five-fingered sex with your old mother" in one piece (Griffin, *Youth* 40).

Swamping all other subjects, war shaped newsroom priorities. With enlistments and the draft continually reducing staff, thirty-year-old "Pete" Wellington, assistant city editor, became de facto managing editor. Energetic and dutiful, Hemingway worked hard, despite his hallmark irrepressible sense of humor at times marring efficiency. He embraced Wellington's gospel as enunciated in the 110 "dos and don'ts" of "The Star Copy Style": "Use short sentences. Use short first paragraphs. Use vigorous English. Be positive, not negative." He wrote simply, accurately, objectively. Grounded in acceptable contemporary colloquial language and, not infrequently, exploiting both narrative and dialogue, he emphasized local color and the character sketch, enlivening the purely factual "who, what, where, when, why." Writing home, he described as live drama both mission and minutiae anchoring this work: "Get all the facts and in the correct order, make it have snap and wallop and write it in fifteen minutes, five sentences at a time to catch an edition" (Paul 125).

Hemingway's few confirmed pieces, initially only a paragraph or two and absent any byline, illuminate contemporary social-cultural moments. Prescient, sister Marcelline observed in these brief early texts a characteristic by-product of Hemingway's reporting that became crucial later. A typical example is "Would 'Treat 'em Rough,'" one of five contemporary "dramas" Hemingway recorded in a series on military recruitment:

> Four men stood outside the army recruiting office at Twelfth Street and Grand Avenue at 7:45 o'clock this morning when the ser-

geant opened up. A stout red faced man wearing a khaki shirt was the first up the stairs.

"I'm the treat 'em rough man," he bawled. "That cat in the poster has nothing on me. Where do you join the tankers?"

. . . The fat man waited outside the door. By 9 o'clock thirty men crowded the third floor hallway. The stout man was nearest the door. Just behind him was a gray haired man wearing a derby, a well cut gray suit . . . and a silk handkerchief. . . .

"I'm over draft age. . . . I never really wanted to get into this war before, but the tanks are different. I guess I can treat 'em rough."

The crowd grew steadily. By 10 o'clock there were forty applicants. . . . The stout man, perspiration pouring down his face, held his place next to the door. He tried to whistle, but his lips wouldn't pucker. He stood on one foot, then the other. He mopped his face with a handkerchief, and finally bolted out through the crowd.

"He looked pretty hot but he got cold feet," a mechanic in overalls commented. (April 18, 1918)

Hemingway's finest among his confirmed *Star* texts—"Kerensky, the Fighting Flea" (December 16, 1917), "At the End of the Ambulance Run" (January 20, 1918), and "Mix War, Art, and Dancing" (April 21, 1918)—foreshadow later achievements in his minimalist style, for example, the Boyle and Drevitts ("Chapter VIII") and Sam Cardinella ("Chapter XV") vignettes of *In Our Time* (1925).

The most dramatic of these early *Star* snapshots, "Mix War, Art, and Dancing," he described as "very sad, about a whore":

Outside a woman walked along the west street-lamp lit sidewalk through the sleet and snow.

. . . Three men from Funston were wandering arm in arm along the wall looking at the exhibition of paintings by Kansas City artists. The piano player stopped. The dancers clapped and cheered and he swung into "The Long, Long Trail Awinding." An infantry corporal, dancing with a swift moving girl in a red

> dress, bent his head close to hers and confided something about a girl in Chautauqua, Kas. In the corridor a group of girls surrounded a tow-headed young artilleryman and applauded his imitation of his pal Bill challenging the colonel, who had forgotten the password. The music stopped again and the solemn pianist rose from his stool and walked out into the hall for a drink.
>
> A crowd of men rushed up to the girl in the red dress to plead for the next dance. Outside the woman walked along the wet lamp lit sidewalk.
>
> . . . The pianist took his seat again and the soldiers made a dash for partners. In the intermission the soldiers drank to the girls in fruit punch. The girl in red, surrounded by a crowd of men in olive drab, seated herself at the piano, the men and the girls gathered around and sang until midnight. The elevator had stopped running and so the jolly crowd bunched down the six flights of stairs and rushed waiting motor cars. After the last car had gone, the woman walked along the wet sidewalk through the sleet and looked up at the dark windows of the sixth floor. (April 21, 1918)

Clear in this early reporting-as-narrative, Hemingway consciously understood mature techniques he would specifically articulate only later: "a skilled writer may omit things he knows, yet make the reader feel them as strongly as if he had actually stated them." Notable here, also, the patterned repetition and counterpoint in contrasting people not included at the party with those present at the dance (Meyers, *Biography* 25–26).

Beyond Wellington, the "Star Copy Style," and his own ever-on curiosity, Hemingway observed and consistently interrogated veteran *Star* journalists. Most impressive among these figures was the colorful Lionel Calhoun Moise, at twenty-six already a legend among his fellow reporters. Moise's otherwise off-putting personal excesses—drinking, brawling, womanizing—proved tolerable quirks given the dramatic appeal in the breadth and quality of his work product. Most impressive, Moise as outsize rewrite man: he "could carry four stories in his head and go to the telephone and take a fifth and then write all five at full speed to catch an edition. There would be something alive about each one" (Baker, *Life* 35). Without idealizing this phenom per se, Hemingway did develop a broadly "rose-colored vision" touching a "newsman's life." Particularly when writing Marcelline, he continuously romanticized news gathering, dramatizing his personal reporting successes while extolling the shared work and camaraderie among the "swell newsroom gang."

• • •

Growing up in Oak Park, young Ernest routinely concocted—often later reshaping and retelling—personal narratives of derring-do in the Michigan woods. Lewis Clarahan, senior among his high school compatriots and a Michigan hiking-fishing companion, recorded numerous instances. Even when still boys, absent any real experience, the slightly older Clarahan could easily distill the limited truths among his friend's tall tales—recognizing then, memorializing later—more than a few dramatic Hemingway plots and actions as wholesale fabrications.

Away from Oak Park, Hemingway continued shaping imaginary personal narratives: for example, convincing *Star* colleagues of his eleven attempts to enlist, being rejected by the army, navy, and marines because of a weak left eye. (The *Star* later printed the claim of eleven enlistment attempts.) Enhancements of various sorts, not all limited to professional work, leavened his Kansas City writings. An increasingly "creative" Hemingway drafted texts of two types: news and features for the *Star;* equally important, letters to his family—these latter often lengthy nuancings of both simple feelings and powerful emotions. Unalike, each genre reveals much—not least the developing "imaginative" impulse underpinning a newsman's otherwise direct reporting.

The principal audience for his enlistment details and routine personal hyperbole lived primarily in Oak Park—senior family, particularly his mother and father, but including older sister, Marcelline, then a student at Oberlin. For the former, he adopted an altogether responsible voice—albeit playing "fast and loose" with truth as early as his first letter home, claiming it to be the second, and reporting three pieces in the paper his first workday. Writing to each individually, he routinely exaggerated both the experience and his developing sophistication, with Marcelline "stretching" claims of achievement beyond the more reality-anchored, albeit carefully crafted, texts for Grace and for Clarence.

Evolving "adult, tale-spinner" Hemingway suggested to Marcelline routine access for himself to both social and political gatherings among city power brokers: "I can tell mayors to go to hell and slap police commissioners on the back!" He learned, he claimed, to differentiate, "sans the use of the eyes," "chianti, catawba, malvasia, Dago Red, claret, and several others." More, he described himself quite seriously as having to carry a pistol, as in Old West Kansas City (Sanford 272–73).

Much among such details smacks of simple good fun. Regardless, Marcelline, barraged with exaggerated, often wholly invented, dramas, generally accepted—as Clarahan, for example, had not—at least Hemingway's man-of-many-parts persona. This impressive character emerged as the central player in prose overflowing with a mixture of incontrovertible truths apportioned variously with partial or complete fabrications. The result, as comprehended from Marcelline's point of view: "Ernest liked Kansas City. His letters to me and to the family . . . told of his excitement at being a real reporter on a real newspaper at last. . . . Ernie was learning a lot; he told us about his new friends on the paper, many of them men years older than he. He met a movie star and he wrote me three pages of raves about her. . . . He was feeling very grown-up to be so independent. My letters to him seemed kiddish in contrast, as all I could write him about were my activities at Oberlin. Instead of being older than he, I now felt younger, as Ernest's new experiences made him seem so much more a man of the world" (Sanford 156).

Exaggeration and language play also personalize elder brother Ernest in "domestic" texts specifically designed for his younger siblings. "Crafted" altogether differently from his exchanges with family adults, they suggest a developing fictionist playfully scattering hyperbole. More important, they humanize Ernest's seniority by broadening and fleshing out a sympathetic lighter side. Typical is a missive written to all the children after being a month away: "Hi Nunbones, Howdy Urra, How are you Nubs, well how is the Bipehouse?" Describing himself variously as your "large and brutal brother," "burley brother," "fraternal brother," and "great litterateur Stein," he kids them about himself: "He is supposed to be laboring. Is he? He is not."

He then singles each one out for an individual comment: "Mr. and Mrs. Edgar . . . did not know the Bipehouse or Nubs but they were sure they must be great being related to the great litterateur Stein and the Noted Ukalaliest Nunbones and the Noted Smiler and Latin Shark, Ura." He closes by urging them, in return for the canceled streetcar transfers he has forwarded, to send him "many Christmas, Thanksgiving and any other presents that are fitting" (Ernest Hemingway Collection, John F. Kennedy Presidential Library and Museum; hereafter cited as "JFK Library"). This large, burly, overwhelming, older brother certainly dominates, albeit possessing a wholly benign persona. Experienced and in charge, he is also tender toward each child, whom he addresses by his or her family nickname.

Regarding his mother, Hemingway carefully praised the various baked delicacies she routinely forwarded to him and his cohorts. He was less flexible—albeit this thread is short-lived—regarding her concerns about religion and his friends Carl Edgar and Bill Smith, both Kansas City residents and companions from shared Michigan summers. Edgar is "a sincere Christian"; Smith believes in "God and Jesus Christ" and has "hopes for a hereafter and creeds don't matter" (*Letters* 1:76–77). Subject closed.

More numerous, respectful, and wide-ranging were carefully wrought texts exclusively addressing paterfamilias Clarence. For his father, Hemingway appeared a uniformly serious, industrious, clever, responsible (fiscally, in particular) adult—an increasingly successful writer and a professional journalist on one of the nation's most respected newspapers, in which Theodore Roosevelt himself had a byline.

This Hemingway possessed both focus and energy, for example, scooping his colleagues to talk with an army officer passing through Union Station about troop transportation. He interviewed sportswriters and Grover Cleveland Alexander, a new member of the hometown Chicago Cubs, additionally claiming that this article was picked up by both the Associated Press and United Press International. He continually sent home *Star* pages, his work circled. He reported on Guard activities and his desire to enlist. He detailed personal emotional responses: sympathy for Black prisoners under heavy guard passing through Union Station at night; anger over malfeasance among hospital administrators and politicians on the Health Board—incompetence, political corruption, graft. Not least, he described plans to leave Kansas City and the *Star* in time to return home and to Walloon Lake before committing personally to the war effort.

For Clarence, Hemingway lessened the fabrication and exaggeration he sent to Marcelline, although untruth and hyperbole abound: the Alexander article was not carried by the wire services; he exaggerated his role in print coverage of the corrupt hospital board and the number of column inches he filled daily with this story. His motives for stretching the truth to his father differed from his purposes with Marcelline and the children. His older sister he wished to impress and dominate—at least partly in jest. His other siblings he wished to impress and dominate—entirely in jest. Eager for approval, he wished to impress both parents. Clarence, particularly, must behold a son worthy of and commanding paternal pride. These audiences allowed for experimental narratives and language craft, and Hemingway purposely stretched the credible in wild (and wily) wordplay.

• • •

Shared work on a major newspaper among productive veteran reporters provided Hemingway with "indispensable" conditions: both independence and an opportunity to mature—as a person and as a writer crafting both fact and fiction. At the most basic, he successfully presented, among credible colorations, contemporary cultural moments and their characteristic human actors. Certain of his personal Kansas City realities he recorded as journalism, with some few of his experiences later appearing in his fiction collections: "Chapter VIII (*In Our Time*, 1925); "The Pursuit Race" (*Men Without Women*, 1927); "God Rest You Merry, Gentlemen" (*Winner Take Nothing*, 1933). A singular anomaly regarding Hemingway's journalism career as it intersects his later published fiction centers in Nick Adams. Hemingway's fullest developed fictional character, Nick appears in at least fifteen stories across the three fiction collections. The anomaly: unexpectedly, this Nick Adams saga "ignores altogether" Hemingway's Kansas City experiences (Paul 10).

Regardless, Hemingway and "fiction" coexisted in Kansas City. He was not "promoted" within the first two weeks, as he claimed. Genuinely patriotic, as his Oak Park upbringing virtually assured, he sought to participate in the war (joining the Missouri Home Guard almost immediately), but he was not rejected by the three military service branches. Regularly covering Union Station, he did interview military officers, politicians, and other "names," including baseball star Grover Cleveland Alexander. However, and importantly, he never met the starlet Mae Marsh. (About her he raved to Marcelline, later even to his parents, concocting an imagined love *and* marriage proposal—just before shipping out from New York for the war front—shocking his sister, horrifying his parents.) And assuredly, at no point in Kansas City could he, as he bragged to his sister, "tell mayors to go to Hell and slap police commissioners on the back." Important, too, despite an interest in unsavory neighborhoods and his extensive hospital coverage—reporting on victims of violence and pursuing white-collar corruption among hospital bureaucrats—no assignment ever required that he carry a Colt revolver.

Ironically, these drama-filled fictions—enhanced and reshaped from actual experiences and mailed home in personal letters from Kansas City—proved pale precursors of details received on that home front only a short while later from Red Cross volunteer Hemingway, wounded in war-torn Italy.

• • •

With the war effort omnipresent in each *Star* edition, Hemingway talked incessantly of battle and ways of getting overseas. He had joined the Missouri Home Guard. Omnipresent and numerous spokesmen proffered powerful inspiration and direction, particularly Hemingway's early hero, the iconic Theodore Roosevelt: "[A] terrible thing that our loved ones should face great danger, but . . . a far more terrible thing if . . . they were not treading the hard path of duty and honor" (Paul 121). Brother wrote sister Marcelline about joining the Canadian army after spending one more summer in Michigan. Jolted to greater consciousness in December by the fiery rhetoric of Billy Sunday (who proclaimed that able-bodied men who do not serve are "traitors"), son wrote parents describing marine and air corps options. Hemingway even encouraged Clarence to think about joining the marine reserves and repeated claims he had made to his sister about being unable to face those who fought if he did not. These problems resolved finally through friends in the newsroom, particularly Theodore Brumback, and the presence in Kansas City of Red Cross recruiters seeking individuals unable to pass the physical for the American army but, even therefore, willing to "commit to the fight" by driving ambulances on the Italian front.

Brumback joined the *Star* in the late fall. Four years older than Hemingway, he was a member of a prominent local family—his father a judge in the Jackson County Circuit Court system. A student at Cornell, 1913–15, Brumback had lost an eye when hit by a golf ball. Leaving the university after the 1916–17 academic year, he enlisted with the American Field Serves in France as an ambulance driver, seeing active duty July–November 1917.

Brumback later recorded his first meeting with the young Oak Park man. Awaiting orientation and assignment, he had watched Hemingway pounding away at his typewriter. When finished, Hemingway spoke: "That's rotten copy. When I get excited this damn type mill goes haywire on me. Sometimes I can't even read what I've written. The copy reader may call me over to the desk in a minute to translate. They kid me a lot, but they print my stuff just the same" (quoted in Bruccoli, *Cub Reporter* 3).

Soon fast friends and aware of the limitations of his own poor left eye, Hemingway attended to Brumback's stories of life under fire in the ambulance corps. Coincidentally, in late February, Red Cross recruiters seeking drivers for the Italian front arrived in Kansas City. Patriotic Hemingway and experienced Brumback, each technically "unfit" for regular service, soon proved ready, eager, to sign on.

Inarguably, a genuine patriotism inspired Hemingway's embracing of the Red Cross ("I couldn't face anybody after the war and not have been in it"). His parents were pleased. Clarence wrote, "proud" of his son's "success" in Kansas City, prophetically observing that Hemingway had in seven months gotten a profession he can take with him "anywhere in the world and earn a living." Both parents judged his decision on how to proceed with life at this moment in time to be "good" (JFK Library).

• • •

Understanding of his upcoming Red Cross wartime experiences would clarify for Hemingway only later and only slowly. Not so his writing confidence. These skills developed inordinately in Kansas City, notable and noted in the newsroom. At his departure, fellow *Star* reporter Tubby Williams exhorted: "Write at war! It will be the making of you—a career. You read human interest and you can tell it" (quoted in Paul 134–35).

Educating himself, professionalizing his writing, and sharpening his inherently keen imagination via exposure to a broad variety of human experience constitute the most obvious long-term residuals of Hemingway's Kansas City education. Moreover, this professional development effected a broader, consequential growth. Using freedom from Oak Park's boundaries, both physical and metaphorical, he began explicitly to craft *in words* an adult Hemingway, a persona not yet completely coherent nor fully credible or public but of much greater breadth than the wit he had affected in high school. From this time, development as a writing professional became his life's creative work.

Eagerly resolved for and signed on with the Red Cross by the first week of May 1918, Hemingway departed Kansas City for Oak Park—soon to New York and the inception of his service. When home, he purposefully visited English teacher Fannie Biggs. Speaking no longer as her student Ernest but as the now prescient adult and continuously evolving wordsmith Hemingway, he tasked his earliest intellectual mentor: "If it comes to a death notice of me, I want *you* to write it, because you'll tell it the way it was and no gushing" (Mellow 613 n. 49).

• • •

Traveling from New York to Bordeaux and then to Paris required eight days. From Paris, Hemingway, Brumback, and now good friend Howell Jenkins departed for Milan. These three, with fellow Chicagoans Fred Spiegel and Bill Horne, were assigned to Red Cross Section IV at Schio, 150 kilometers east of Milan.

Before reaching their destination, however, Hemingway and others volunteered for an emergency "body detail" at a munitions factory at Bollate, twenty-five kilometers outside Milan. A violent explosion had destroyed a building, killing all thirty-five female workers, literally shredding fourteen bodies. As their first medical action, Hemingway and the other Red Cross volunteers disentangled human parts from a barbed wire fence, collecting additional remains from the field beyond.

On June 9, the men arrived at Schio, and training began: driving ten miles to the front; negotiating the hazardous roads around seven thousand–foot Mount Pasubio; gathering casualties; returning them safely to Schio. Initially, the need for ambulances proved light, affording time for sports and simply "shooting the breeze." Such leisurely living caused drivers from other units to dub Section IV, "the Schio Country Club."

Unsurprisingly, Hemingway soon began rhetorically reconfiguring this new reality. Free time and his irrepressible sense of humor prompted him to contribute to *Ciao*, the sporadically published Section IV newsletter. His eight hundred–word Lardner imitation "Al Receives Another Letter," much in the manner of his earlier *Trapeze* "Lardners," constitutes Hemingway's only published writing during the war after his leaving the *Star:* "Well Al I am now an officer and if you would meet me you would have to salute me. What I am is a provisional acting second lieutenant without a commission but the trouble is that all the other fellows are too. There ain't no privates in our army Al and the Captain is called a *chef.* But he don't look to me as tho he could cook a damn bit. . . . I can tell you we've been in two battles Al. The Battle of Milan and the Battle of Paris. That is a joke Al and maybe you can't understand it but it will show you anyway I am the same old joker Huh Al . . . ?" (Griffin, *Youth* 69–70).

• • •

Early in July, Hemingway wrote to former classmate Ruth Morrison in Oak Park. Exercising an increasingly usual bravado, he enhanced basic realities: saying that he had left the Red Cross for a period to be a second lieutenant in the Italian army (actually a courtesy rank extended to all Red Cross drivers); imaginatively creating, detailing, his brief residence in a house so close to the front that it had been seriously damaged by shelling ("bombs go scheeeeeeeek Boom and every once in a while a machine gun goes tick a tack a tock"); and describing his personal horde of captured items—an "Austrian officer's automatic pistol . . . German helmets . . . junk" (*Letters*

1:113.) Ironically, the uniformly hyperbolic untruths in these words written to Morrison remarkably anticipate details of his actual—imminent—reality.

Settled in at Schio, along with Horne and Jenkins, Hemingway volunteered to operate a rolling canteen along the lower Piave River, supplying frontline Italian soldiers in trenches with coffee, cold drinks, chocolates, soup, cigarettes, magazines, postcards, and water. Engaged thus in the early hours of Monday, July 8, 1918, he was seriously wounded by an Austrian muzzle-loaded trench mortar—dubbed an "ash can"—a canister (approximately five-gallon size) filled with steel and other metal fragments that, when exploding, scattered a powerfully destructive force at ground level.

The soldier nearest him died instantly. Others were seriously injured. Hemingway, in shock and semiconscious during evacuation and initial field treatment, was sent by ambulance to Treviso. His wounds: a machine-gun bullet in the right knee and another in the right foot, fracturing his big toe; numerous flesh wounds from shrapnel—over two hundred pieces of shell—none lodged above the "hip joint" (Griffin, *Youth* 74–76; Mellow 60–62; Villard and Nagel 216–19).)

Brumback reassured Oak Park. On the authority of an unnamed Italian officer, he reported that the felled Hemingway soon roused himself to carry a badly injured soldier on his back to safety and first aid—despite the ongoing action and despite himself being seriously hurt in both legs. Hemingway would claim not to remember. An Italian official told him about it the next day, adding that he would be recommended for a medal specifying bravery under fire (Lynn 81). (No independent evidence confirms that Hemingway carried a wounded soldier to safety, and the very real machine-gun bullets in the right knee and foot, in addition to the numerous flesh wounds, make his history in this version unlikely, albeit enduring.)

Grateful, relieved, Grace wrote, rejoicing that "in the eyes of humanity my boy is *every inch a man*. . . . You thought more of others than yourself and so will be marked forever as a *brave* man. God bless you, my darling, you are worthy to be Ernest Miller, named for great noble souls—your grandfather and grand uncle and their noble forefathers. . . . It's great to be the mother of a hero" (JFK Library).

On his birthday, July 21, Hemingway wrote home about his wounding, the newsman in him pointedly underscoring the "headline" fact: "I'm the first American wounded in Italy and I suppose the papers say something about it" (*Letters*, 1:118). Indeed, the *Kansas City Star* touted and neatly contextualized this news: "Ernest M. Hemingway, formerly a reporter for the *Star*, has been wounded while on ambulance duty with the Italian Army—the first casualty to any of the *Star*'s 132 former employees now fighting with the Allies" (Sanford 161–63; *Star*).

Where Hemingway was known, the press made much ado—often attributing to him heroic acts. Before he arrived in Italy, the high school *Trapeze* began printing continuous updates. Later the school paper credited him with assignment as a "special war correspondent" for the *Star*, his newspaper work continuing even while "serving as a lieutenant in the Italian Ambulance Corps." Many reading of his actions and reflections reacted personally to his descriptions and judgments. Michigan and St. Louis buddy Bill Smith, accepted into the marine air corps, wrote in early August, reinforcing Hemingway's oft-expressed feelings about those unwilling to fight: "Lord, they make me sick."

Faithful longtime Oak Park pal Lewis Clarahan wrote on July 30:

> I hope this reaches you before you recover from the bites of the flying pig. However I don't mean to imply that I don't want you to recover before you get it, unless you have good American nurses, the kind that make a person want to postpone getting well indefinitely. ($5 reward to the person who can make any sense out of that sentence.)
>
> Seriously tho, we are real proud of the first member of the Hiking Club to get wounded in action. I just read in the paper that you had been decorated. Congratulations. It was certainly a nervy thing to do—I only hope I will have that much nerve in such a place.

> I am in hopes of getting in the service by September. There is hardly a soul left in Oak Park that could go to war. I'll have to get in just for company.
>
> Don't feel obligated to write. I know what it is to work 17 hours a day.

The unintended irony of Clarahan's words regarding American nurses was unfolding in Milan even as he wrote and would prove powerful, indeed.

• • •

Unsurprisingly, Hemingway's reflecting on his "heroic" self quickly proved fertile. Writing home, he pondered his reputation for a "charmed life," having been "shelled by high explosives, shrapnel, and gas" and shot at by "trench mortars, snipers' machine guns, and . . . an aeroplane machine-gunning the lines," no one of which that day kept him from carrying out the wounded soldier (*Letters* 1:147). Mentally unaffected and ambulatory on crutches, this gregarious, high-energy, tale-telling persona soon became a favorite among medical staff (not least with the nurses) and uniformly among his few fellow wounded in the newly opened Red Cross hospital in Milan.

Following some extended time and space for both afterglow and serious reflection, still-recovering Hemingway directed a letter, on October 18, to his father particularly, albeit certainly affecting a proud mother as well. His bravado in a voice responsible, self-aware, implies a wisdom dearly purchased: no job, no salary (he suggests fifteen thousand a year) could bring him home now. Confident, he knows his role. Despite being physically unfit to fight, his conscience remains clear: ambulance driving, albeit dangerous, is necessary and certainly "no slacker's job"—unquestionably worth taking up again. Now an experienced veteran, he would even accept a second wounding because of the "satisfactory feeling" of being "beaten up in a good cause." That said, he opposes giving "special credit" to those wounded, personally claiming to care not a whit about public glory for himself—his sacrifices having been anchored in a simple patriotism.

Perspective proves critical. Hemingway's remarks turning unexpectedly to the home front, his bravado briefly risks excess, a slipping into "sound over sense," when he claims that the toughest wartime assignment actually devolves to those at home, particularly within the family circle. Earlier, *Oak Leaves* had printed Brumback's July 14 letter to the family recounting Hemingway's wounding, then, despite his own injuries, heroically assisting the Italian soldier. The *Oak Parker* also published those patriotic acts, but in its November 16 edition, it additionally emphasized Hemingway's "those at home" focus in the "go[ing] out in a blaze of light" reflections he sent to his parents on October 18: "The real heroes are the parents. Dying is a very simple thing. I've looked at death and really I know. If I should have died it would have been very easy for me. Quite the easiest thing I ever did. But the people at home do not realize that. They suffer a thousand times more. When a mother brings a son into the world she must know that some day the son will die, and the mother of a man that has died for his country should be the proudest woman in the world, and the happiest. And how much better to die in all the happy period of undisillusioned youth, to go out in a blaze of light, than to have your body worn out and old and the illusions shattered" (*Letters* 1:147).

Regardless, in the broader world, the *Kansas City Star* promptly reported the wounding of its former junior reporter: "Italy Honors E. M. Hemingway. Grade of First Lieutenant Given Man From the *Star* Abroad." In November, following the Armistice, the *Chicago Herald* printed Hemingway's letter describing his wounding and the soldier's rescue. In December, it wrote of his support for the Italian soldiers at the front, part of the final, winning effort to "settle the Austrians."

One may easily imagine Hemingway's Oak Park peers, and even persons older and younger than he who did not know him personally, impressed by his (albeit partially fabulist) narratives and by them moved to enlist or to make some other "commitment" to the war effort.

• • •

Despite such intensities, high seriousness varied dramatically in the texts of this accomplished tale-spinning Lardner imitator, not least when touching on the "woman question." On August 8—a month to the day following his wounding, Hemingway penned a "directive" query to Marcelline: "Why do you not dip the quill and sling me a screed yourself?" A lack of female correspondents constitutes both subject and theme: "Dear Ivory, call up on the telephone all my former sweet hearts! Tell them that the master woodsman, now known as The Heero of the Peehave, loves them with an undying love, coming to them my undying fealty and filial devotion. Tell them that I will return, God willing, and woo and perhaps wed them all. Inform them that it is only lack of interest that keeps me from writing them. Write me their replies. . . . Also call up Frances Coates and tell her that your brother is at Deaths door and that she will please, no excuses, write to him. Make her repeat the address after you so that she will have no alibi! Tell her I love her or any damn thing!" (*Letters* 1:128).

This voice perfectly intoning the playful journalist "Ernie" of his high school *Trapeze* days (and the older brother in Kansas City to his at-home siblings) ultimately centers on Frances Coates, Hemingway's earlier infatuation with her known to Marcelline. In truth, she may stand in here, quite fortuitously, not only as herself but for all others among his high school "sweet hearts." Coates did write Hemingway in early November, urging, "Please wallop 'em all for me—hard." She mentions the "wonderful write-ups you've been getting." He should be "immensely proud—if you're one-hundredth as proud as we are of you." Finally, "please go easy on . . . the attractive bits of French and Italian and English femininity roaming around loose" (JFK Library).

Regardless, by early fall, the girls of home were past history as much as the "master woodsman" merit badge mentioned to Marcelline—her brave brother now Hemingway, "the Hero of the Piave," and more. Coates, an attractive Oak Park young woman, at nineteen his exact contemporary, now paled with all others of her sex in the stark light of twenty-six-year-old Red Cross nurse Agnes von Kurowsky.

• • •

Agnes graduated from New York's respected Bellevue Nurses Training School in 1917. At Bellevue, all activity emphasized dedication and professionalism: its women uniformly ladies; *respectability* the governing criterion for any and all social interaction. With experience both as instructor and supervisor, Agnes volunteered for the Red Cross Nursing Service in January 1918. Recommendation materials describe her as attractive and self-possessed: "5′8″; 133 pounds," deep-brown hair (Reynolds, *First War* 189–91). Committed, dutiful, Agnes had adjusted well to Bellevue's training and conservative lifestyle. In July 1917, she recorded in her diary: "I've been practically 3 years without the least bit of sentiment or romance & very little attention." She did form an informal attachment to an older doctor—but four days at sea from New York en route to wartime service in Milan, she noted, "I'm afraid I'm forgetting 'Daddy' already" (Villard and Nagel 52).

Mutual attraction between the wounded, but rapidly recovering, Hemingway and nurse Agnes was in place by late August (dinner in town alone, August 31; giving him her "home ring" September 7). Letters chart an increasing emotional involvement, but physical longing effects only stolen kissing and hugging. Moreover, Agnes professed love and referred to herself periodically as "Your Missis," but also, and importantly, she retained a continuing awareness of his youth—still in his teens—addressing him as "Mr. Kid," "Dear Boy." Regardless, at the end of September, he then relaxing in Stresa, she repeatedly saluted him possessively: "Kid, my kid," "My dear boy," routinely signing herself, "'Yours til the war ends' (from love letters of a rookie) Aggie." Salutations include: "Oh—Brushwood Boy-o'-mine"; "Mister Kid"; and a seemingly over-the-top series of concluding epithets: "Your poco idiot—(but yet—yours—so you can't kick); Von—(otherwise known as Ag—Aggie—Agony—Artless—Curiosity—Vonny Agnes—Kid—Mrs. Kid and a few others)" (Villard and Nagel 92–97).

The relationship between nurse and patient prospering thus, on November 23, Marcelline again received current "woman-question" news, concluding with both effusion and direction: "Really Kid I'm immensely older . . . you wouldn't know me. I mean to look at or talk to. . . . Always I've wondered what it would be like to really meet the girl you will really love always and now I know."

Marcelline is directed to say nothing to their parents. Hemingway's plan: to marry Agnes in two years. Should their parents disapprove of Agnes or this future, he will cease visiting home after the marriage (Sanford 299–300).

This high plain once achieved could *not* be held.

• • •

Following the November Armistice, Hemingway sailed home to America aboard the *Giuseppe Verdi* in January 1919, expecting Agnes to follow in a few months. Separated but professing love, even hoping he will send her copies of his stories—Hemingway now determined to be a writer—Agnes wrote as the new year dawned, her tone and content complex: "You are to me a wonderful boy, and when you add on a few years and some dignity and calm, you'll be very much worthwhile" (January 1, 1919). Before long, however, both content and tone sharpened—she was no longer eager to get home and blithely remarking about being teased regarding her unmistakable "fondness for Italian officers." Such ideas continued, only underscoring those touching her plans for future travel and work, from Torre di Mosta in February, for example: "fonder every day of life in furrin' parts." A fortune teller having predicted that she is “going to travel a lot,” she queried her young “intended,” who was in the American Midwest struggling with his family, his early writing, the future: “How do you like the idea?” (February 5, 1919). Agnes could go to Rome “for a year” with fellow nurse Cavenaugh, but she “prefers the Balkans” (February 15, 1919).

March opening, she directed, personally and ominously, that he “shouldn’t write so often”; she is not unhappy where she is—in fact, having “the time of my life and never lack for excitement; . . . learning to smoke and gamble . . . not at all the perfect being you think I am. But, as I am, I always was, only it’s just beginning to creep out. I’m feeling very [wicked] tonight, so goodnight, Kid, & don’t do anything rash, but have a good time. Afft, Aggie” (March 1, 1919).

March 7, 1919: Closure.

“Ernie, dear boy” opens her “Dear John” letter. She admits that she will “hurt” Hemingway here but not “permanently”:

> For quite a while before you left, I was trying to convince myself it was a real love-affair, because, we always seemed to disagree, & then arguments always wore me out so that I finally gave in to keep you from doing something desperate.
>
> Now, after a couple of months away from you, I know that I am still very fond of you, but, it is more as a mother than as a sweetheart. It’s alright to say I’m a Kid, but I’m not, & I’m getting less & less so every day.
>
> So, Kid (still Kid to me, & always will be) can you forgive me some day for unwittingly deceiving you? You know I’m not really bad, & don’t mean to do wrong, & now I realize it was my fault in the beginning that you cared for me, & regret it from the bottom of my heart. But, I am now & always will be too old, & that’s the truth, & I can’t get away from the fact that you’re just a boy—a kid.
>
> I somehow feel that some day I’ll have reason to be proud of you, but, dear boy, I can’t wait for that day, & it is wrong to hurry a career.
>
> I tried hard to make you understand a bit of what I was thinking on that trip from Padua to Milan, but, you acted like a spoiled child,

& I couldn't keep on hurting you. Now, I only have the courage because I'm far away.

Then—& believe me when I say this is sudden for me, too—I expect to be married soon [to Domenico Caracciolo, an Arditi artillery lieutenant from Naples and heir to an Italian dukedom]. And I hope & pray that after you have thought things out, you'll be able to forgive me & start a wonderful career and show what a man you really are.

Ever admiringly & fondly,
Your friend, Aggie

(Villard and Nagel 163–64)

Hemingway wrote to friend and confidant Bill Horne on March 30: "Oh, Bill, I can't kid about it and I can't be bitter because I'm just smashed by it. . . . I've loved Ag. She's been my ideal. . . . I forgot all about religion and everything else because I had Ag to worship" (*Letters* 1:177). In a follow-up letter to Horne on July 2, Hemingway reported closure via a successful process of cauterization: "'Ag' doesn't recall any image to my mind at all" (1:195).

• • •

Agnes von Kurowsky cannot accurately be described as *frivolous, degenerate, fickle,* or *really bad*—at various times her own self-descriptors. As James Nagel demonstrates throughout his *Hemingway in Love and War,* the overriding concerns of Agnes's diary and letters, far surpassing references to romance, are discovery of her own identity, her personal and professional growth, and future prospects within her profession. Like many educated middle-class women in these years, Agnes sought for herself a professional career—at least for a time. Her Bellevue background and work in Italy suggested conscientious commitment to nursing as a profession. Following the war, she devoted eleven years to the Red Cross in Hungary, Romania, and Haiti. Taken thus broadly, Ernest Hemingway finally played but a part in her personal history.

Agnes sent Ernest one final letter. Dated December 22, 1922, she congratulated him on his marriage and urged him to "think of what an antique I am at the present." He never mentioned her to Hadley, nor Pauline, nor others in his Paris years, though hers is an overt presence in Hemingway's developing art: Ag in chapter 10 of *in our time*, 1924; similarly, Ag, now Luz, in "A Very Short Story" of *In Our Time*, 1925; partially, yet recognizably, in Catherine of *A Farewell to Arms*, 1929; and finally, prominently, albeit briefly, in one of the Paris memory vignettes of "The Snows of Kilimanjaro," 1936.

• • •

Hemingway's personal exposures to war—his attending to the bodies of women killed in the munitions factory explosion; his wounding by shell shrapnel—failed to create that sensitive awareness of war's horror and waste prominent in his writing beginning the next decade. Initially, his original witness and injuries served principally as had the Kansas City journalism—to refine and proclaim his consciously developing persona as an experienced, sophisticated, accomplished adult. Luck helped. He had been where most had not, arguably proving himself as most would not. Yet these details prompted no serious questions or deep reflection. Acclaim for patriotism and decoration for bravery simply strengthened Hemingway's confidence and charisma.

Over a fast-paced eighteen months, roughly 550 days—from October 1917, when he arrived in Kansas City, to mid-March 1919, when he understood that his relationship with Agnes had become for him simply biographical history—a still teenaged Ernest Hemingway partially mastered a steep learning curve revealing how the world thought and acted. He had not yet located his place in that world, but he was discovering the power in words—as journalism, as fiction—to present himself compellingly and, importantly, as he wished others to see him.

Loosed from Oak Park, he began to portray himself to those left behind as an experienced, sophisticated, successful adult—in Kansas City an accomplished newspaperman, virtually an equal among *Star* professionals. In Italy, his wounding effected the good fortune of being decorated and lionized, fleshing out this persona further. His real-world experience exceeded most other men's: the elemental drama of war, albeit anchored in fortuitous, unexamined sacrifice, produced a persona possessing unquestioned heroism—and soon impatiently readying to go "public."

Back in Oak Park in 1919, despite vociferously protesting a lack of privacy, Hemingway capitalized on his celebrity status, marked not least by his earning $172 in speaking fees. He consciously honed reality, *verbally* shaping actual personal experience into derring-do, imaging a mature, sophisticated adult. In fact, this developing "persona" constituted the premier product of his experiences. He had received Agnes's "break-up" letter on March 13. Losing Agnes was bitter, but his detailed, carefully wrought public guise reduced and concealed the pain. The following week, he made his second dramatic speaking appearance at Oak Park and River Forest High School, exuding strength and confidence.

Popular and in demand, he consistently proffered fictional wartime narratives as his truthful, personal, on-scene reporting. He stretched reality's boundaries in that sophisticated, worldly-wise witness he had been cultivating since early Kansas City reporting. He appeared in interviews with the *Oak Parker* and other local press outlets; in adult study groups (including Grace's favorite, the Nineteenth-Century Club) and, less formally, in women's and church societies; and, several times, in high school rallies. Perhaps the grandest moments occurred early on (February 16) in a singularly formal "recognition and appreciation" evening, involving medals and a citation, presented by the Italian government at his home—the large gathering filling Grace's music studio (Baker, *Life* 57, 574; Griffin, *Youth* 104). Twenty years of age, a still youthful Ernie had proven himself: Ernest Hemingway, a young man of consequence—wounded *and* decorated in the Great War.

Going forward: the need to "get away," to establish "a change of scene." Hemingway's resolve for summer and fall 1919: therapeutic escape to northern Michigan, "the last good country," there to write—these crafted *fictional words* to become the former journalist's first published stories.

• • •

In Petoskey, Michigan, May–December 1919, Hemingway did write stories, particularly eyeing the *Saturday Evening Post.* Unfortunately, his reimaginings of Kansas City, Milan, and Chicago proved unpublishable. Moving to Horton Bay characters, although unsuccessful, suggested promise, particularly in his 250-word vignette "Pauline Snow": A beautiful young girl raised by a trusting older couple is unprotected from Art Simons, whose "thick blunt fingers" touch her when they talk. Her innocence surfaces one sunset: "Don't you think that's awfully pretty, Art?" Her future unfolds in his response: "We didn't come here to talk about sunsets, kiddo!" Albeit Hemingway's technique is not yet fully under control, action and setting, realistic dialogue, and understated irony here anticipate the narratives of *In Our Time* (1925)—specifically, as in this singular story, which he took to Paris in December 1921 and transformed into "Up in Michigan" by February 1922.

In time present, the lack of published success writing fiction in Michigan over the summer and fall of 1919 did not interrupt Hemingway's tale-telling war adventures. In Petoskey, his several neatly nuanced and rehearsed oral warrior narratives much impressed well-connected Canadian Mrs. Ralph Connable. Through the auspices of her husband, head of the F. W. Woolworth chain in Canada, she indirectly effected Hemingway's return to journalism. Initially, Hemingway was hired as "companion" in Toronto to the couple's partially paralyzed teenaged son; through Ralph Sr., this connection led to assignments and positions with the *Toronto Star Weekly* and the *Star,* February 1920–January 1924. Ernest Hemingway—initially, freelance reporter, then roaming European correspondent, even briefly, staff writer—published 191 pieces.

# 3

There's no one thing that is true. They're all true.

—*For Whom the Bell Tolls*

## Paris, 1920s

### THE JOURNALIST TURNS TO FICTION, THEN NONFICTION

Arriving in Toronto, January 1920, Ernest Hemingway moved into the luxurious Ralph Connable residence as companion to nineteen-year-old, Ralph Jr., while other family members vacationed in warmer climes. The younger Ralph was partially disabled (underdeveloped right hand and limb, effecting a general withdrawal and apathy). Their closeness in age suggested that the older, athletic, Hemingway might prove an excellent companion and role model for the younger man. Continuing a favorite of Mrs. Connable, who had initiated this now broadening relationship with the family, Hemingway stayed on through May. He particularly enjoyed the young man's sister, Dorothy. At twenty-six, this short, dark-eyed brunette possessed multiple charms: intelligence (she was an avid reader); experience (in war with the Red Cross in 1918, she helped establish a YMCA for the Sixth Division, then remained in Germany aiding the occupation army). Not least, she proved an able sportswoman. Dorothy and friends shared their outdoor enthusiasms with Hemingway, his background predisposing him to relish the tobogganing, skiing, and snowshoeing (Burrill 27–37).

Another bond of sorts existed with Ralph Sr., also a high energy sportsman and inveterate prankster among family and friends. More importantly, he assisted Hemingway in securing freelance work for the *Toronto Star Weekly* beginning in February. Submissions passed for approval through the hands of editor-in-chief J. Herbert Cranston. At a half-cent per word initially, Hemingway worked up to five dollars per article. He wrote primarily for the *Weekly,* thirty-three pieces through December 1921, then also for the *Daily Star.* As European correspondent based in Paris, from February 1922 through August 1923, he produced seventy-eight articles for the *Star,* seventeen for the *Star Weekly.*

• • •

In Toronto, Hemingway's *Weekly* fare emphasized human interest magazine features: entertainment, social sightings, and offhand "authoritative" observations—a genuinely surface "reporting." If each piece expressed a Canadian viewpoint, Cranston exerted little content control.

Hemingway's *Weekly* back pages texts constituted a broad-stroke miscellany. A wry, omniscient narrative voice sometimes memorialized, sometimes deconstructed, the contemporary human comedy—representative activities, fashion crazes, popular slang. Offered free choice of material, he fused journalism and fiction while characterizing the times. Subjects ranged among personal favorites: fishing, camping, eating, money, travel, politics, war. Subheadings centered perspective: "How to Be Popular in Peace Though a Slacker in War"; "Toronto Women Who Went to Prize Fight Applauded the Rough Stuff"; "Why Not Trade Other Public Entertainers among the Nations as the Big Leagues Do Baseball Players?" "The Wild West Is Now in Chicago."

*Tone* keyed details. Hemingway's second piece, "A Free Shave" (March 6, 1920), captured *one* early voice. Following overt allusion to the United States as the "land of the free and the home of the brave," Hemingway wryly addressed contemporary Canada: "The true home of the free and the brave is the barber college," where a free shave may require "the cold, naked valor of the man who walks clear-eyed to death." Answering why his hand was extraordinarily bandaged, the apprentice barber explained: "Darn near sliced my thumb off with a razor this morning."

Such details establish the narrative's ultimately lighthearted purpose—an after-the-actual-fact emotional reflection: "The shave wasn't so bad. Scientists say that hanging is really a very pleasant death. The pressure of the rope on the nerves and arteries of the neck produces a sort of anesthesia. It is waiting to be hanged that bothers a man." This "profound" reflection regarding contemporary "free post-war social services" is matched here by the narrator's concluding advice. Should one wish to claim the whole of available free services—board, room, and medical attention: "Walk up to the biggest policemen you can find and hit him in the face." Of course, the resulting free, state-sponsored largesse may well "depend on the size of the policeman."

Somewhat more seriously, Hemingway's expertise regarding the outdoors centered primers on camping, fishing, boating: "When You Camp Out, Do It Right"; "Trout Fishing," "Trout Fishing Hints," and "The Best Rainbow Trout Fishing"; even, for November 20, 1920, on indoor fishing, "Bigger Trout are taken around the tables in King Street cafeterias than win the prizes offered by the sporting magazines."

Firsthand knowledge and experience characterized these semi-instructive essays, details highlighting contemporary wordplay (including slang) and featuring representative "character" types. As their subtitles suggest, these entertaining sketches emphasized "color," visually unpacking, from varying angles, everyday realities: "Lieutenants' Mustaches the Only Permanent Thing We Got"; "Keeping Up with the Joneses, the Tragedy of the Other Half." For readers, the observing and the sharing effect camaraderie—this feeling constituting the principal interaction. From February through June 1920, Hemingway produced nineteen such *Weekly* visuals, vignettes wry or mildly satirical, most simply entertaining—any actually "enlightening" commentary purely fortuitous.

• • •

Hemingway's major development as a journalist came more directly with the *Daily Star*, especially from Paris after February 1922. Nevertheless, maturing intelligence and sensibility did appear among his later *Weekly* pieces and did reflect growing sophistication—in content, style, and purpose. Two widely disparate examples appeared nineteen months apart: "Black Novel—a Storm Center" (March 25, 1922); later Hemingway's detailing his initial exposure and emotional engagement with Spanish *torero*, in two consecutive *Weekly* articles, "Bullfighting a Tragedy" and "Pamplona in July" (October 20 and 27, 1923).

"Black Novel" centers on *Batouala*, by African author René Maran, awarded the Goncourt Academy Prize for "best novel of the year by a young writer"—one powerfully indicting French imperialism in Africa. The reader "gets a picture of a native village seen by the big-whited eyes, felt by the pink palms, and the broad, flat, naked feet of the African native himself. You smell the smells of the village, you eat its food, you see the white man as the black man sees him, and after you have lived in the village, you die there. That is all there is to the story, but when you have read it, you have seen Batouala and that makes it a great novel: Batouala old and with stiff joints of his age, cruelly torn by the leopard that his spear missed, lying on the earth floor . . . feverish and thirsty, dying while his mangy dog licks his wounds. And while he lies there, you feel the thirst and the fever and the rough, moist tongue of the dog." Incipient fiction writer Hemingway credited this volume's prize-winning value to its powerfully memorializing intellectual and emotional content in sensuous detail.

Similarly, in "Bullfighting a Tragedy," Hemingway captured the dramatic emotional response characteristic of first experiencing *la corrida*. In visual and visceral detail, he recorded the physical moments of the Spanish bullfight, unwittingly capturing his own earliest emotions regarding what would become a lifelong obsession, culminating as subject and theme in his final published writing, "The Endless Summer," *Life*, September 1960.

Here, at the beginning for the *Star Weekly:*

> Then ducking his head . . . a bull came out into the arena. He came out all in a rush, big, black and white, weighing over a ton, and moving with a soft gallop. . . . The sun seemed to dazzle him for an instant. He stood as though he were frozen, his great crest of muscle up, firmly planted, his eyes looking around, his horns pointed forward, black and white and sharp as porcupine quills. Then he charged. As he charged, I suddenly saw what bullfighting is all about.
>
> For the bull was absolutely unbelievable. He seemed like some great prehistoric animal, absolutely deadly and absolutely vicious. And he was silent. He charged silently and with a soft, galloping rush. When he turned, he turned on his four feet like a cat. When he charged the first thing that caught his eye was the picador on one of the wretched horses. The picador dug his spurs into the horse and they galloped away. The bull came on his rush, refused to be shaken off and in full gallop crashed into the animal from the side, ignored the horse, drove one of his horns high into the thigh of the picador, and tore him, saddle and all, off the horse's back. (October 20, 1923)

• • •

Hemingway's time with the Connables ended, he returned to Oak Park in mid-May 1920, thence to Michigan for a summer further distancing himself (ultimately more than he intended), both intellectually and emotionally, from his parents.

He was joined in Horton Bay for a time by Chicagoans Bill Horne and Charles Hopkins and Kansas City (also Michigan) friends Bill and Kate Smith and Ted Brumback. These adult visitors, reduced to Brumback by July 21, Hemingway's twenty-first birthday, engaged in various festive doings. One midnight these included careless unchaperoned, albeit innocent, swimming and fireside behavior with his young sisters, Ursula and Sunny, and their neighbor's (Loomises) daughters, resulting in mother Grace expelling both men from the summer cottage. Explicitly in a lengthy letter to Hemingway, she detailed among his known excesses and immaturity: "your lazy loafing and pleasure seeking, borrowing with no thought of returning, spending lavishly and wastefully on luxuries for yourself . . . neglecting your duties to God and your savior Jesus Christ" (Baker, *Ernest Hemingway* 72). More than regretful, Hemingway was resentful.

• • •

In the fall, living with Bill Horne in Chicago, Hemingway continued drafting attempts at publishable fiction. In October, still writing intermittently for the *Weekly*, he signed on as writer-editor for the *Cooperative Commonwealth* (a magazine publication of the socialist Cooperative Society of America); essentially a mouthpiece for an illegal (fraudulent) enterprise, this publication ceased in December 1921.

During this Chicago period, Kate and Bill Smith introduced Hemingway to (and within the year, he became engaged to) St. Louis friend Hadley Richardson. Twenty-eight, attractive, and a talented pianist, she was seven years his senior. Living then with Kate, Bill, and their brother Y.K. also advanced Hemingway's fledgling literary prospects. Through them, he met Sherwood Anderson. The latter's "letters of introduction" would prove singularly key professionally, following Hemingway's marriage to Hadley—in Horton Bay, Michigan, September 3, 1921—and the couple's arrival in Paris in January 1922.

In October 1921, Hemingway had accepted, beginning January 1922, a stringer position in Europe, based in Paris, for the *Toronto Daily Star:* seventy-five dollars a week, plus expenses when on assignment; otherwise, freelance rates—a penny per word. For John Bone, managing editor, Hemingway became the initial *Star* roving European correspondent. The first of his seventy-eight articles from abroad appeared on February 4, 1922, and addressed the developing postwar political setting: "Poincaré's Folly: France Now in Hands of Old Professionals."

• • •

Reporting from Paris, Hemingway sharpened both his sensibilities and his focus. He witnessed the ethical chaos prefigured in Yeats's "Second Coming" (1919): "Things fall apart; the center cannot hold; / Mere anarchy is loosed upon the world." Echoing Yeats in Paris were writers and journalists Hemingway had read in postwar Chicago—Sherwood Anderson, Theodore Dreiser, Robert Frost, Ringgold Lardner, Vachel Lindsay, Edgar Lee Masters, Carl Sandburg.

In February 1922, apart from their living quarters, Hemingway rented a sixth-floor walk-up room solely for his writing—mornings, while accomplished musician Hadley played her piano in their fourth-floor walk-up apartment at 74 Rue du Cardinal Lemoine, a working-class neighborhood. Beginning with arranged introductions, including with the indispensable Shakespeare and Company bookstore owner, Sylvia Beach, Hemingway began establishing relationships with contemporary literati—peers-teachers-patrons: Morley Callaghan, John Dos Passos, Scott Fitzgerald, Ford Madox Ford, James Joyce, Harold Loeb, Ezra Pound, Gertrude Stein, Edmund Wilson.

Using Anderson's introductory letters, he met Stein and, through her, Joyce and Pound. The latter soon forwarded six of Hemingway's Chicago poems to the *Dial.* (They were declined.) Other important contacts, some occasioned by his *Star* assignments, followed: publishers, correspondents, journalists—Bill Bird (owner, Three Mountains Press), Max Eastman, Ford Madox Ford (*English Review*), Guy Hickok (Paris bureau chief, *Brooklyn Eagle*), Robert McAlmon (editor-publisher, Contact Editions), Paul Scott Mower, Edward O'Brien (editor, *Best Short Stories,* an annual), George Seldes, Lincoln Steffens.

*Star* reporter Hemingway, covering the International Economic

Conference in Genoa over three weeks in April 1922, forwarded fifteen articles. From Constantinople after September 25, he reported on the Greco-Turkish war, particularly his witnessing the Greek retreat into Thrace and Macedonia in October 1922. He memorialized this event in three articles in October and November: "Christians Leave Thrace to Turks"; "A Silent, Ghastly Procession Wends Way from Thrace"; "Refugee Procession Is Scene of Horror." Later in November 1922, Hemingway covered the peace conference in Lausanne. On the move in Germany during March 1923, he sent the *Star* ten articles from the Ruhr valley describing French and Belgian occupation. (A misstep, and not a singular instance in this period, he was reprimanded for using a pseudonym to share his *Star* data and texts with Hearst's International News Services.)

Postwar conference coverage, particularly appearances and actions by England's Lloyd George, France's Clemenceau, Russia's Tchitcherin, and most seriously, Italy's Mussolini darkened his vision. Mussolini prompted in Hemingway both rational and emotional judgments and feelings. Early examples appeared in two pieces, datelined Milan, both appearing June 24, 1922: "Fascisti Party Now Half-Million Strong" and "Pot-Shot Patriots Unpopular in Italy," the first in the *Weekly*, the second in the *Star*. In the latter, he described the Fascisti Party as "black-shirted, knife-carrying, club-swinging, quick-stepping, nineteen-year-old pot-shot patriots." After Mussolini became premier on October 31, 1922, Hemingway continued to mock what he genuinely feared—"Mussolini: Europe's Prize Bluffer, More like Bottomley than Napoleon" (January 27, 1923). A decade later, Mussolini still haunted the prescient Hemingway: "France is a country and also Great Britain . . . but Italy is a man, Mussolini. . . . A man . . . rules until he gets into economic trouble; he tries to get out of this trouble by war" (*Esquire*, September 1935).

Yeats's "Second Coming" describing a general postwar ethical collapse suggests the evolving and sharpening awareness and judgment in the formerly patriotic (as wounded noncombatant) Hemingway. After April 1922, his *Toronto Star* pieces—recording witness of postwar conferences and limited group interview interactions with world leaders—constituted Hemingway's professional publication success in the half-decade following his wounding. These experiences, the journalism they inspired, reshaped his perspective—it was no longer personalized nor optimistic.

• • •

*Star* reporting required much "business" travel. From the outset, both Ernest and Hadley proved venturesome wanderers. They ranged widely—by train, on foot—in Switzerland, France, Germany, Italy, and Spain (hiking together and he, principally, hunting, fishing, skiing). Walking expeditions proved as various as their settings: from Lake Geneva and the Swiss Alps to Fossalta (site of his war wounding), Rapallo (Pound's residence), and the Black Forest. Enthusiasts at Paris racetracks, both Hemingways also soon became regular passionate observers of that singular, crowd-involved Spanish spectacle—*torero.* Beginning in summer 1923, following his bullfight experience at San Fermin in July, memorialized in the *Weekly* in October, bullfight study (its formal history) and attendance quickly became "necessary," annually in outings centered in the Fiesta de San Fermin in Pamplona but also in Madrid, Seville, Ronda, Granada.

Throughout his personal travels—sandwiched among both newspaper reporting and *torero*—Hemingway also began seriously to focus on drafting publishable creative texts.

• • •

A first major step in the fall of 1922: Hemingway broached with managing editor John Bone his returning to Toronto as full-time salaried reporter. He proposed late 1923, consciously planning a larger career shift: toward imaginative writing, specifically, publishable fiction. Then a seriously negative note. On December 2, Hadley, traveling to Lausanne to join Ernest covering the peace conference, had a suitcase stolen in the Gare de Lyons train station. The contents: Hemingway's earliest in-progress fiction manuscripts.

At this time, he had completed two of three stories for Robert McAlmon's Contact Press—"Up in Michigan" (critiqued by Stein) and "My Old Man." Additionally, Edward O'Brien had persuaded Hemingway to allow him to publish "My Old Man" in his *Best Short Stories* annual for 1923. A third story, "Out of Season," soon completed, McAlmon published Hemingway's first book, *Three Stories and Ten Poems,* 300 copies, in August 1923. Also, in 1923, the *Little Review* published six "snap-shop" vignettes titled "In Our Time." With this vignette progress completed at eighteen sketches, Bird's Three Mountains Press published the collection as *in our time,* 170 copies, in March 1924.

• • •

McAlmon had welcomed Hemingway's ten poems to complete the slender volume *Three Stories and Ten Poems.* Hemingway's serious efforts with poetry actually proved brief and uncomplicated. As early as February 1922, Pound submitted several pieces from Hemingway's Chicago days to *The Dial;* they were rejected. A year later, in January 1923, Harriet Monroe's *Poetry: A Magazine of Verse* (Chicago) published six poems as "Wanderings." Generally speaking, while Hemingway's prose soon appeared sporadically among the little magazines in Europe and America—*Little Review, Poetry, The Exile, the transatlantic review, This Quarter, transition,* the *Double Dealer,* and *Der Querschnitt*—only *Der Querschnitt* accepted him as a serious poet.

Aspiring writer Hemingway's poetic self and intentions in the 1920s reflect his associations with Stein and Pound, the Paris poems serving essentially as "stylistic exercises and vehicles for quick satire" (Gerogiannis, *Complete Poems* xv). Regarding *Three Stories and Ten Poems,* Edmund Wilson wrote: "Mr. Hemingway's poems are not particularly important, but his prose is of the first distinction," while Ford Madox Ford's *transatlantic review* ignored the poems altogether: "a dismissal indicating to Hemingway that they had served their purpose—as fillers for his first book. From then on he wrote only satirical verse for the little magazines and a personal brand of poetry that was not meant for publication at all" (xv).

• • •

Hadley now pregnant and Hemingway offered the reporter position he had planned for, the couple sailed to Canada, arriving September 4, 1923. Hemingway's work in Europe was known and highly respected, and his Toronto return had been officially anticipated in the paper under John Bone's well-intentioned but much-exaggerated praise for Hemingway's foreign correspondent breadth and history. An official blurb "trumpeted his exploits as a foreign correspondent, his language mastery, his service with both French and Italian forces, 'even wounds and decorations'" (Burrill 154).

Beginning his *Daily Star* reporter work on September 10, Hemingway began immediately to regret his decision to return. After checking the assignment ledger the first morning, "he whirled and stomped out of the office, having just begun to feel what was commonly acknowledged as 'the Hindmarsh treatment.'" Canadian novelist Morley Callaghan, whom Hemingway came to know well later in Paris, was then a part-time *Star* cub reporter. He checked the ledger on Hemingway's first day and was shocked: "Five inconsequential jobs such as I might be asked to do myself! . . . They were piddling. Just junk assignments" (154). Indeed, going forward in their brief relationship, *Star* assistant managing editor Harry Hindmarsh at the beginning, but for reasons not fully clear, disliked Hemingway and limited his reporting to "cub" subjects and out-of-town events—with which he often found fault.

Hadley delivered John Hadley Nicanor "Bumby" Hemingway on October 10, 1923, while Ernest was away on assignment. Immediately following this "last straw," Hemingway contacted Sylvia Beach to locate a Paris apartment—they would now return there as a family of three.

After publishing *Three Stories and Ten Poems* in the summer of1923 and having arranged publication of *in our time* for early 1924, Hemingway, fledgling author, left Europe for Toronto and the *Star.* Following his resignation, effective December 26, the Hemingways returned to Paris in January 1924.

• • •

Journalism would total roughly a third of Hemingway's published work. At this point, he willingly paused the nonfiction. He began crafting an altogether new writing, a fictional prose that brought him success and, soon, worldwide renown. His initial resolve: fiction, with an emphasis on short stories.

After six months of writing no fiction, he resumed in February 1924—working in congenial Paris cafés on stories, including "The Doctor and Doctor's Wife," "Cross-Country Snow," "Soldier's Home," and "Mr. and Mrs. Elliott." He began work with Ford Madox Ford as unpaid assistant editor of *the transatlantic review,* in which, in April, "Indian Camp" appeared, even as Bird's Three Mountains Press *in our time* showed up in Sylvia Beach's bookstore.

Then, for Hemingway, annus mirabilis 1925–26 changed everything.

*Professional relationships* began: Fitzgerald, Perkins, the House of Scribner; and they ended: Anderson, Boni and Liveright.

*Personal relationships* became strained—increasingly with family in Oak Park: Hemingway's father returned copies of *Three Stories and Ten Poems* over the sexual explicitness of "Up in Michigan," and his mother expressed public disgust over action and character by all principals in *The Sun Also Rises;* soon, in Paris, growing and warranted mistrust developed in wife Hadley vis-à-vis attractive, energetic Pauline Pfeiffer, Paris editor of *Vogue.*

*Public readership* of his soon five fiction volumes began and grew steadily, initiating both critical renown and financial success. By 1930, Hemingway's major work—*In Our Time,* 1925; *The Torrents of Spring,* 1926; *The Sun Also Rises,* 1926; *Men Without*

*Women*, 1927; *A Farewell to Arms* (1929); and *In Our Time*, reissued with an introductory vignette in 1930, appeared under the Scribner aegis.

At Scribner, Hemingway joined distinguished contemporaries (and a respected traditional firm, then experiencing, by design, a new direction from its senior editor, Maxwell Perkins—a direction particularly realized in its best-selling, short fiction writer, Scott Fitzgerald).

At this time, New York publishers boasted numerous successful fictionists—Zane Grey, Sinclair Lewis, Booth Tarkington, Edna Ferber—and a vigorous younger community of writers-publishers was developing, some successfully competing among senior houses like Charles Scribner's Sons. In 1925, both variety and distinction proved abundant—*Dark Laughter; The Professor's House; Manhattan Transfer; An American Tragedy; So Big* (Pulitzer 1925); *The Great Gatsby; Arrowsmith* (Pulitzer 1926).

Hemingway belonged? He could compete?

• • •

In 1925, Sherwood Anderson helped place *In Our Time* with his publisher, Boni and Liveright. Unfortunately, a tepid advertising campaign irritated Hemingway: in its three ads, taken together, no discernible effort was made to distinguish the bookseller from the book buyer, to create a campaign tailored to this new author, or to address a recognizable audience. Further, untrue was Liveright's claim for the *In Our Time* collection: "tells utterly *new* stories in a new way with a new simplicity"; all but four of the fifteen stories had been previously published.

A chance meeting in Paris with Fitzgerald that spring—during *Gatsby*'s extravagant early popularity—followed by his intense personal lobbying convinced Hemingway to change his publisher to Scribner. The argument: Scribner meant manuscript control by gifted senior editor Maxwell Perkins *and*, potentially, one's stories appearing, even one's novels serialized, in the highly regarded *Scribner's Magazine.* Fitzgerald would intercede.

Encouraged by Fitzgerald and by his own reading of *in our time,* Perkins approached Hemingway, only to discover that Liveright had first option on his future work. Attracted to Scribner following this expression of genuine interest by Fitzgerald and Perkins, a determined Hemingway—in a few short weeks preceding the Christmas holidays in 1925—drafted *The Torrents of Spring,* a twenty-eight-thousand-word satire of Anderson's style, especially in *Dark Laughter.* Liveright could not publish this "elaborate and extremely witty parody . . . of Sherwood Anderson in particular" (*NYTBR,* June 27, 1926), of a Boni and Liveright principal author, a fact soon freeing Hemingway from any contractual obligations, allowing him to join Scribner.

Hemingway and Scribner would become a lifelong team beginning in May 1926 with *The Torrents of Spring*—published quickly, essentially without editorial changes. It stabilized in the marketplace as a "rollicking satire," and Scribner reprinted it in 1926, 1928, and twice in 1930. Most important, the prize manuscript Perkins (and Fitzgerald) had sought—*The Sun Also Rises*—appeared from Scribner in October 1926. The novel's success for both publisher and author was variously demonstrable: favorable reviews and, not least, its numbers: ten printings the first year, fourteen overall—and sales of 36,140 copies (Trogdon 259–60). Less attractive in this affair, his treatment of Anderson revealed another side of Hemingway's character.

• • •

Beginning with the *Star* pieces, particularly later coverage of the postwar Genoa and Lausanne conferences, Hemingway's publication history and experience in the half-decade following his wounding significantly reconfigured his personal perspective, his vision of the war and its aftermath increasingly according with Yeats's.

His maturing view produced a fictional style (e.g., in the eighteen *in our time* vignettes from 1924) reflecting his journalism: simple sentences relatively free of adjectives and adverbs and of explicit authorial moralizing. The reader must determine meaning in these early Yeats-influenced narratives exposing a world irrational and violent—at base characterized by the failure of love, often of simple communication, and captured as/in "pointillistic glimpses of violence" (cover of Cohn, *Hemingway's Laboratory*). Clarity regarding the war and civilian life postwar sharpened across *In Our Time,* 1925; *The Sun Also Rises,* 1926; *Men Without Women,* 1927; and *A Farewell to Arms,* 1929. Criticism has long considered as major subject and theme in this early Hemingway fiction man's "insensitivity," even "inhumanity," regarding his fellows.

Important today, because often overlooked in earlier critical scrutinizing of "man's" plight in these linked stories, was Hemingway's early focus and achievement centered in contemporary female characters. Rhetorically, his texts inscribe a remarkably explicit vision emphasizing women, many "wounded" by war and/or other contemporary verbal and physical violences: collectively with *In Our Time* and *Men Without Women;* more obliquely in *The Sun Also Rises;* again directly in *A Farewell to Arms.*

• • •

The thirty *In Our Time* (1925) narratives—fifteen vignettes, fifteen stories—individuate, often freeze-frame, forty-plus female characters, the adults both with and without children. Many facing wartime stresses remain nameless, even wordless. In the three *In Our Time* vignettes in which women appear, none speaks: in "Chapter II," a young woman goes into labor in an overloaded wagon amid the chaos of wartime mass evacuation; in "Chapter VI," a young girl's iron bedstead hangs twisted and exposed from her bedroom, a formerly safe domestic space now destroyed by war; and in "Chapter VII," a coward soldier, with a nameless, state-sponsored prostitute in hand, flees war's terror.

The explicit, aptly titled second stories volume, *Men Without Women* (1927), focuses on adult women, its contemporary issues generalizable beyond war, its specific focus destructive male-female miscommunication: young, pregnant Jig confronts her irresponsible lover ("Hills Like White Elephants"); a pending, heartbreaking, albeit unmentioned, divorce saddens a mature American wife and no less her not-insensitive husband ("A Canary for One").

Among the *In Our Time* narratives, the thematically paired "A Very Short Story" and "Soldier's Home" further establish Hemingway's broad representation of women in wartime or affected by war, here, pointedly, at home, the focus specifically on the domestic.

No character speaks in the retrospective "A Very Short Story." In Italy, a wounded soldier and nurse pray and plan marriage. Home in Chicago, he concentrates on work—pursuing *their* future. Unexpectedly, she writes: theirs was just a boy-girl love. She is now engaged to an *Arditi* major. Devastated, the soldier in a taxicab with a nameless salesgirl contracts gonorrhea. Important, also, the nurse's planned future disintegrates: "The major did not marry her in the spring . . . or any other time." An American commoner, she perhaps threatened the Italian major's social "class system." Regardless, as enunciated in the second of these paired stories, for some, this painful history surely prefigures postwar threats to America's social and class values and mores.

Harold Krebs's mother in "Soldier's Home," an exception to Hemingway's voiceless females, fully captures a matriarch's embodying, and articulating painfully and in extenso, American core values she believes are threatened postwar. Her son, a returning soldier, apparently "lacks ambition." She "knows" that wars reveal "how weak men are," that "there can be no idle hands in [God's] kingdom," that "all work is honorable," that other boys are becoming "really a credit to the community." Her greatest fear: "civilized" values—domesticity (marriage, family), community (ambition, work), patriotism and religion ("For God and Country")—will weaken following the war.

In the second stories volume, *Men Without Women* (1927), Nick

Adams, the principal character in Hemingway's three collections (1925, 1927, 1933), appears with experiences focused on female wartime voicelessness, even absence, as subject and theme.

An Italian major's sharpening of Nick's language skills anchors the principal action of "In Another Country," as both men rehab war wounds. Unexpectedly, the major's ill young wife—nameless, voiceless, off scene—dies. Drawing upon courtesy, duty, even grammar, the tearful major's controlled suffering provides Nick a powerful lesson in male courage unrelated to war and physical wounds: for example, to display feeling is not to express weakness. More broadly, the major's young wife, silent and unseen, contributes to the elaborate mosaic of Nick's continuing "life lessons" across the story collections, lessons increasingly centered in male-female relationships.

"Now I Lay Me" again finds Nick wounded and hospitalized. Fearing loss of control in sleep, he stays awake by invoking cherished childhood memories, particularly of himself fishing. From childhood, too, he remembers "control" issues between his mother and father. As with Krebs, these memories emphasize a dominant woman in a domestic role, here captured in a single telling act. Mrs. Adams discards Nick's father's unique childhood collection of Indian artifacts by burning them on the lawn: "I've been cleaning out the basement dear." Like Mrs. Krebs, Nick's mother assumes a seat of power in her traditional role and would oppose any postwar threat to her beliefs.

In wartime present, his mother's long-ago act does not affect wounded Nick's mental fishing. Regardless, childhood shapes adulthood. Subliminally, remembering over time his parents' fractious relationship has compromised Nick's vision of women, eliminating any desire to marry. Now, responding to exhortations from his happily married orderly, he reviews all "girls I have ever known." They blur, becoming "rather the same," while the fishing continues, exciting, ever new.

Beyond representative males Nick and Harold, Hemingway's early readers also encountered two Helens, each a conspicuously active and positive postwar influence regarding contemporary male-female relations.

The critical female in *Soldier's Home,* finally, is not Harold's mother, Mrs. Krebs, but his youngster sister and baseball pitching "phenom," Helen. She innocently idolizes her brother, even wishing he could be her beau. Such genuine effusiveness constitutes the "shell-shocked" Harold's first postwar experience of feminine human warmth, prompting the emotionally stunted soldier to agree to watch her pitch. A female wholly unencumbered by Mrs. Krebs's traditional religious, domestic, community "baggage," Helen proffers both attention and affection, moving Harold to focus and to act—now for her, his sibling; prospectively for him—pulling himself together, seeking a job, building a postwar life in Kansas City.

The second Helen's importance is extraordinary—not least because she never appears, never speaks, is never quoted. Regardless, as Nick's pregnant wife, she helps shape the two closing *In Our Time* narratives.

A core domestic value—parenthood—dominates the postwar "Cross-Country Snow." Nick has chanced love, marriage, fatherhood, with Helen. Equal partners, they experience no rivalry as skiers, and both regret having to abandon European slopes to allow their child to be born stateside. This decision-making clearly registers Nick's emotional growth at Helen's hands regarding women and marriage. In a union characterized by maturity and successful communication, Nick and Helen constitute a postwar couple becoming family.

And Helen, specifically, as a female character? In "Big Two-Hearted River," following immediately "Cross Country Snow" and the final *In Our Time* narrative, we note that as with many women in the preceding stories, Helen is voiceless, wordless—moreover, actually absent, nameless, even unmentioned, exactly like the war itself. Critically important, however, albeit unseen, unheard, we know she partners a fruitful postwar marriage (with child), Helen as critical for Nick as his overtly acknowledged "need for thinking," his "need to write." Nick—soldier, husband, father, aspiring author—represents his, the, wartime generation. Helen, unseen and unheard, actively conveys hope, stability. She does so, the reader imagines, in an intelligent, humane voice.

• • •

As with these short story narratives, so with the centrality and critical import of female presences in Hemingway's earliest novels. Gertrude Stein's epigraph in *The Sun Also Rises*—"You are all a lost generation"—underscores fears evidenced earlier in matriarchs Mrs. Krebs and Mrs. Adams, and these anxieties echo among the female principals in the first major novels, *The Sun Also Rises* and *A Farewell to Arms*.

Characters *are* "lost" in *Sun:* Cohn (and Frances), Mike, Brett. Brett loses two lovers in the war—one to dysentery, one to what was then called "traumatic neurosis" (today as PTSD). Irresponsible, alcoholic, promiscuous (also sometimes witty and charming), she is irrecoverably lost, unsuitable for Jake, and while a major character, not a representative female across the social spectrum in Paris in 1925. Important, male figures not lost in *Sun* actually are numerous and include Jake, Bill, the Count, Harris, Montoya, Romero, the American family and the religious pilgrims on the train, the Spanish peasants on the coach.

Jake, narrator and traditional male, would like to recover his Catholicism and, despite an emasculating war wound, would like to find love, even marriage. His subconscious routinely (and instinctively) processes the domestic vision he aspires to but rarely acknowledges—*even to himself.* For Jake, throughout the novel, certain women—nameless, wordless, most simply passersby personally unknown to him—constitute a metonymic chorus. They include Aloysius Kirby's daughter, coworker Krum's wife and children, the family on the train, and a loving couple Jake and Bill observe upriver from Notre Dame. In San Sebastian, Jake subconsciously records, and approves, nurses tending children and youthful lovers sunning on a raft.

Like Nick, Jake embraces the traditional, especially the familial. Unlike Nick's, Jake's prospects for love, marriage, family, even religion—although present or prospective for many moving about Paris in 1925—because they are tied loosely to Brett, continue to be seriously uncertain for him at novel's close.

In *A Farewell to Arms,* guilt-ridden at her fiancé's death, Catherine Barkley abandons traditional religion. Gradually, at first, then more steadily, she becomes again whole by redefining the spiritual, by realizing the young priest's words—"to do for, to sacrifice for, to serve"—in human terms. She discovers both self and purpose in committing to emotionally stunted Frederic—spiritually, the two becoming one. After Catherine's death, the exhortation to seize life that she epitomized continues for Frederic—initially, perhaps unutterable because inchoate, but finally accessible, increasingly articulable: "I never think and yet when I begin to talk I say things I have found out in my mind without thinking." Frederic's retellings of their story allow him to move forward amid meanings still unfolding: life-affirming, spiritual, and grounded in human love.

Catherine's death completes a larger secular parable that defines and anchors Hemingway's recurring purpose with his principal female characters at this time: particularly for Nick and Helen in the stories; for Jake, in *The Sun Also Rises,* not with Brett, literally, but associatively, with the numerous other women leading meaningful lives that he passes among and silently captures in his consciousness; for Frederic, with Catherine in *A Farewell to Arms.* With these women and among other briefly appearing three-dimensional female characters centering the early narratives, Hemingway shapes and renders intelligible the central conundrum of his time: Given a postwar world of discredited or destabilized values, how to live, what to believe—now?

• • •

Whether writing journalism or fiction, Hemingway told stories: imagination shaped his journalism; experience grounded his fiction. Regardless, these narratives differed fundamentally.

Fiction's imagined "realities," its experiential "truths," relate to but are other than, sometimes even beyond, the actual, the everyday, the mundane. Hemingway later described his method for purposeful creation and communication of his realities, his fictional objective, truths: "If you make it up instead of describe it you can make it round and whole and solid and give it life; you create it, for good or bad" ("Monologue to the Maestro," *Esquire*, October 1935).

Echoing among his earliest fictions—the *in our time* vignettes (1924), *In Our Time* (1925), and *The Sun Also Rises* (1926)—are earlier *Toronto Star* and *Star Weekly* pieces detailing both war and *torero.* During this period, Hemingway developed perspective and a personal "meaning" touching both subjects and, particularly regarding *torero,* an ever-growing understanding of and attraction to Spain's cultural history and its contemporary religion and politics. Intellectual and emotional impetus from these two sources and radical changes in Hemingway's personal life key his writing in directions that were unexpected at decade's turn.

• • •

In 1930, Scribner, now copyright holder, reissued *In Our Time.* A new, introductory vignette, "On the Quai at Smyrna," sounds the domestic alarm uniting this volume's numerous voiceless women as it draws upon Hemingway's *Star* reporting regarding the Greek retreat into Thrace and Macedonia. Hemingway had earlier memorialized this event in *Star* articles in October and November. These details from Smyrna specifically document one kind of contemporary female horror and terror: on a pier illuminated by ceaseless shelling, mothers—most wordless, albeit crying hysterically—hold languishing infants, who, in death, are violently wrenched away.

Amid these unarticulated, even inarticulable, details, this excruciating preamble to the *In Our Time* collection again presents Hemingway's hallmark fictional characters of this era—courageous and resilient women, named and nameless. Such female figures surely would attract contemporary readers to similar Hemingway texts describing the troubled socioeconomic time-present beginning in 1929–30.

But no . . .

• • •

Early in 1929, before Depression-era financial and social upheaval gripped America, history choreographed a brief snapshot moment: Max Perkins, soon named Scribner senior editor and an indispensable lifelong Hemingway friend, reported immediately after reading, then rereading, the manuscript of "A Farewell to Arms" while on a train returning to New York from Key West: "It's a most wonderful book . . . full of lovely things." Indeed, Perkins continued, it was all he could do "not to buttonhole someone and make them read it." Instead, he took to the train's bathroom with "the bottle of absinthe Ernest had bestowed" and there drank a "lonely health to you" (Dearborn 272).

What neither man could appreciate at the time, for Hemingway going forward in the 1930s, the theme was redirection: a deliberate, serious reorienting of his writing subjects, purpose, and style amid and following major personal changes: divorce (Hadley) and remarriage (Pauline) in 1927; children: Jack (Bumby), 1926; Patrick, 1928; Gregory, 1930; and not least, a radical altering of both fiscal and physical realities—broadly in a national Depression, more narrowly in Key West, a land that time forgot.

# 4

# Economic Instability and Professional Redirection, 1930–1933

Economic instability greeted Hemingway and family in the new decade. Facing a shrinking income, he possessed no continuous funding source: royalties from *The Sun Also Rises* and prior work now went to Hadley, following their divorce in 1927; *A Farewell to Arms* book profits had lessened following serialization in May–October 1929. As the new decade approached, that novel's history already had produced much of the unexpected: the second and third monthly installments (June, July 1929) had been banned in Boston; then Laurence Stallings's Broadway stage adaptation, in September 1930, failed after two weeks. Finally, even more unexpectedly, in November 1930, Paramount Studios paid eighty thousand dollars for the movie rights, Hemingway's share a sizable twenty-four thousand dollars.

Partly in response to the uncertain economic future but not least because of his genuinely broadening sportsman's instincts, Hemingway established an inexpensive residence in Key West, the southernmost populated island in the Florida Straits—tiny at eight square miles, just ninety miles north of Cuba. Technically his family's home base for a decade after 1928, *home* proved an elastic term throughout the 1930s.

Extensive travel characterized even the earliest period, 1928–30: Piggott, Kansas City, Chicago, New York; and abroad, Spain, France, Switzerland. Pauline's wealthy Uncle Gus, serving as financial godfather, underwrote numerous early travel excursions, picking up both related and unrelated expenses (travel details, even including the "outfitting" of Hemingway, bear hunter, in Wyoming). The largest and longest-lasting evidence of this largesse: the purchase, in April 1931, and remodeling of the permanent Key West home at 907 Whitehead Street.

• • •

Hemingway's writing career at Scribner's was genuinely advantaged because it was shepherded by Maxwell Perkins. As a junior editor in 1920, Perkins had successfully argued for publication of Fitzgerald's *This Side of Paradise,* and thereafter, he steadily reinforced a paradigm shift at the traditional (conservative) publishing house: "We can't go on publishing Theodore Roosevelt and Richard Harding Davis and Henry Van Dyke and Thomas Nelson Page forever, you know" (Bruccoli, *Sons* xxiii). Moreover, Perkins steadily promoted women in the Scribner current authors' list, for example, Taylor Caldwell, Dawn Powell, Caroline Gordon, and not least, Hemingway's fellow Floridian novelist and naturalist Marjorie Kinnan Rawlings.

Vice president and editor-in-chief by 1932, Perkins continued to redefine American literary popular culture and Scribner's corporate culture. His editing genius—focusing on structure and character presentation, only rarely on manuscript minutiae such as line editing or reading proofs—ideally suited Hemingway, regarding both personal interactions and issues touching his texts. Surprisingly, their twenty-plus-years relationship unfolded largely as epistolary, the author answering roughly five hundred of his editor's seven hundred letters (Bruccoli, *Only Thing* 26). They did meet occasionally—fishing in Key West, even hunting in Arkansas, but regarding business, invariably in New York.

"Business" letters constituted their most serious exchanges, these most often initiated or furthered by Hemingway. Wide-ranging, they often centered on inappropriate and/or unprintable language, potential libel, and, in a seemingly constant flow touching the author's "needs," money. Topics unfolded under various heads: promotion, serialization, illustrations, reprints, negative reviews. Regarding publisher "promotion," for example, Hemingway complained to Perkins about the handling of his *Men Without Women* stories collection (1927): "Of course I know nothing about it but after the first of the year—when Men Without was still selling well—it seemed as though they were satisfied with the sale and pretty well laid off" (May 31, 1928, *Letters* 3:389).

Ironically, financial issues often distracted the author from numerous, genuinely disappointing gaffes in Scribner's early marketing: in the dedication to *Torrents of Spring,* S. Stanwood Menken's name was misspelled; reference in capital letters to mistitled "IN OUR TIMES" marred the cover of *The Sun Also Rises;* the *Men Without Women* jacket claimed thirteen stories, six unpublished (actually there were fourteen and four, respectively); on the jacket flap of *A Farewell to Arms,* Catherine Barkley's name appeared as "Katharine" (Hanneman 12, 15, 21, 24); the initial blurb for Scribner's *In Our Time* claimed, inaccurately, that the stories had been "completely revised"; ads reported the number of *Death in the Afternoon* photographs to be eighty, eighty-one, and eighty-four; early *Green Hills of Africa* ads failed to identify Hemingway as the primary character and that the book dramatized events involving real persons.

Regardless, the publisher proved timely, exact, and exemplary when called upon to defend its increasingly praised, thus increasingly prized, author. The second and third *A Farewell to Arms* monthly installments, in June and July 1929, were banned in Boston—for "salacious material" and for content-purpose as an "anti-war tract." The publisher's unequivocal response came promptly:

“The very fact that *Scribner’s Magazine* is publishing ‘A Farewell to Arms’ . . . is evidence of our belief in its validity and integrity. Mr. Hemingway is one of the finest and most highly regarded of modern writers. . . . ‘A Farewell to Arms’ is in its effect distinctly moral. . . . [Moreover,] Mr. Hemingway set out neither to write a moral tract nor a thesis of any sort. His book is no more anti-war propaganda than are the Kellogg Treaties” (Bruccoli, *Only Thing* 107 n. 1).

• • •

In April 1928, Hemingway and Pauline had returned to America, sailing from Paris to Cuba, then on to Key West—she was seven months pregnant with Patrick. The car Uncle Gus had ordered for them to drive north to Piggott, Arkansas, had not arrived and did not for some weeks. Hemingway soon took up fishing from docks and bridges, educating himself about saltwater keepers. In this pursuit, he met and immediately befriended Charles Thompson (a “conch” and one of Key West’s wealthiest citizens: owner of a fish company, icehouse, ship’s chandlery, hardware and tackle shop) and his wife, Lorine, soon a favorite with Pauline. Bonding among this foursome dramatically reoriented Hemingway’s geographical perspective and the couple’s domestic plans.

Key West was, even then, strapped economically, wholly apart from the impending financial straits soon furthered by the unfolding national Depression. Earlier, following completion of the Flagler Railroad in 1912, the Key West population had risen to twenty thousand, and the area prospered through World War I. The 1920s, however, proved ruinous: the population halved; blight savaged the sponge beds; cigar factories folded or moved elsewhere; the steamship line closed; commercial shipping relocated to New Orleans; commercial fishing waned, crippled by necessarily continuous capital investment; the naval base was deactivated.

Language in the streets—English, Cuban Spanish, and Caribbean Creole—characterized the island’s working-class and itinerant diversity. Sub-rosa economic and personal interactions ranged broadly: liquor smuggled from Cuba erased Prohibition; a general lack of policing allowed much unsavory and/or illegal activity to develop essentially unmonitored—beyond major smuggling and gambling, other staple, illicit interactions and entertainments as varied as cockfighting and prostitution flourished. For writer and developing sportfishing enthusiast Hemingway, however, Key West's poverty-driven "frontier" openness appealed. One lived as one wished and, important for this author, away from newsmen, critics, even the pestering public.

Although distinctly a "place out of time," Key West also included the everyday "normal"—a simple, relaxed, *traditional* reality existed, and when needed or desired, so did connections to the larger world: ferry service to Havana; twice-daily train service to the mainland; a fledgling Pan American airline passenger operation, albeit flights principally served the mails. Hemingway wrote to Waldo Peirce in 1930: "My simple idea of coming to Key West [was] to write and see no one and fish when through writing." Thus began Hemingway's most physically active and intellectually and imaginatively varied decade.

• • •

Beyond rediscovering male friendships—his *sine qua non* for functioning fully, for keeping mental health intact and sharp—Hemingway experienced a resurgence of writing potential. Soon this indefatigable outdoorsman with a high-energy personality discovered the "perfect" physical activity in this remote land for one such as he: deep-sea sportfishing. In time, the "call" to fish with those from among his varied, ever-growing gang, his "Mob," would expand into serious at-sea outings, some exceeding a month at a time—in the Dry Tortugas, Bimini, and Cuban waters.

Routinely, also, and with a constantly shifting cast of companions, Hemingway at home did simply party. Dominating this latter pursuit, from 1931 to 1936, a varied gang of "out-of-towners" came and went from Key West. Principals included artists Henry Strater and Waldo Peirce; St. Louis–Michigan friends Bill Smith and sister Kate, she now married to novelist John Dos Passos; poet Archibald MacLeish and wife, Ada; Scribner editor Max Perkins; and after 1933, *Esquire* founding editor Arnold Gingrich; socialite Jane Mason; American bullfighter Sidney Franklin.

Rhythm mattered. When writing, work came first—from early morning until early afternoon. Following that, Hemingway fished until dinner, then ate, drank, told lies and swapped tales with his cronies. Among the actual "locals," and beyond the Thompsons, were Josie Russell, who owned and operated Sloppy Joe's Bar, Hemingway's in-town hangout, and charter boat captain Bra Saunders. Toby Bruce, whom he first met at Pauline's family home in Piggott—and who was eighteen years Hemingway's junior—also became a lifelong friend in Key West. Over time, Bruce served faithfully and variously, initially as secretary and driver. Soon he was charged as overseer with homesite renovations, including the island's first swimming pool, and later, beyond maintaining the property, as chief mechanic for Hemingway's fishing yacht, *Pilar*.

• • •

Professionally, for successful author Hemingway after 1930, the theme was change. He determined to write less fiction and to develop more broadly into the writer as literary figure—as "man of letters." He worked nearly two years planning, researching, crafting, a professional *redirection*—shaping for both article and book publication a personalized nonfiction: this multivarious journalism to explore male thoughts shaped by a male imagination playing over male things and expressed as male texts.

Familiar writing subjects—fishing (now deep-sea) and hunting (soon African big-game)—would assume primacy, replacing war and war's aftershocks. Then, too, another earlier interest, never absent—Spanish history and culture surrounding *la corrida*—resurged, in new presentations and emphases, most dramatically as the volume-length *Death in the Afternoon* (1932). There, eighty-one photographs freeze-frame timeless rituals: preparatory, spectacular, inexorably grim, then final.

Following Gertrude Stein's igniting his fascination with the bullfight in Pamplona, in July 1923, Hemingway took up this subject, even in widely varied outlets—early, in the *Star Weekly* (2); later, in *the transatlantic review* (1). In these texts, he established a singular critical reality: *la corrida* is not "sport" but "tragedy." Immediately, then consistently, he began exploring this fundamental truth throughout his major fiction, 1924–29.

Spanish bullfight rituals and traditions first appeared dramatically within Hemingway's fiction as six chapters of *in our time* (1924), these texts then repeating as interchapters for *In Our Time* (1925). *La corrida* anchors the San Fermin thread in *The Sun Also Rises* (1926), and matadors are the specific subject of "The Undefeated" and "Banal Story" in *Men Without Women* (1927). Despite certain positive, exceptional matadors—Villalta, Pedro Romero, Manuel, and Maera—these fiction narratives record, recapitulate, the actual and widespread postwar collapse of prewar traditional values: with *la corrida,* age-old rites, both aesthetic and spiritual, become increasingly unstable before modern violence, dishonor, and death.

• • •

Hemingway's initial attraction to the bullfight—intellectual, emotional, historical—broadened continuously between 1930 and 1932. It fostered intellectual growth, inspired professional focus, and spurred transition to a new writing mode and a further shaping of his nonfiction content. These multiple investigations and subsequent written presentations of *la corrida* illustrate the continuous interdependence between his journalism and his fiction—after 1929, nonfiction assuming priority.

Hemingway began the 1930s professionalizing his interest in the bullfight as a nonfiction subject. The twenty-five hundred–word article "Bullfighting, Sport and Industry" is essentially a news and business feature in the premier issue of *Fortune* (March 1930). He opens confidently, explicitly affirming his subject: the Spanish bullfight is "an art, a tragedy, and a business." Financially centered, the article explores the panoply of costs associated with *la corrida:* the bulls and horses; on-scene actors such as picadors; behind-the-scene players, particularly ranchers and promoters. Representative facts include that the intense bull-matador drama typically unfolds over approximately twenty minutes; that in Spain, May is the "fatal" month (i.e., the largest number of formal killings). American bullfighter Sidney Franklin, whose experience included both Mexico and Spain, sourced background here. Franklin, to become a longtime Hemingway friend, concluded the article's noneconomic details dramatically with this "highlight": "There was always a way to avoid being gored," which was, after all, "simply a matter of a man goring himself on the bull by some mistake in technique."

This journalism furthered Hemingway's ever-broadening attraction to *la corrida.* Learning the day-to-day business issues and decision-making processes impressed him with its multifaceted character. While including some cultural history, "business" details centered this magazine piece on economic issues. Regardless, his developing nonfiction bullfight impulses pressed beyond the economic into broader dimensions—historical as well as contemporary. The result: Hemingway's comprehensive *Death in the Afternoon* (1932) reflects an aficionado's depth of interest and combines the professional research and writing of *both* journalist and historian.

• • •

Hemingway's volume-length literary-historical portrait of taurine action and artistry demonstrates "authoritative" knowledge and "authorial" experimentation. Subjects and storylines unfold in multiple voices from various perspectives—at the extreme, consequentially aided by humorous, often "non-sequitur," "asides." Additionally, as a veritable sightseeing guide to Spain, a review of Spanish food and wines, a compendium of formal pronouncements both describing and historicizing *la corrida,* the volume constitutes an apologia for a Spanish tradition wherein "meaning" anchors in "courage" and unfolds in a stylized, age-old ritual—a tragic "dance of death."

Not unexpectedly, sidebars *repeatedly* underscore the writer's "craft," Hemingway anticipating the substantial negative criticism of himself, his interests, and his art triggered here. Throughout *Death in the Afternoon,* he centers himself as writer and authority: he lectures, often pontificating. Genuinely knowledgeable, he explicates with photographic assistance the artistry unfolding in the *torero*'s choreography. Watchful regarding the reader's attention span, he dramatically takes up queries and objections, even inventing a feisty, voluble female presence—an "Old Lady" interlocutor.

Her observations and multiple confusions regarding *la corrida* afford humorous "relief"—a purposeful rhetorical distancing between the reader and the often graphically detailed subject matter. Further, she prompts fertile authorial asides. (Certain of these interchanges develop into what will be the full-length story "A Natural History of the Dead"—this modified text then included in the *Winner Take Nothing* collection of 1933.) At one point, the Old Lady denominates a reflection by her interlocutor as "very sad." Hemingway responds seriously, in words oft-quoted later by literary critics glossing his recurring fictional subjects, particularly those expressing darker themes: "Madam, all stories, if continued far enough, end in death, and he is no true story-teller who would keep that from you. . . . If two people love each other there can be no happy end to it" (Robert Coates, *New Yorker,* October 1, 1932; Meyers, *Critical Heritage* 161–62).

Most consequential in *Death in the Afternoon,* an authoritative Hemingway takes up *la corrida* directly, his arguments describing, contextualizing, *justifying,* its formal rituals. A voluble masculine voice tracks the drama in broad strokes, exploring, often in minute detail, the artistry and aesthetics of this "timeless action." Captured in eighty-one action photographs, the principal actor—matador, bullfighter, *torero*—is freeze-framed (literally photo-enhanced) in these "portraits of the artist." Larger "meanings," "truths," "art" of *la corrida* center in masculine control, death faced in a stylized, tragic action dramatizing and attesting to courage in a world challenging, even cynical.

For American critics-reviewers, "values" in such ritualized acts and unfoldings proved debatable, prompting widely disparate critical assessments. Max Eastman, for one, was clearly unaccepting: "To drag in notions of honor and glory here, and take them seriously, is ungrown-up enough and rather sophomoric. But to pump words over it like tragedy and romantic conflict is mere romantic nonsense and self-deception crying to heaven. It is not tragic to play mean tricks on a beautiful thing that is stupid and stab it when its power is gone" (*New Republic,* June 7, 1933, 94; Meyers, *Critical Heritage* 175).

Following inordinate success with his fiction, 1925–29—stories, *In Our Time, Men Without Women;* novels, *The Sun Also Rises, A Farewell to Arms*—Hemingway's professional redirection prompted extensive reaction and response. Ranging among critique, speculation, even supplication, critics expressed judgment-laden fears of losing a contemporary storyteller now uniformly recognized as among *the* leading American literary figures. His wide-ranging interest in *la corrida* prompted concern among professionals regarding its meaning for his going forward.

Whether or not purposely laying down a "new marker," Hemingway did address in *Death in the Afternoon* the attraction to *la corrida,* his being drawn to the bullfight as inspiration and subject. In part, *la corrida* furthered in him an understanding *as a writer* of both act and action, principally, in how to inscribe what "actually happened" and what stimulated the specific "emotion experienced." Recognizing "teachable moments" touching these critical points, Hemingway became explicit in the book, offering a writer's truth beyond any question of subject matter: "If a writer of prose knows enough about what he is writing about he may omit things that he knows and the reader, if the writer is writing truly enough, will have a feeling of those things as strongly as though the writer had stated them. The dignity of movement of an ice-berg is due to only one-eighth of it being above the water."

Perhaps the most consequential among the variety of reactions to this compendium—to the critical issues these exchanges generated—was Hemingway's "authoritative," unequivocal, response establishing and defending both credentials and subject matter, especially going forward. His was no superficial interest in the bullfight. Insisting on that recognition—by both critics and the general adult reader—he demanded and achieved a broader, purposeful design.

Hemingway's role as author now legitimately transcended any simple version of the "professional writer" epithet. He had clarified a broad desideratum, his personal perspectives defining the writer-as-artist. In *Death in the Afternoon*—a multi-varied, sometimes spectacular, tour de force—he addressed certain issues among those most pressing for the contemporary man of letters. For Ernest Hemingway, specifically, these centered, as here, in a masculine courage defining and evidencing *purpose* in literature and art—particularly in troubled periods, such as time present.

Indisputably, he understood—himself. In the future, he would voice that multifaceted self from numerous perspectives: as global traveler, connoisseur, insider-expert: literally, as a/the magister.

• • •

Apart from this singularly detailed historical, cultural, and financial treatment of *el torero* and *la corrida* in *Death in the Afternoon,* the bullfight remained a recurring presence in Hemingway's writing to the end of his life, initially in three short stories—"The Mother of a Queen," in *Winner Take Nothing* (1933), and in *Esquire,* "The Friend of Spain" and "The Horns of the Bull" (1934, 1936). The bullfight appeared in *For Whom the Bell Tolls* (1940). He opened the 1950s with a fairy tale, "The Faithful Bull" (*Holiday,* 1951), and concluded with the reporter's factual "A Matter of Wind" for *Sports*

*Illustrated* (1959). Notably, Hemingway's final journalism centered on contemporary bullfighting, specifically on Spain's most famous living matadors: "The Dangerous Summer," a three-part serial in *Life* (September 1960).

• • •

In time present, the ever-deepening Depression resulted in steadily declining sales and Scribner's need throughout the 1930s to respond with ever more varied and creative advertising. The publisher drafted fuller, postpublication copy, stressing Hemingway the *fiction* writer. A full-page ad in the *New York Times Book Review* on October 9, 1932, promoted *Death in the Afternoon* ("Third Big Printing") among ten primarily fiction titles, including Zelda Fitzgerald's *Save Me the Waltz* and Morley Callaghan's *A Broken Journey*. A month later, Scribner claimed *Death in the Afternoon* as "a best-seller" in the "leading bookstores in New York, Chicago, Philadelphia, and points West" (*NYTBR*, November 13, 1932).

The *Winner Take Nothing* stories volume—fiction planned to underwrite the "new" Hemingway nonfiction persona—was published in October 1933. The modest success of *Death in the Afternoon* (five printings, sales of 20,780) had encouraged Scribner's belief in a uniformly positive name recognition carryover. A Hemingway short fiction volume could reasonably be expected to generate substantial sales.

Regardless, despite Scribner's *NYTBR* ad claiming, "Among these fourteen stories, practically every reviewer has found several that he considers 'Hemingway's best work,'" and despite the genuine achievement of such stories as "A Clean Well-Lighted Place" and four "Nick Adams" narratives, including the final, paired "A Day's Wait" and "Fathers and Sons," the *Winner Take Nothing* collection foundered at a single printing of 20,300 copies in October 1933. (For comparison: The earlier *Men Without Women* stories volume, in 1927, had sold 23,815 copies—five printings in its first year.)

Consistent with Hemingway's two previous collections, initially most striking about the *Winner Take Nothing* narratives are the presence of and the emphasis on various boundary-challenging male-female relationships. Notably, as with both the *In Our Time* and *Men Without Women* narratives, authorial sympathy resides with women suffering, especially from insensitive or otherwise unaware males, whose authority controls everyday civil, social, and religious realities. Although this thematic emphasis parallels its import in the earlier story volumes, within *Men Without Women,* the subject, "male-female relations," soon morphs significantly, becoming major now because registering among the final Nick Adams narratives.

• • •

In "One Reader Writes," the shortest narrative at a mere 435 words, a young wartime wife and mother writes to a newspaper columnist–doctor for help, hers a simple, albeit powerful plea for clarification and direction. Mental anguish humanizes this confused young woman painfully fearful about how to act regarding her returning soldier's "malady"—that is, syphilis. Although she is ill educated and at points ungrammatical, humanity focuses her text: no writing errors; no crossings-out; no rewritings. Her hunger for love, understanding, and direction has become threatened amid issues centered in female *respectability*—a crucial conventional norm defined here, as it typically was, by male authority figures: her personal physician (she has a child at home); a newspaper doctor (she seeks his help, anonymously); her husband; her father; her pastor.

Empowered male voices and actions fail her, although any patriarch from the list of male authority figures might help. Her distress is compounded by prejudicial ignorance, as expressed by her father, who once claimed that anyone with this malady might "well wish themselves dead." Concepts such as "proper," "right," "respectable" are male defined. Moreover, capital letters here highlight the force of their enactors—"Father," "Husband," "Pastor." Ironic, albeit possibly a direct result of pastoral homilies touching female respectability, she, herself, fails to seek *Jesus.* At story's end, her emotional needs—personal, private, grave, by now effectively long-standing—are dramatized most painfully outside her letter.

Alone in bed, she verbalizes her desire, a desperate hunger to rescue human love, not least in its physical expressions, from her husband's malady. (Repeating that formal term three times underscores how formidably this issue exists in her mind.) The actual "failure" here is essentially male and devolves from the meaning of *respectability* as it touches both the human and the divine: "It's a long time. And it's been a long time. My Christ it's been a long time. He had to go wherever they sent him, I know, but I don't know what he had to get it for. Oh, I wish to Christ he wouldn't have got it. I don't care what he did to get it. But I wish to Christ he hadn't ever got it. It does seem that he didn't have to have got it. I don't know what to do. I wish to Christ he hadn't got any kind of malady. I don't know why he had to get a malady."

Christ's presence in her words emphasizes His absence in her life. Mentioned four times, not once prayerfully, He becomes here, albeit faultless, another failed male. A need for the emotional and the physical presses. In her loneliness now, any otherworldly (male) succor is genuinely secondary.

Notably, among Hemingway's other fictional women in this volume, female voices and points of view are not so uniformly silenced or otherwise frustrated as in "One Reader Writes." In "A Sea Change," the more worldly young woman speaks up for herself. In so doing, she "educates" her sophisticated male companion: broadening his sexual perspectives by clearly articulating her own; justifying these needs by clarifying them as essentially the equal to his own.

In everyday parlance, a "sea change" generally implies an "improving" situation. Thus, the title "A Sea Change" predisposes the reader toward sympathy for its young woman principal and her request: permission from her male lover—in this 1920s setting—to have a same-sex physical experience. Her argument draws upon his own sometimes illicit acts, these experiences sought, then justified, because undertaken by him acting as "a writer." Having understood and supported his need for "varied experience," she sums up her position in a challenging affirmation: "I'm sorry. But when we do understand each other there's no need to pretend we don't." An added justification: her planned same-sex encounter will be brief—experiential behavior not unlike his own "experimenting." Important, too, because sincere, she avers: "I'll come back if you want me."

And he? He "releases" her, albeit not without an uncharacteristically harsh rejoinder: "And when you come back tell me all about it." His voice, he notes to himself, "sounded very strange." Moreover, after she departs from the bar where they are meeting, he ponders his own vagaries—impulses sought, surrendered to. As writer, he understands her needs and plans, but as a man, not yet.

Reflecting thus and in the fuller context of overhearing chatter among three men at the bar, each probably homosexual—the bartender certainly—he recalls Alexander Pope's "An Essay on Man." Earlier, he had hurled at her specific lines from the poem—then upset, he recalled them only incompletely. Now, again remembering, he addresses the bartender: "Vice is a very strange thing, James." This second reference prompts the reader to ponder Hemingway's purpose (as applied to *this* man) in the specific allusion to Pope's text:

> Vice is a monster of so frightful mien,
> As, to be hated, needs but to be seen;
> Yet seen too oft, familiar with her face,
> We first endure, then pity, then embrace.

This quatrain, quoted completely, requires that the reader apply these words to the story's action as a whole—not simply to the young woman's wishes. Progression of thought in Pope's poem clearly suggests the thinking of the present male (she called him "Poor Phil") regarding her wishes, and it parallels his own unconventional thought and action patterns. Appearing where they do, might the poet's words suggest future action by the current speaker?

At story's end, Phil, a writer who sometimes experiments with the illicit, looks into the mirror at the bar: "He saw that he was really quite a different-looking man. The other two at the bar moved down to make room for him."

Albeit unalike as contemporary character studies, these two stories highlight the humanity of their unnamed female principals—a sympathetic understanding also characteristic of women depicted in Hemingway's early major fiction. Indeed, empathy with the emotional needs of "contemporary" women centered his published narratives as early as 1923 (e.g., "Up in Michigan"), then throughout the groundbreaking plots, techniques, and themes of his first major fiction, 1925–30.

• • •

Singularly important, the *Winner Take Nothing* volume concludes the Nick Adams saga. To varying degrees, the author's alter ego, Nick, appears in the collections—*In Our Time, Men Without Women, Winner Take Nothing*—in at least fifteen of forty-two stories (and probably in several other narratives in which the major figure is nameless, as, e.g., in "An Alpine Idyll"). Inarguably Hemingway's most fully realized "fictional" character overall, Nick is the principal figure in four of the fourteen *Winner Take Nothing* stories. These individual narratives chronicle key moments, both emotional and intellectual, as Nick develops from his late teens to middle age, many details roughly paralleling his creator's own life. (In "Fathers and Sons," the final narrative, Nick is thirty-eight, while Hemingway at that time is thirty-four).

Specifically in its Nick Adams narratives, this volume marks a critical shift in Hemingway's male-female subjects and themes. These changes initiated, then highlighted, conclude with "snapshot" moments in the Nick Adams biography across three generations.

• • •

In "The Light of the World," teenagers Nick and Tom "ride the rails" in northern Michigan. In a train station, they encounter the irrational in verbal sexual violence, most memorably involving three whores: initially, a bartender threatens the boys using sexual slang, calling them "punks"; wanting to amuse them, a lumberman harasses a gay cook; then, usurping control, albeit in a "soft voice," Alice, a 350-pound whore, "lights up" this stunning, godless "world." After shocking a fellow professional into silence, she modulates her voice, effecting a "poetic" moment by intoning a corrupt former lover's encomium: "You're a lovely piece, Alice." Nick, overlooking the sterile in the dramatic physical, embraces timbre over content: Alice's "prettiest face . . . her smooth skin . . . her lovely voice." Breaking the spell, Tom grabs Nick, and he hustles off both male innocents.

In "A Way You'll Never Be," Nick, older—now soldiering in war—suffers a serious head trauma. Under medical care, he frequently hallucinates—from images of racy Parisian women and song to dramatically, fleetingly, seeing himself shot in battle. No women appear in time present, but this war includes, can even center in, violence to women. Nick experiences this horror bicycling through a battle zone, where he witnesses, littering the road, numerous enemy propaganda postcards depicting soldiers raping civilian women. Among such detritus, also scattered about are genuine photos and letters between lovers and among family members, these latter honest sentiments and pictorials memorializing domestic bonds—painfully, many nonexistent now, their principals lost.

• • •

Critical because effecting an overt shift of perspective both within and without this third story collection, a *new* Hemingway narrative voice moves content and vision unmistakably from the "female," often domestic, to explicitly "masculine things" and "male perspectives." These changes will develop principally as journalism. Regardless, initially they do include Hemingway's fiction. This new emphasis on male things and points of view appears unmistakably at the end of the Nick Adams saga—highlighted explicitly and dramatically in the masculine focus of "A Day's Wait" and "Fathers and Sons."

In "A Day's Wait," Nick strengthens the bond with his nine-year-old son, "Schatz." Generational affection here centers "family" values in the masculine. The boy's grandfather was a great hunter, and Nick's relationship with that male figure is complex. Regarding Schatz, he is an actively loving father and mentor touching male things. Particularly regarding nature and the natural world, he develops in the youth a masculine, sportsman's vision.

In the story, Schatz is sick and in bed. Also in bed, the boy's stepmother. This female character—wordless, uninvolved in the story's action—is mentioned only once.

Young Schatz has confused Fahrenheit and Celsius. Insufficiently attentive as father, Nick allows the silent youngster to believe that his temperature reading ensures death to be inevitable, even imminent. Waiting for the doctor and unaware of the boy's confusion, the father attempts comfort—giving medicine, talking, reading stories. Anticipating death, the lad silently retains a heroic composure for hours before the misunderstanding is corrected.

Professional *writer* Nick misses the obvious in the lad's looks and in his unfocused, non sequitur responses. An instance revealing Nick's ineptness in this "crisis" occurs during a lull when he takes time to hunt quail. Wintertime, the ground "varnished with ice," his dog "slipped and slithered"; Nick, in fact, falls "twice, hard, once dropping my gun and having it slide away." The father's foolishness trying to hunt in these clearly unsafe elements highlights the son's courage: Nick lying on the ground, having dangerously lost control of his gun; young Schatz lying on his "deathbed," "holding tight onto himself." Fortunately, relief for both follows quickly upon the lad's ultimately clarifying question: "About how long will it be before I die?" Inept and embarrassed, Nick immediately clarifies and engages as the loving father and caregiver that he is.

The genuine bond shared by Nick and his son proves critical for understanding the multigenerational *male* Adams family relationships across Hemingway's three fiction collections. In the final narrative, "Fathers and Sons," Nick, now thirty-eight, reflects as writer and father on his family. As the title suggests, except as memories, no women appear. Maleness/, masculinity, centers emphasis *not* on husbands, nor lovers; not on the domestic, nor on male-female love, but on fathers and sons.

Estranged while still young from his mood-driven father—a Dr. Adams, who sees only literally, "making him both sentimental and cruel"—now mature, thirty-eight-year-old Nick, focused on young Schatz, unspools a retrospective analysis covering much Adams family interactive unhappiness, not only his own. This male-oriented reverie accepts that each family member "betrayed" his father "in their various ways." Yet regarding the future *and* prospects with his own young son, Schatz, Nick remembers that beyond the conflicts always came genuine good times with his father: the outdoors, the restorative rhythms of nature, the actual hunting and fishing. Adult Nick "loved to fish and shoot exactly as much as when he had gone with his father."

In time present, not yet able to write about that man as father, author Nick can and does praise that man as grandfather to his young grandson, notably, in answering the boy's query: "What was it like, Papa, when you were a little boy and used to hunt with the Indians?" Responding to this eager, inquisitive ten-year-old, Nick honestly, accurately, describes a "superb hunter, who had lived among Indians." Moreover, despite painful, irreversible differences with this male figure, Nick reaches for the positive, proudly reporting: "I'd rather see him shoot than any man I ever knew." Young Schatz, eager to hunt with his own first gun in the year upcoming, proudly embraces his grandfather, a patriarch and "peerless marksman who walked with Indians."

Assessing Nick's character—his strengths and weaknesses as a writer when last seen—is important. His words, as words, reveal both character and talent. Nick *can* write, and Nick *will* write. Two spontaneous, unrelated, only loosely focused, word strings are indicative: these brief reveries include mindless acts (e.g., Nick's purely physical sex earlier with the Ojibway fellow teen, Trudy); and more seriously, his sensitive reflection on both the historical and contemporary pain and loss suffered by Ojibway families and culture in the area of his own family's summer home in Michigan.

Reflecting on both, Nick's imagination, the writer's imagination, free-associates in streaming words—these first framing the "good"—as he mindlessly understood it as wholly sexual with the teen, Trudy: "tightly, sweetly, moistly . . . fully, finally, unendingly, never-endingly, suddenly ended, the great bird flown"; then, more realistically, the "bad": "when you go . . . where Indians have lived you smell them gone and all the empty painkiller bottles and the flies . . . do not kill the sweetgrass smell, the smoke smell, and that other like a fresh cased martin skin. . . . Long time ago good. Now no good." Beyond the capacity of his strictly moral father to appreciate, adult Nick has mastered language, *his* profession—using words powerfully, imaging in these words new meanings, fuller realities.

*Winner Take Nothing*, Hemingway's last original story collection, concludes the Nick Adams saga—fifteen stories unfolding across three volumes, 1925, 1927, 1933, and ending with "Fathers and Sons." Collectively, the stories constitute snapshots of Hemingway's developing art and mindset. They conclude at an "evolutionary" moment in change that will reshape a worldview—for the nonce, a consciously masculine vision soon to be formally expressed in/as a *personalized* journalism.

• • •

Critically important for Hemingway—also in October 1933—*Esquire* published its initial issue. His personal role would prove crucial in establishing and sustaining the magazine's immediate and, in his time, extraordinary success. Hemingway's initial presence and continuing voice (twenty-five essays, 1933–36; six short stories, 1936–39) offered this monthly an authoritative *male* speaking in troubled times in soon-to-be-characteristic "Hemingway" journalist voices: "sportsman, manly man, exposer of sham, arbiter of taste, world traveler, *bon vivant,* insider, stoic and battle-scarred veteran, and heroic artist" (Raeburn 44).

# 5

# The Launch of *Esquire: The Magazine for Men*

Widely varying images of Hemingway, writer, unfold in multiple voices in the 1930s, particularly in newly launched *Esquire* magazine, beginning in the fall of 1933—sportsman, wartime journalist-essayist, and literary figure. Regarding Hemingway's fiction, perhaps his two finest short stories appear back-to-back: "The Snows of Kilimanjaro," *Esquire,* August 1936; "The Short Happy Life of Francis Macomber," *Cosmopolitan,* September 1936. Regardless, his sole novel published in this decade, *To Have and Have Not,* in 1937, was uniformly panned.

Many considered the Hemingway who returned to America from Paris in 1928 a "Left Bank expatriate" writer. Widely varying pro and con public images of "man" and "literary figure" interchanged steadily over the following decade, his portrait as author achieving its fullest positive dimensions following publication of *For Whom the Bell Tolls* in October 1940.

Throughout the 1930s, Hemingway's life teemed with action. During the early Key West years, his marriage to Pauline continued to supply indispensable financial assistance through her Uncle Gus, specifically his underwriting their extended travel: important here, Hemingway's first African safari, December 1933–February 1934. When the couple returned to the United States in late March 1934, they had been abroad for nearly nine months.

Despite such seemingly continuous travel, for Hemingway, writer, the 1930s constituted his most prolific and varied publishing period: in the decade's first half, books—*In Our Time* (reprinted 1930), *Death in the Afternoon* (1932), *Winner Take Nothing* (1933), and, drawing from the safari, first fruits, the narrative-memoir-apologia *Green Hills of Africa* (1935). Then came two short stories, each among his finest: "The Snows of Kilimanjaro" and "The Short, Happy Life of Francis Macomber."

• • •

After three years of journalistic silence, Hemingway, in periodicals at mid-decade and later, detailed from direct personal witness a world much in flux. Regarding the "winds of war," he wanted America to remain neutral, as clear in his two articles for *Esquire* in fall 1935: "Notes on the Next War" (September) and "The Malady of Power" (November). His most sympathetic words for the political "Left" appeared in three *New Masses* pieces: "Who Murdered the Vets?" (1935), powerfully rendering government irresponsibility in the deaths of over four hundred World War I vets killed in the Labor Day hurricane at Matecumbe Key; "Fascism Is a Lie," politically charged remarks before the American Writers' Conference in New York (1937); then ideas and arguments much lauded by the *New Masses* editors, "On the American Dead in Spain" (1939).

In 1937, Hemingway's political-editorial contributions to the Spanish Civil War documentary film *The Spanish Earth* were acknowledged in its premiere for the Roosevelts at the White House, July 7. Fellow writer-reporter Martha Gellhorn was present for this showing, and she and Hemingway were again together in Spain in August, where he initiated his on-scene war reporting for the *North*

*American Newspaper Alliance* (thirty-one dispatches in 1937–38). These latter pieces appeared in over sixty American and European newspapers and periodicals under such broad titles as "Hemingway Reports Spain," "Shelling of Madrid," and "Tortosa Calmly Awaits Assault" (collected, reprinted in *Hemingway Review,* spring 1988).

In America, Depression-era suffering continued serious and widespread. Hemingway's multivarious publications capturing the dark days of 1937 abroad concluded with his embracing painful domestic realities—literally at home. In a Key West homage of sorts, he took up the nation's economic woes with the novel *To Have and Have Not.*

Despite expectations raised by these numerous, varied texts, Hemingway's support for formal "causes" often, as here, proved subject to continuous modification. His apparent commitment to the Left, as understood and then expressed in reviews of *To Have and Have Not,* was considered indicative regarding his much anticipated *For Whom the Bell Tolls* (1940). But no. Although Hemingway predicted "the next war," he continued wanting the United States to remain neutral. His novel condemned the Communist leaders in the Spanish Civil War. Moreover, his artist's voice at the earlier American Writers' Conference proved predictive regarding issues dramatized in *For Whom the Bell Tolls:* "It is very dangerous to write the truth in war and the truth is also very dangerous to come by."

• • •

A return to fiction, especially to the short story, dominated these decade-ending years: in his comprehensive collection *The Fifth Column and the First Forty-Nine Stories,* 1938; in *Esquire,* 1938–39, a trilogy of Spanish Civil War narratives—"The Denunciation," "The Butterfly and the Tank," and "Night Before Battle"; in *Ken,* "The Old Man at the Bridge"; and in *Cosmopolitan,* "Under the Ridge." Moreover, even at home, writing amid the inordinate economic hardships characterizing America across the decade, Hemingway never lost focus on his much-beloved, war-shattered Spain. He dramatized realities and his own experience there via his play *The Fifth Column* (published in 1938; on Broadway with Lee Strasberg directing, eighty-seven performances in 1940).

Important, also, the breadth and quality of Hemingway's short fiction—in the collected *First Forty-Nine Stories* (1938) and, immediately following, in the Spanish Civil War narratives—offered supporting evidence of career excellence during Pulitzer Prize considerations for 1940. Assessments of writers formally under review for the fiction prize suggest, in judgments confirmed and underscored by support for the nomination of *For Whom the Bell Tolls*, that, at decade's turn (although no prize was awarded for 1940), many literary experts deemed Ernest Hemingway America's "major living author."

• • •

Despite this late burst of fiction, nonfiction characterized and centered Hemingway's published writing throughout the 1930s, these years also witnessing his continuous and singular evolution as a writer.

At mid-decade, the range of venues for the author's personal voice(s) proved inordinate: in books initially, *Death in the Afternoon* (1932) and *Green Hills of Africa* (1935). The latter volume, which was serialized, with illustrations, presents much scattershot activity. Hemingway, "greenhorn frontiersman," learns to kill "cleanly." Expertise established, content moves to ideas—from Hemingway's personal opinions regarding classic American authors (e.g., Twain's genius) to polemical judgments unpacking the present literary scene—that is, many writers ruined by money or a compromised self-image owing to critics (they "angleworms in a bottle" feeding off each other). Regardless, for Hemingway, an unsuccessful reality: *Green Hills of Africa*, with two printings, sold just 12,532 copies.

Then, returned to journalism, Hemingway spoke from varied

perspectives and locales: under fire, metaphorically, at home for his "insufficient" or "incorrect" reaction to the Depression's social realities; by 1937, under fire, literally, in Spain, reporting a Civil War at firsthand.

• • •

Beginning in October 1933, lasting especially through the decade's middle years, 1933–36, Hemingway developed an extraordinary chance opportunity to express in singular public voices his own idiosyncratic opinions. Specifically, that month, he began his foray into a "personal" journalism, committing to and accepting the role as principal in a new, singularly "masculinized" periodical—*Esquire: The Quarterly for Men.*

Founding editor Arnold Gingrich superintended all dimensions of *Esquire,* the product and design of his creative genius. Throughout the periodical's early years, then extending across the editor's decades-long career with the magazine, "Ernest Hemingway" proved both a singular, predominant author and, no less, a popular subject. For Gingrich, early and late, Hemingway constituted a genuine, unique touchstone, and a lasting "connection" began between and among author, editor, and magazine.

Hemingway's vision, intent, with his nonfiction *Esquire* essays became quickly apparent. They proved grist for a wide-ranging, carefully calibrated, first-person "public" voice. Designed to secure a broad audience, shaped to thwart increasing criticism, and perfected to capture *the inimitable* Ernest Hemingway in his own words, the author crafted personal multivocal texts as "informal," albeit unmistakably "educational," letters. Early pieces even included photos, sixteen in the initial essay, "Marlin Off the Morrow." Six other essays presented detailed illustrations. Both clarifying and heightening meaning(s), the visuals, principally rhetorical in their purpose, offered dramatic silent testimony and tribute to Hemingway's expertise.

These broad magazine texts anchored authentic, contemporary subjects in authoritative commentary. Topics ranged from sport (in greatest detail, marlin fishing in the Gulf and African big-game hunting) to both national and European economic and political straits—particularly emphasized, the prospects for civil war brewing among Spanish factions. In twenty-five *Esquire* essays, Hemingway explored an inordinate range of subjects and, these, not least, in a "controlled" emotional expression, especially during the increasingly troubled years through mid-1936: his words sometimes "unfolding" as information, sometimes "unspooling" as "charged" personal testimony.

• • •

Of his twenty-five *Esquire* "letters," Hemingway devoted twelve to fishing the Gulf Stream: the first and last; the most controversial; the most often reprinted; an explanation of his preference for deep-sea fishing over other sports; and not least, exposition of his writing aesthetics. These letters affirm and demonstrate his knowledge of the Gulf Stream and his expertise in big-game sportfishing. He speaks from diverse perspectives, most often as an aficionado possessed of scientific and environmental interests and more—as both sportsman and literary artist.

Each essay is informational, Hemingway's voice ranging widely. Usually informal, the "I" refers to himself as "your correspondent" and regularly adopts the second-person personal pronoun. His mood varies from relaxed, even contemplative, to an instructional tone that approaches formal lecturing. The memorable extreme occurs when Hemingway speaks out self-defensively on craft—regardless of whether as sportsman or as writer. These latter pieces can be caustic, coarse, even obscene, particularly in their humor. Regardless, at their best, the Gulf Stream letters achieve the simplicity and directness of good feature writing.

• • •

In the mid-1930s, Hemingway's *Esquire* essays attracted spirited, often disproportionately "spleen" over "keen" reader responses—a truth that developed early. Harsh reader missives "fired off" steadily to "the Editor" appeared in one or another of the magazine's sections—"Backstage with *Esquire*"; "Editorial Comment"; "The Sound and the Fury"; "The Publisher's Page." Some printed reader letters certainly challenged "good taste," not to mention libel limits. Occasionally, editor Gingrich "stepped in" to a dispute among letter writers, attempting to modulate the moment in some substantive manner. Other times, he did so only to "interrupt" momentarily the flow of vitriol, to effect a pause, then to "duck out," as, for example, in a piece during an extended period of Hemingway's sparring with noted newspaper critics: "*Esquire* enters the ring only in the capacity of announcer, not as referee or judge . . . and bows discreetly out before the first punch" ("Editor's Comments," September 1934, 11).

Important, too, certain of Hemingway's expatiations and explications, drawing readership "ire and fire" were, arguably, simple, unintended misunderstandings. The author's intensity sometimes distracted from, even obscured, his primary purpose—for example, his legitimate attempt, particularly in certain Gulf Stream fishing essays, to demonstrate for the reader that and how wealth, leisure, even art, can and do meaningfully address contemporary socioeconomic issues.

• • •

*Nominal* subjects in Hemingway's personalized *Esquire* essays—beyond fishing the Gulf Stream and hunting big game in East Africa—included cultural commentaries, often critiques, touching contemporary art, politics, sports, travel, literature, and writing. Even so, and inarguably, the *actual* subjects of these essays—the multifaceted Ernest Hemingway.

Knowledgeable, directive, Hemingway intoned the first-person voice of teacher and insider, world traveler, connoisseur, sportsman, and disciplined professional. These self-referential *Esquire* texts offered commentary "authoritative," often strident, their meanings intoned by a knowledgeable contemporary. Understandably, such essays provoked both positive and negative reader responses, including fiery "summary judgment" critiques from professionals: both literary critics and newspaper pundits.

Collectively, Hemingway's essays present and defend his personal vision of the "complete" man of letters and, more specifically, of himself in that role amid the broad contemporary "scene." Having witnessed the recent past as a reporter for the *Toronto Star*, he is a knowledgeable, "credentialed" writer in *Esquire* regarding the European economy, the rise of fascism in Italy, the power struggles in Spain, including the central role of the Catholic hierarchy. He predicts the "next war," and he wants the United States to remain neutral.

However comprehended in their immediate time present, the twenty-five *Esquire* essays, collectively, and now viewed retrospectively, constitute a singular writing achievement for the author in this decade.

Regardless, the critical question touching the *Esquire* Hemingway at the outset, albeit both then and now phrased variously: What happened to the author of *The Sun Also Rises*, *A Farewell to Arms* . . . the creator of Nick Adams, Jake Barnes, Catherine Barkley?

Answers began and developed from an initial chance meeting and fortuitous intellectual embrace between two creative geniuses.

• • •

In the beginning . . .

The year 1933 presented urgent economic pressures on Hemingway. He needed to reestablish and sustain both the readership and income levels that closed out his 1920s. *Death in the Afternoon* (1932) had not, and *Winner Take Nothing* (1933) would not approach those earlier sales figures.

Going forward, such economic challenges might have nullified any positive Hemingway response to Arnold Gingrich's unexpected and singular invitation: to join—as a major figure—his planned fall launch of *Esquire: The Quarterly for Men.* Obvious disqualifying (?) negatives touching this proposal: a national Depression; in spring 1933, *Esquire* was still only a concept, a venue soon to be but not yet finally shaped nor published; a quarterly "magazine for men" anticipating a readership among males of wealth and/or leisure (a realistically broad and viable readership in the mid-1930s?).

For Hemingway, the question of taking up *Esquire* arose amid undeniable personal pressures on him for change. His acceptance, more or less immediate as it turned out, anchored in and depended for success directly upon the fortuitous conjunction of two events: Hemingway's genuinely seeking a *new* direction (including economic) for his writing; Gingrich's arrival on scene, *the* editor to facilitate and fund that new writing direction. The editor's already-planned and in-place "brainchild," *Esquire: The Quarterly for Men,* was scheduled to begin publishing in fall 1933.

The magazine's October 27 launch (ironically, coincidental with publication that month of *Winner Take Nothing*) proved so successful that by January 1934, *Esquire: The Quarterly for Men* was no longer a quarterly but, as today, a monthly—and retitled, *Esquire: The Magazine for Men.*

• • •

Following the disappointing sales of *Death in the Afternoon* and *Winner Take Nothing,* Hemingway sought to establish distance between himself and the continuous largesse of Pauline's Uncle Gus. This dedicatee of *A Farewell to Arms* had gifted Hemingway with numerous materials from Spain assisting his taurine research for *Death in the Afternoon;* moreover, such gratuities proved continuous: several automobiles; eight thousand dollars for the Key West house; twenty-five thousand dollars for the African safari.

Then, in 1934, Hemingway borrowed—not from Gus—more than five thousand dollars (combined) from Scribner editor Max Perkins and his new editor at *Esquire*—Arnold Gingrich (from the latter, thirty-three hundred dollars as an advance against twelve essays). These dollars helped fund purchase of his fishing yacht *Pilar.* Effecting both status and some personal financial security for Hemingway, such borrowings occurred as Key West declared its own "state of emergency," July 2, 1934: half its population was then on federal relief (Curnutt and Sinclair xxii).

• • •

Arnold Gingrich's vision, willingly shaped to *feature* Hemingway, and his timely largesse proved irresistible for the author because indispensable—at the time presenting essentially nothing less than a positive, career-altering, thus life-changing, opportunity. Hemingway accepted Gingrich's offer: a "founder's" role as the principal contributing writer for *Esquire: The Magazine for Men* (to appear monthly via a "letter" essay beginning in January 1934).

This serendipitous opportunity would help Hemingway underwrite personal travel and other expenses regarding planned, some already developing, nonfiction writing projects. Such sustained funding also would help assuage the author's disappointment, even anger, over increasingly-in-print criticism of his lifestyle and his subjects and viewpoints. *Esquire* would provide a platform for rebutting both readers and professional critics, the latter upset that his fiction "failed" to face social issues, much less expose and address their underlying causes.

By exploring unlimited handpicked subjects, occasionally fleshed out with photos and/or illustrations, Hemingway could, he believed, directly explain and image his values and document a personal vision in his *own* voice—actually, his own many voices: hardworking artist and sportsman; man of letters; man of action; man of leisure. He could and would range across art, sports, travel, to European unrest, even war. Regarding "sport" as a specific subject—he expatiated on deep-sea fishing, big-game hunting, bullfighting, boxing. Soon he began developing a *personal voice* and tone on topics and in viewpoints entirely his own: his persona "an authoritative figure speaking casually, and not writing and revising" (Stephens, *Hemingway's Nonfiction* 332).

Hemingway's twenty-five such letters, undeniably a format that was new in many ways, unfolded in an article journalism offering information expressed with the accuracy and clarity of sophisticated feature writing. His *Esquire* journalism took up the contemporary moment uniquely, anchoring it in numerous unexpected vantage points entirely his own.

• • •

Critical background regarding *Esquire*'s founding in spring and fall 1933 centered, at the outset, in the acumen and business insight of Arnold Gingrich. Phi Beta Kappa from the University of Michigan (1925), Gingrich had joined the Men's Wear Service Corporation. In 1931, he created *Apparel Arts* to rival trade publication *Men's Wear*. Then, in 1932, he focused on what would become *Esquire*—a periodical magazine he conceived as the "male counterpart" to *Vogue* and *Harper's Bazaar* (Gingrich, *Treasury* xi)—specifically, a quarterly publication for (wealthy) men.

His bold idea: "Conceived at the darkest moments of the depression . . . born at the dawn of the New Deal," this periodical would target men "unimpeded by financial worries, the first to buy new styles . . . new models . . . to take up new vogues" (Gingrich, *Treasury* xi). Not least, it would assume a cultured cachet for the "serious reader attracted to *Esquire*'s lettered side" (Gingrich, *Armchair Esquire* 21).

While engaged with this planning, Gingrich fortuitously encountered Ernest Hemingway in Louis Henry Cohn's New York bookstore, the House of Books. Gingrich's being a collector of Hemingway titles proved instrumental in moving conversation forward, soon effecting a publishing agreement: Hemingway would be *Esquire*'s "principal" contributor—and not least, he would help attract other writers.

For each edition, Hemingway agreed to write a letter averaging roughly fifteen hundred words on any subject, from any location, absent editorial interference (except for questions of libel—as determined by Gingrich). Hemingway's payment: two hundred dollars per article, twice that given any other writer—and, by 1936, increased to five hundred dollars (Gingrich, *Nothing But People* 271).

In the initial edition, "Autumn," in October 1933, Hemingway headed up a distinguished cast of writers, including, in alphabetical order: Erskine Caldwell, Morley Callaghan, John Dos Passos, James T. Farrell, Dashiell Hammett, and Ring Lardner; and an eclectic range of writers of different stripes: Douglas Fairbanks Jr., Harry Hirschfeld, Bobby Jones, Gilbert Seldes, Gene Tunney—their wide-ranging texts surrounding one, "Poor Man's Night Club," by founding editor Arnold Gingrich.

• • •

In that premier edition, *Esquire: The Quarterly for Men* announced its raison d'être: "to become the common denominator of masculine interests, to be all things to all men." Under several headings, Gingrich suggested more fully, and in no uncertain terms or risk of confusion, its specific purpose—"giving the masculine reader a break": "The general magazines, in the mad scramble to increase the woman readership that seems to be so highly prized by national advertisers, have bent over backward in catering to the special interests and tastes of the feminine audience. This has reached a point . . . where the male reader looking through what purports to be a general magazine, is made to feel like an intruder upon gynaeric mysteries. Occasionally features are included for his special attention, but somewhat after the manner in which scraps are tossed to the patient dog beneath the table" (*Esquire,* fall 1933, title page).

This interest in and proportioning of all things male was enhanced by another of the editor's claims in the magazine's opening moments, specifically in response to the anticipated question, "How will you be able to sustain this ambitious project that is *Esquire?*" To such "doubting Thomases," Gingrich replied "that the first issue of *Esquire* is meant to be a low mark rather than a high one, and that it will be not merely equaled but surpassed in every issue from here on out."

While conceived as a quarterly, the magazine's initial dramatic sales success dictated an immediate course correction. Monthly publication began with the second issue, in January 1934.

Between that date and August 1936, except for three months without an article, Hemingway published, as "the lead-off man," a total of twenty-five essays—some including photos or illustrations to image and explain this "writer" as a man of action and a man of letters. These texts document deep-sea fishing from Bimini, Key West, Cuba; hunting from Tanganyika; postwar Paris and Spain; writers and writing from New York and Key West. And although not part of the initial agreement, Hemingway would add six short stories for *Esquire,* beginning with "The Snows of Kilimanjaro" in August 1936. Gingrich publicly applauded this story—and more; he arranged for Hemingway a financial bonus: one thousand shares of *Esquire* stock (Merrill 35).

Beyond his own specific "material" contributions to the magazine, Hemingway, the constant, headed a distinguished revolving cast of contributors (Gingrich soon becoming known as the "headhunter of famous authors"), including in the years 1934–38, among others, Havelock Ellis, Ford Madox Ford, Aldous Huxley, Thomas Mann, Bertrand Russell, Leon Trotsky; and American writers Erskine Caldwell, John Dos Passos, Theodore Dreiser, Scott Fitzgerald, Dashiell Hammett, Langston Hughes, H. L. Mencken, George Jean Nathan, John O'Hara, Ezra Pound, John Steinbeck, Thomas Wolfe.

• • •

From the outset, Gingrich had conceptualized the ideal *Esquire* reader: an educated, financially secure, semi-sophisticated urban *fellow,* a male "character type" that over time *Esquire* did attract, identify, characterize, and nurture.

While any such reader portrait must be, at best, a snapshot

generalizable in its details, and thus at a certain point inexact, the broad-stroke middle-aged figure characterized evolved from the magazine's own (periodic) questionnaires seeking to capture or describe or present the "typical" *Esquire* reader. The portrait coincides with the last of Hemingway's twenty-five essays and with his first of six short stories (1936–39)—specifically, "The Snows of Kilimanjaro."

The typical *Esquire* reader at that moment in time:

> You're a married man, thirty-six years old. You'll be thirty-seven on the twenty-first of September. You look at your copy of this magazine on an average of four or five times a month, and ten other people look through it during the month. You play bridge, go to night clubs, and you may enjoy dancing. At any rate, you dance. You wear your tailcoat once a month, and your dinner jacket half again as often. You belong to a country club. You left college in your junior year. But you own your own home, which is more than the average college graduate can say at your age. You buy 1.42 books each month. On all purchases that run over a hundred dollars, you and your wife have the habit of talking it over together before deciding. You are three times more frequent a violator of this rule than she is. Since the bank holiday you've both been a little more impulsive about parting with your hard-earned money for purposes of comfort and the enjoyment of living than you ever were before. Your favorite spectator sport is football, while your favorite active sport is golf, with tennis a fairly close second. You'd rather go to the theatre than the movies, and you'd rather do either than dance. Your favorite authors are Sinclair Lewis and Ernest Hemingway, practically in a dead heat for first place in your literary rankings. The author for whose work you seem to care least is Ben Ames Williams. Your favorite actress is Helen Hayes, although you like Katherine Cornell so well that it's hard for you to decide between them. Your favorite actor is Leslie Howard. As for the screen you just can't seem to see anybody but Charles Laughton among the men and Myrna Loy among the women. When it comes to radio entertainers, you rank Jack Benny off by himself,

and the only trouble you have is deciding whether Woollcott annoys you more than Burns and Allen. It's even money that you won't read this, as your feeling about this space seems to be that you take it or leave it alone, and you skip it just about as often as you read it. That's too bad, because for this once, at least, we'd enjoy having you look yourself over in this mirror of your own manufacture. (*Esquire*, September 1936, 5)

As this detailed "reader snapshot" touched Hemingway, man and author, in late summer 1936, its timeliness proved extraordinary. It captured a specific time in the magazine's history when and where it overlapped with Hemingway's own history, that "moment" also a critical juncture for each—that is:

—the last one of Hemingway's twenty-five *Esquire* essays appears, May 1936;

—"The Snows of Kilimanjaro," arguably Hemingway's finest short story, appears, in *Esquire*, August 1936;

—this comprehensive survey of "the *Esquire* reader" creates a broad spectrum of that (male) reader's individual characteristics as these exist and are "describable" specifically in September 1936 (and if these collocations are not enough: even as "The Short Happy Life of Francis Macomber" appears this month in *Cosmopolitan*).

Hemingway's status as an accomplished author across genres (journalism, essay, fiction) is reported on as understood among an *identifiable, educated, contemporary, adult, male* readership. These "snapshot" details capture the typical *Esquire* reader whose individual characteristics are identified or suggested here and who currently prompts monthly *Esquire* sales to average above 500,000.

This representative *Esquire* male reader (a man of education and means) accepts Hemingway's status as essayist and fiction writer. Recognized as a distinguished author, Hemingway is a reader favorite appreciated, even paired, with fellow American midwestern novelist and Nobel laureate Sinclair Lewis. Notable also: in 1936, this positive assessment of Hemingway's importance is registered in *Esquire* well before publication of *For Whom the Bell Tolls* and that novel's widespread support for the Pulitzer Prize nomination in 1940.

• • •

As Gingrich had hoped at the outset, Hemingway became the magazine's most "talked about" feature. His name helped raise and sustain monthly sales exceeding all expectations, despite its Depression-era price of fifty cents. Among the magazine's specific, continuous principal attractions: Hemingway's freelancing on art, literature, writing, sports, national politics, European unrest . . . war. Regarded as an expert on these subjects, his voice guaranteed attention, proving informational, conversational, and often, when topical, potently controversial.

Hemingway's awareness and understanding regarding contemporary "issues"—his addressing economic and social realities, every bit as much as his ignoring them—generated strong reactive controversy among journalists and other public figures regarding the writer's role in times such as the present. Much of what he said reflected, too, his "understanding" and fear regarding how American writers are "destroyed": "They read the critics. If they believe the critics when they say they are great then they must believe them when they say they are rotten and they lose confidence. At present we have two good writers who cannot write because they have lost confidence through reading critics. If they wrote, sometimes it would be good and sometimes not so good and sometimes it would be quite bad, but the good would get out. But they have read the critics and they must write masterpieces. The masterpieces the critics said they wrote. They weren't masterpieces of course. They were just quite good books. So now they cannot write at all. The critics have made them impotent" (*Green Hills of Africa* 23–24).

Hemingway sharpened his vision, taking public stock of himself as writer. He responded both to issues and to reader reactions printed in the magazine. Doing so, he addressed (sometimes even "calling out") other writers by name; some examples included fellow fictionist Ring Lardner; journalists Heywood Broun, H. L. Mencken, Gilbert Seldes, Westbrook Pegler, William Saroyan, Alexander Woollcott, even major literary critic Edmund Wilson—each a fellow professional critical of Hemingway's lifestyle, social conscience, and, not least, artistic integrity.

• • •

Assuming a nuanced first-person persona in *Esquire,* Hemingway often explained, argued, judged, the "contemporary moment" in distinctly iconoclastic voices: teacher-insider; sportsman; celebrity; connoisseur; literary artist; journalist. His subjects ranged from deep-sea fishing and big-game hunting to politics, economics, and war. Each article, at base informational, often proved in its tone and summary details both instructive and *authoritative.*

An impressive example of such intellectual content: the Philadelphia Academy of Science was interested in Hemingway's theories about marlin. He believed that marlin are like jewfish, ending life as females, no matter how they began. He invited ichthyologists from the Philadelphia Academy of Science to fish with him, even presenting them a blue marlin, then only the second of its species to be caught in the Gulf Stream, for the Philadelphia Museum. Recognizing this assistance to scientific research, in action described in the *Proceedings of the Academy of Natural Sciences of Philadelphia,* a species of fish was named after him: the *Neomerinthe hemingwayi* in 1935 (Fowler, *Proceedings* 41–43).

Four of the twelve Gulf Stream letters include photographs, illustrations accompanying the texts of six others. Sixteen photos appear with the first *Esquire* article, "Marlin Off the Morro," including two of Hemingway's record black marlin—twelve feet, eight inches, 486 pounds—"the biggest catch of this season, brought to gaff by E. H. in 65 minutes." The rhetorical effect of the photos accompanying these texts is to offer drama, silent testimony, and tribute to active expertise. Only once in these Gulf Stream essays does Hemingway specifically reference a photo—here capturing a large marlin shown mutilated by a shark before it could be landed (July 1935, 23).

In a more characteristic and applicable example of his concern with *craft,* professionalism, and that not least among sports fishermen, Hemingway concluded another Gulf Stream letter with an argument stressing the *environment:* "Bimini needs a good smoke house. . . . The fisherman could pay a fee for having the fish cured and take the meat himself or it would revert to the government [bringing in] a steady revenue to the town. . . . At present it is disgusting and sickening to see edible game fish slaughtered and wasted. Killing fish . . . allowing their meat to waste, should be an offense punishable by law" ("The President Vanquishes," July 1935, 167).

This responsible concluding detail—to an essay with an altogether different primary focus—calls attention to Hemingway's sensitive treatment of the social *responsibilities* between contemporary man and the natural world. Such responsibilities are underscored here as compared with the kind of broad "attack" from contemporary naysayers that his interest and activity in Gulf Stream fishing could produce:

> This is a beef against Hemingway. This fishing that he thinks makes the gong ring isn't even a tinkle. . . . There were about thirty Plushbottoms and Hemingways there—all gone simple over fishing. . . . I went out alone . . . and by the afternoon the Captain didn't have enough flags for the sailfish I hooked. . . . But this wasn't my entire catch. The boat was loaded with grouper, amberjack and barracuda—plenty pounds of fish. At the dock, a flunkey unloaded the catch, weighed the big ones to see if you broke some sort of record, somebody took some pictures, then the flunkey tossed the whole catch off the dock to the sharks. Great sport, eh feller? Any sap can catch a boatload nearly every day. It's about as tough as catching flies around a garbage can with fly paper and just as sporting. (Liberman, "Deep-Sea Low-Down," May 1935, 12)

Usually informal (referring to himself as "your correspondent" and regularly using the second-person personal pronoun), Hemingway's mood varies from relaxed, even contemplative, to an instructional tone that approaches formal lecturing: "This fish was hooked on a trolled cero mackerel bait, on a 12/0 Pflueger swordfish hook, No. 13 piano wire leader, Hardy 20 oz. tip and Hardy 6-inch reel with 500 yards of 39-thread line and was gaffed and taken on board one hour and twelve minutes from the time he was hooked. He jumped twelve times and was a male fish" ("Genio after Josie," October 1934, 21).

Despite his responding to sometimes savage criticism of such content in these pressing economic times, his letters, at their best, *present* Ernest Hemingway, a man with values held both as an individual and as an artist. On the whole, the twenty-five essays underwrite an artist's apologia. The twelve Gulf Stream letters, half the total number of his *Esquire* essays, demonstrate the simplicity and directness that characterize Hemingway's excellence in feature writing: "The Gulf Stream and the other great ocean currents are the last wild country. . . . You are more alone than you can ever be hunting and the sea is the same as it has been since before men ever went on it in boats. In a season fishing you will see it oily flat as the becalmed galleons saw it while they drifted to the westward; white-capped with a fresh breeze as they saw it running with the trades; and in high, rolling blue hills the tops blowing off them like snow as they were punished by it" ("On the Blue Water," April 1936, 31).

Hemingway's journalist writing is idiosyncratic, deliberately effecting, as he intended, a new "prose." Enacting the writer's craft, particularly when engaging technical matter as "round and whole and solid" and "true"—he produces the *poetic* in otherwise purely mechanical details, as, for example, when describing this interaction with a giant marlin:

> He can see the bulk of him under water, great blue pectorals widespread like the wings of some huge underwater bird, and the stripes around him like purple bands around a brown barrel, and the sudden

> upthrust waggle of a bill. . . . [When] hooked . . . the drag loosed now, to go off jumping, throwing water like a speedboat, in those long, loping rhythmic, pounding leaps of twenty-feet and more in length. To see that happen, to feel that fish in his rod, to feel that power and . . . great rush, to be a connected part of it and then to dominate it and master it and bring that fish to gaff, alone and with no one else touching the rod, reel, or leader, is something worth waiting many days for. ("Out in the Stream: A Cuban Letter," August 1934, 19)

• • •

In "Monologue to the Maestro," Hemingway, addressing his own writing technique, offers a writing maxim—later published and oft-quoted. His interlocutor, Arnold Samuelson, is a young man who hitchhiked from Minnesota to Key West to learn about writing from Hemingway. After making him the night watchman for the *Pilar*, the author shares with this acolyte an introductory credo of writing "do's and don'ts," including: "Always stop when you're going good and you know what will happen next; read everything so you know what you have to beat; watch what happens . . . and write it down making it clear so the reader will see it too and have the same feeling that you had; get in somebody else's head for a change; listen and observe (You should be able to go into a room and when you come out know everything that you saw there and not only that. If that room gave you any feeling you should know exactly what it was that gave you that feeling)."

Along the way, he offers numerous truisms and nuggets of advice touching the role of the imagination:

> It is the one thing besides honesty that a good writer must have. The more he learns from experience the more truly he can imagine. If he gets so he can imagine truly enough people will think that the things he relates all really happened and that he is just reporting.
>
> If it was reporting, they would not remember it. When you de-

> scribe something that has happened that day the timeliness makes people see it in their own imaginations. A month later that element of time is gone, and your account would be flat and they would not see it in their minds nor remember it. But if you make it up instead of describe it you can make it round and whole and solid and give it life. You create it for good or bad. It is made; not described. It is just as true as the extent of your ability to make it and the knowledge you put into it.

And the writer should have read everything, so "he knows what he has to beat: . . . *War and Peace, Madame Bovary, Buddenbrooks, Dubliners, Tom Jones, Huckleberry Finn*" and all the good Kipling and Maupassant, Henry James's short stories: "There is no use writing anything that has been written better before unless you can beat it. What a writer in our time has to do is write what hasn't been written before or beat dead men at what they have done. . . . Most live writers do not exist. Their fame is created by critics who always need a genius of the season, someone they understand completely and feel safe in praising, but when these fabricated geniuses are dead they will not exist. The only people for a serious writer to compete with are the dead that he knows are good" (October 1935, 21).

• • •

Memorable moments occur in the *Esquire* essays when a self-defensive Hemingway speaks out on craft—whether the sportsman's or the writer's. Such pieces, sometimes humorous, can be caustic, coarse, even obscene. A knowledgeable figure, one who "suffered fools" almost not at all, Hemingway often took on his critics, minimizing their critiques via his own rhetorical flourishings—for example, regarding criticism of his African safari in 1934: *"Their clients get record heads, record tusks and super lions year after year. They simply happen to be super hunters and super shots.* (There are too many supers in these last two sentences. Re-write them yourselves lads and see how easy it is to do better than Papa. Thank you. Exhilarating feeling, isn't it?) *Both mask their phenomenal skill under a pose of nervous incapacity which serves as an effective insulation and cover for their truly great pride in the reserve of deadliness that they live by.* (All right now, better that one. Getting harder, what? Not too hard you say? Good. Perhaps you're right)" ("Notes on Dangerous Game: The Third Tanganyika Letter," July 1934, 19).

While these excerpts "explode" personal attacks on both his subjects and writing style, Hemingway also can and does defend the broader writing profession—he the litterateur as well as author-journalist. An ironic, even "brutal," example is his unsparingly negative assessment of famous Scribner contemporary Ring Lardner, whose work Hemingway repeatedly imitated in his own high school journalism. He writes here on the occasion of the senior writer's death. His issue:

> Ring Lardner has not been dead long enough for anyone more interested in literature than in the personality of his friends to criticize him with the impartial scalpel of the post-mortem examiner. But when it is done, and it will take a finely ground and disinterested scalpel to post him properly. . . . it will be stated that what kept Ring Lardner from being a great writer was the very thing for which Mr. Pegler praises him . . . [not using dirty words]. It was not that he did not care for the human race . . . but he felt superior to the part of it he knew best [sports figures]. . . . Take the matter of dirty words. I doubt if a day has passed in my life in which I have not heard what Mr. Pegler calls dirty words used. Therefore how could a writer truly record any entire day and not use dirty words?" ("Defense of Dirty Words: A Cuban Letter," September 1934, 19)

Put succinctly: Lardner is not a master. No writer can write anything truly great when he feels superior to the people he writes about, regardless of his compassion. Hemingway believed that Lardner "with never a dirty word wrote of those who make it with their hands in the nightly tragic somewhere of their combat, distorting the language that they speak into a very comic diction, so there's no tragedy ever, because there is no truth" ("Defense," 158B).

Pegler was not alone in his distress regarding Hemingway in *Esquire* on the now-deceased Lardner. Columnist Gilbert Seldes observed: "Mr. Lardner despised people, if he did, because they were swine; Mr. Hemingway sneers at people because they are not bulls. I stick to Mr. Lardner, considering his attitude of mind more civilized" ("The Prize-fighter and the Bull," November 1934, 174).

Perhaps understandably, Hemingway could not let these matters stand thus. His follow-up was an off-color *ad hominem* response to this personal criticism: "The magazine, it seems, is coming out early, a break for all of us who cannot wait a whole month to get another shot of Gilbert Seldes. (*It's a vice with me. I tried to break it off. They said all it would bring was blindness, insanity, and death but I said no, I'd paid the fifty cents. . . . Let me read Seldes if I want to. It's no worse than a bad cold and if you get it at the start you can knock it with this stuff I'm going to give you*)" ("Notes on Life and Letters: Or a Manuscript Found in a Bottle," January 1935, 21).

Despite the unpleasantness of general reader complaints in the "Sound and Fury" sections of the magazine and regardless how intense these could become, the professional voices, both inside and outside the magazine's pages, were the most consistently brutal and unforgiving overall.

Early following Hemingway's seeming dismissal of Ring Lardner's work, Heywood Broun, in his "It Seems to Me" column in the *New York World Telegram*, August 18, 1934, lashed out at Hemingway, dismissing the author's achievements and importance: "I do not like the man, and yet I must admit that I know no other phony in the whole course of English letters who could write so well concerning things about which he had not the slightest comprehension [i.e., bullfighting and boxing]. . . . I feel that in the current year and in the seasons to come there is going to be an increasing demand that authors know their stuff. . . . The Proletarian Novel" (13).

• • •

The multi-varied Hemingway "persona" voiced in his *Esquire* texts is only partially invented. A genuine *self* speaks. His words, no less when he is fiercely angry or brutally ironic, mark him as sympathetic and reliable in the contemporary moment. His widespread personal experiences are still unfolding in these years and on three continents. Again—after more than a decade away from formal journalism—his reporting effects a serious, sympathetic sense of place and time, these credentials offering a critical anchoring in the tortuous economic time present.

In the midst of an increasingly dehumanized world, Hemingway writes in *Esquire* of personal ideas, values, ideals—not acts but beliefs, the author on authorship and on himself:

> The hardest thing . . . is to write straight honest prose on human beings. First you have to know the subject; then you have to know how to write. Both take a lifetime to learn and anybody is cheating who takes politics as a way out. . . . All the outs are too easy and the thing itself is too hard. . . . Books should be about the people you know, that you love and hate, not about the people you study up about. . . . If the book is good, is about something you know, and is truly written and reading it over you see that this is so you can let the boys [critics] yip and the noise will have that pleasant sound coyotes make on a very cold night when they are out in the snow and you are in your own cabin that you have built or paid for with your work. ("Old Newsman Writes: A Letter from Cuba," December 1934, 26)

No less important for the serious writer is a critical "barometer" to assess, shape, and control personal reflection and memory: "Some of the best shooting I remember was in Tolstoi and I have often wondered how the snipe fly in Russia now and whether shooting pheasants is counter-revolutionary. When you have loved three things all your life, from the earliest you can remember; to fish, to shoot and, later, to read; and when, all your life, the necessity to write has been your master, you learn to remember and, when you think back, you remember more fishing and shooting and reading than anything else and that is a pleasure. You can remember the first snipe you ever hit walking on the prairie with your father" ("Remembering Shooting-Flying: A Key West Letter," February 1935, 21).

• • •

Given the particular "time present" of these texts, Hemingway's *Esquire* subjects range from deep-sea fishing and big-game hunting increasingly to politics, economics, and war.

Experience establishes his authority. Hemingway has seen the developing tragedy in Europe via his earlier *Star* reporting (in 1922, he was among the first American newsmen to interview Mussolini). He followed, often witnessing the rise of Fascism and Nazism, the revolution in Spain, the Communist riots in Paris, the overthrow of Machado in Cuba in 1933 and the counterrevolution in 1934, the Depression in America, and Mussolini's incursion into Ethiopia in 1935.

In *Esquire,* his pertinent observation: "*We must keep out of it*" ("A Paris Letter," February 1934). In a similar piece, his informed sensitive intelligence led Hemingway to voice what many would soon discover and painfully come to understand:

> Many in Italy today . . . remember the last war as it was; not as they have been taught. Many . . . have been beaten because they opened their mouths, some were killed, others are in prison . . . and some have left the country. It is a dangerous thing in a dictatorship to have a long memory. You should learn to live for the great deeds of the day. As long as any dictator controls his press there will always be great daily deeds to live for. . . . Mussolini's sons are in the air where there are no enemy planes to shoot them down [in Ethiopia]. But poor men's sons all over Italy are foot soldiers, as poor men's sons all over the world are always foot soldiers. And me, I wish the foot soldiers luck; but I wish they could learn who is their enemy—and

why. ("Wings Always Over Africa: An Ornithological Letter," January 1936, 174–75)

• • •

Overt reaction to the especially political dimensions of Hemingway's *Esquire* letters as expressed by fellow professionals—from authors to newspaper columnists—proved ubiquitous and most often sharply critical. Taking up Hemingway, man and writer, and linking his public acts and ideas to *Esquire,* columnists—especially widely read commentators such as Broun, Mencken, Woollcott, judged *Esquire* "low-brow" or worse: "like having Thomas Mann or Ernest Hemingway read from their works at a burlesque show" (Pringle, *Scribner's Magazine,* March 1938, 33). This latter voice dives deep into this distortive, albeit colorful morass describing the *Esquire* habitué at length—in part: "He drives too fast. And he swears upon no provocation at all. . . . He hasn't been to church since the last time he ushered at a wedding. And try as we may, we have yet to find a subject which he considers sacred. . . . The *Esquire* man cares not a whit for better wages for the masses, better working conditions, or shorter hours. . . . What he likes is the old leisure of 1929."

Major pundits voiced similar criticisms, even berating Hemingway's own choice of subjects and personal lifestyle—each implying or indicating or accusing Hemingway of deliberately ignoring the nation's economic woes. Edmund Wilson, prominent essayist, literary critic, and fellow Scribner author, whom Hemingway earlier had held in high regard, was utterly dismissive. Wilson described Hemingway as the "*Esquire Man*"*:* he, who "with the sportsman's tan and outdoor grin . . . poses with a giant marlin . . . to exploit . . . in well-paying and trashy magazines . . . the Hemingway of loose disquisitions—arrogant, belligerent, and boastful—the worst-invented character . . . in the author's work" (*Atlantic,* July 1939).

Aside from such professional commentary, general reader objections (essentially uncensored) moil about in *Esquire*'s "Sound and Fury" section: on the one hand, too much matter simply sexual—"popular, slick, cheesecake, smoking car, girlie"; regarding Hemingway, even "*too much* . . . fishing and hunting"; on the other hand, broadly, "*too little* . . . 'big pay' magazine sophistication; social relevance." Missing for many? "Hemingway's renowned fictional voice and style" (Stephens 332–33).

Accusations that he "sold out," "abandoned his talent," "compromised his integrity," are certainly false. Hemingway could have sought venues like *Vanity Fair* and *Cosmopolitan*—at this time, the latter had paid five thousand dollars for a short story (Gingrich, *Nothing But People* 87)—or Hollywood, which had been seeking materials from him since *A Farewell to Arms*. The much-maligned hunting and fishing texts "enlarged his public image as an accomplished, versatile sportsman," a "technically proficient journalist," and a man and a writer "who never tired of exposing the amateur, the 'four-letter man' who failed to measure up to the professional" (Grimes, "Hemingway" 364).

His multifaceted persona is not the exaggerated creation of the Kansas City, Milan, Toronto periods. Albeit casual, the *Esquire* letters offer an extraordinary range of subjects—including the quintessential Hemingway, a man of the *natural* world: "America has always been a country of hunters and fishermen. As many people, probably, came to North America because there was good free hunting and fishing as ever came to make their fortunes" ("He Who Gets Slap Happy," *Esquire*, August 1935, 19).

Hemingway's *Esquire* canon exhibits a lifestyle and career through the multiple voices of a complexly nuanced persona—often very like the "real" Ernest Hemingway. These essays offer his key public testimony in the decade of his greatest productivity and widest range of self-expression.

In sum, for Hemingway, *Esquire* provided numerous possibilities, despite, even from the outset, certain of his views guaranteeing negative reader responses. Particularly censured, his detailing the "sportsman's" lifestyle, these critiques underscoring the absence of any perceived purposeful "political" or "social" content and argument. Subscribers and professional pundits alike questioned his artistic integrity and his social conscience. Previously, many had faulted the "failure" to write fiction offering Left-leaning moral support, that "defect" now greatly aggravated by his *Esquire* persona and the magazine's general content and philosophy. Regardless, whether facing vitriol or praise, Hemingway focused on his *own* acts and ideas absent alteration, explanation, justification.

• • •

Then, important, but at first unnoticed because unexpected, reader reactions to Hemingway's *Esquire* texts (his ideas, the personality he effected) began evolving *from* multifaceted "nay-sayer" objections challenging his apolitical subjects *to* a steadily broadening readership's more sympathetic "mix" of responses. Many among the latter showed awareness and interest in the informational, even intellectual, dimensions of his words and, not least, his subjects: Hemingway, as "lead-off man," always and everywhere—magister. In a "magazine for men" devoted to an affluent lifestyle, he "teaches" how leisure can be rewarding because worthwhile—this value developing in a personal, intellectual, socially grounded sense—as he, himself, exemplified: that is, man of leisure, man of work, man of art.

The principal subject of his *Esquire* essays—unfolding in multiple modes and offering numerous perspectives—is, always, their author, Ernest Hemingway. Moreover, the texts—sometimes outspoken, other times more subtle—are most often impactful because they are political.

Personal experience backgrounds virtually all details possessing teachable import. Hemingway writes from Paris; he writes from Spain. He predicts the next war. He describes the Italian invasion of Ethiopia. A writer knowledgeable, detailed, and astute, Hemingway has traveled. He has seen. He understands. A decade earlier, he reported on—then developing, now actual and dangerous—European political and economic realities. Early in *Esquire,* although informed and experienced regarding both global and national issues, Hemingway revealed himself an energized sportsman.

In short order, however, that authoritative figure also emerged as the dedicated man of letters in touch with contemporary, pressing, real-world issues. Doing so, he defined and sought after a new—for himself—writing mode.

A literary artist, he is serious and concerned about his art's reception and "place" on the contemporary scene. He shapes in his *Esquire* letters an apologia envisioning a new, even original *non-fiction voice:* the author, as insider and artist, expresses, explains, a widely experienced "personal" self—engaged with travel, leisure, and sport as much as other real-world business. Such details, each and all, underpin this writer—both artist and sportsman—at his work.

• • •

While many critics continued to be critical of Hemingway's apparent lack of formal *social import* in his writings given the ever-deepening Depression, more positive responses continued to develop regarding this outspoken sportsman. Hemingway's voice, always singular in attracting readership, even despite reader-written rants "to the editor," began to stimulate interest discernible, indeed notable, as recorded in sales—a measurable barometer of steadily increasing readership. By 1936, at fifty cents a copy (a price four or five times that for most nonspecialized periodicals) and despite harsh times reducing fascination with sport and/or leisure, *Esquire*'s monthly sales had surged from less than 200,000 the first year to 550,000–700,000 (Kaul 106).

• • •

Hemingway's "personalized" *Esquire* perspectives developed across two broad subjects. Early on, he described his ideas, travels, exploits. Later he responded to the personal and professional criticism these subjects generated: a generalized, albeit unyielding critique centered in his downplaying, even "avoiding," social issues—his focus ranging from "bullfights and safaris" to a new obsession, "high-seas" marlin fishing. Regardless, and important for *Esquire,* Hemingway soon attracted genuine, positive, formal (i.e., written) attention from acknowledged experts both among serious sportsmen and some very serious scientists.

Prompted thus and, not least, reflecting his own calibrated self-scrutiny, Hemingway set about in this topical nonfiction for *Esquire* to shape an engaged, newsworthy, public voice and persona. In a deliberate, conscious effort, to a degree similar to that he had initiated earlier with *Death in the Afternoon* (1932), then furthered in *Green Hills of Africa* (1935), he began in the magazine to develop, nuance, and defend—in refrains sometimes oblique, sometimes stentorian—one, indeed the, Ernest Hemingway.

• • •

In *Esquire,* Hemingway accomplished much: he kept writing and publishing; he spoke in tones of familiarity to an *Esquire* audience that bought more than 500,000 copies of the magazine a month by 1936; his work shared space with that of the best literary figures of the period, among others, Erskine Caldwell, Morley Callaghan, e. e. cummings, Ford Madox Ford, John Dos Passos, Theodore Dreiser, F. Scott Fitzgerald, Langston Hughes, Aldous Huxley, Ring Lardner, D. H. Lawrence, Thomas Mann, Ezra Pound; and in the much maligned fishing letters, he worked through material he would turn into *To Have and Have Not* and *The Old Man and the Sea.*

Of greatest import finally: Hemingway's presentation of himself in the letters and the values he held in these years—both as an individual and as an artist, despite sometimes savage criticism of him in each role. As a whole, the twenty-five *Esquire* texts constitute an important personal testament and informal apologia.

Over the many months, editor Gingrich occasionally, necessarily, editorialized (even parried) negative reader reactions to Hemingway in "Backstage with *Esquire,*" "Editor's Notes," and "Publisher's Page" columns. Irrespective of the turbulence generated by certain

Hemingway pieces, Gingrich, as editor, proved an able, understanding, supportive ally—to the last: "They can't forgive his fishing and hunting. They wish he would grow up . . . and face the ugly facts of our changing times. They wish he would show in his writings some awareness of the pock-marked political complexion of our era. In other words, season his literary soup to the moment's taste with a sprinkling of class consciousness, of politico-sociological salt. They forget that politics, as such, is the death of art, that nothing can more damagingly 'date' a work of art for the future than preoccupation with what seem to be serious things of the moment."

And more:

> Shakespeare knew . . . what every artist who survived his obituary notices had to find out on his own: "To Thine own self be true." . . . No artist of our day has learned the lesson any more thoroughly than Ernest Hemingway. To himself ever faithful, he has held true to his long-since self-charted course. . . . It has lost him, these past four or five years, the allegiance of that majority of the critics, those who follow literary "fashions." This falling away of literary camp followers has not surprised him. . . . But it explains why many things are being said of him, and why almost none of what is being said is true.
>
> More completely and consistently the conscious artist than any other writer of our time, he worked . . . on the development of what has become the most infectious literary style in the language. Even then he was not understood. They thought he wrote exactly how people talked, that his style was simply that of an ubiquitous and skillful court-reporter. It wasn't.
>
> It's no trick to copy the Hemingway style. It's almost as easy to duplicate it as it is to parody it. But it is the trick of a lifetime to duplicate the method of seeing with the Hemingway eye for significant and selective detail, to achieve the all-important pattern down to which to strip the so-called "stripped style." This is the thing that makes the Hemingway manner a snare and a delusion for young writers, because it is inseparably inherent in the well-nigh copyproof Hemingway method. ("Reviving Salutes to the Living," February 1937, 5, 28)

Approaching the end of Hemingway's time as a regular *Esquire* contributor, his editor's praise proved unequivocal: "For the magazine's first two years he was its most conscientious contributor. He had to send his copy in from all over the world. . . . He more than once chartered planes . . . to make our monthly deadline. He was in there when we needed him and as long as we needed him. He never needed us" ("A Farewell to the Lead-off Man," June 1937, 5). It is worth mentioning that when he was unable to satisfy *Esquire*'s essay deadline for August 1936, Hemingway sent Gingrich, as substitute, "The Snows of Kilimanjaro," inarguably one of his finest stories.

• • •

Man of letters and "public figure," Ernest Hemingway developed multiple irrepressible and multivocal "selves." These are perhaps no more completely suggested than in the words of distinguished critic, biographer, and literary scholar Matthew J. Bruccoli, who offers a summary exhaustive description and categorization of Hemingway—as both man and artist: "hunter, fisherman, soldier, aesthetician, patriot, military strategist, yachtsman, drinker, womanizer, gourmet, sportsman, philosopher, naturalist, intellectual, anti-intellectual, traveler, war correspondent, boxer, big-game hunter, and author" (*Mechanism of Fame* xix).

*Esquire* captured those Hemingway voices, each and all—Gingrich's personal commitment to both man and artist particularly critical between 1933 and 1939.

# 6

> The world breaks everyone and afterwards
> many are strong at the broken places.
>
> —*A Farewell to Arms*

## Variety and Notoriety

### *TO HAVE AND HAVE NOT* AND *FOR WHOM THE BELL TOLLS*

Ernest Hemingway's 1930s, 1929–40, constitute his most prolific and varied publishing period: principally, *A Farewell to Arms, Death in the Afternoon, Winner Take Nothing, Green Hills of Africa,* thirty-one *Esquire* essays and stories, *The Spanish Earth* (film), *To Have and Have Not,* twenty-eight *NANA* (war zone) dispatches, *The Fifth Column and the First Forty-Nine Stories,* culminating, at decade's turn, in the publication of *For Whom the Bell Tolls*—and the questionable judgments underlying its failure to receive nomination for the Pulitzer Prize.

Snapshots of Hemingway's principal activities in a single year—for example, 1937—suggest both variety (and notoriety) across his in-print "presences" late in the decade. Photographic newspaper and magazine features that year emphasize Hemingway at war, an active journalist; Hemingway at home, publishing his sole novel of the decade, *To Have and Have Not.* Hemingway was the principal in four newspaper interviews and the subject of thirty articles. His published "doings" ranged inordinately—from the "Fascism Is a Lie" address before the Second Congress of American Writers to altogether different headlines, most famously, "Hollywood style" coverage in the *New York Times:* "Hemingway Slaps [Critic Max] Eastman in Face" (August 14, 1937). Unremarked in this latter coverage, was this a pattern of behavior? Hemingway had experienced a similar altercation with poet Wallace Stevens in Key West the previous summer—an out-of-the-way "macho dust-up" that produced no similar public notice.

• • •

Hemingway's published professional writing in this critical decade included certain extraordinary, but not always fruitful, experimentations. As his breadth of focus proved ambitious, sales wavered. Not again—neither in his journalism nor in his creative-imaginative texts—did Hemingway expound in print across so broad a variety of formats and critical voices.

The "experimental" *Death in the Afternoon* (1932) disquisition on Spanish *torero*—braced with numerous asides and eighty-one extratextual "action" photos—became his first volume to yield weak sales. Then the illustrated safari narrative *Green Hills of Africa* (1935), despite serialization preceding volume publication, splintered into a financially disappointing memoir-cum-critical excursus assessing the American literary scene. Within a year, albeit briefly, *serendipity.* The African experience spawned two among Hemingway's finest short stories: "The Snows of Kilimanjaro" (*Esquire*) and "The Short Happy Life of Francis Macomber" (*Cosmopolitan*). But then his novel *To Have and Have Not* (incorporating two previously published stories stressing contemporary economic straits) was deemed by many, and in explicit detail, a failure.

In addition, the Spanish Civil War focused Hemingway's attention across several writing formats. In 1938, with director Joris Ivens, he supplemented his formal on-site journalism by scripting narration of the film documentary *The Spanish Earth.* He further explored and leavened his political wartime experiences with a drama, *The Fifth Column.* (Scribner published the play with Hemingway's collected short fiction as *The Fifth Column and the First*

*Forty-Nine Stories* to generally weak sales in October 1938.) Opening on Broadway in March 1940, *The Fifth Column,* Hemingway's final literary "experiment" of the decade, ran for just eighty-seven performances.

Despite the inordinate variety among these texts and the expected breadth of appeal to their potential audiences, Hemingway sold just 116,000 books in the troubled 1930s—impressive but just 14,000 more than for *A Farewell to Arms* alone (Trogdon, *Lousy Racket* 260).

• • •

At Charles Scribner's Sons in the 1930s, Hemingway shared a "literary stable" growing steadily and producing multiple fiction writers with best-selling volumes. Joining him and established figures like Scott Fitzgerald, new Scribner authors in these years: John Peale Bishop, Eugene O'Neill, Marjorie Kinnan Rawlings, Allen Tate, Edmund Wilson, Stark Young—even Sherwood Anderson and, not least, Thomas Wolfe (*Look Homeward, Angel,* 1929; *Of Time and the River,* 1935).

With Fitzgerald and Hemingway, Wolfe completed the publisher's "Big Three." Their names and works proved ubiquitous: twelve novels (including three serializations); nine story collections; twenty-five pieces in *Scribner's Magazine.* Making the numbers, per se, more stunning: Wolfe's time at Scribner was relatively brief, 1929–37 (then signing on with Harper, he died at thirty-seven, in 1938). Fitzgerald, with Scribner since 1920, also died young at this time—just forty-four—in December 1940.

The period from late 1936 to 1940 also proved critical for Hemingway regarding his continuing relationship with Arnold Gingrich and *Esquire,* despite his ceasing to write a monthly article or letter. He published six stories in the magazine—most significant, "The Snows of Kilimanjaro," in August 1936, but notable also, three interrelated wartime stories, in 1938 and 1939, set in the famous Chicote's Bar in Madrid, directly addressing the strife in Spain: "The

Denunciation" (November 1938), "The Butterfly and the Tank" (December 1938), and "Night Before Battle" (February 1939).

• • •

Hemingway had reported to Max Perkins in July 1936 that Gingrich was positive, indeed "very steamed up," about his progress with a novel and that Gingrich urged him to publish that book before the story collection he was also assembling (Perkins, *Selected Letters* 448). Perkins agreed, and thus matters stood in the fall of 1937. Scribner expected a successful return to the novel form and a reinvigoration of the "Hemingway" audience in the timely and domestic *To Have and Have Not.*

Despite positive expectations, Depression-era fiscal concerns restrained Scribner's advertising roll-out: a full-page ad (*New York Times Book Review,* October 17) listed *To Have and Have Not* first—but among nine titles. It stressed three prepublication printings (boasting 10,000 copies) and heralded a "brilliant novel of life in a grim and gaudy corner of America." Modest success of a sort ensued: four printings; 41,085 copies sold; number 4 on the bestseller list the first month.

Most extraordinary at the outset of this "launch" was a stunning *Time* magazine cover, October 18, 1937, featuring an in-color action painting of deep-sea "angler Hemingway" by his friend and Bohemian expatriate artist Waldo Peirce. The portrait appeared over the edited-for-decency dying words of the novel's principal, Harry Morgan, whom Scribner had captioned: "the most completely *real* masculine character that Ernest Hemingway has created" (*NYTBR,* October 17, 1937).

Underscored in promotion for this Depression-era novel set in Key West and centered on an out-of-luck Conch and his ex-prostitute wife was the "maleness-masculinity" that had characterized Hemingway's journalism in this decade—across the *Esquire* canon and central in his *NANA* and other wartime reporting.

Harry Morgan's last words, as he is dying of gunshot wounds

from a Cuban revolutionary he is smuggling on his boat, highlight the novel's socially conscious "one man alone" theme. His words appear below Peirce's "action" Hemingway portrait. Machine-gunned, now incoherent and dying, Harry sums up: "A man ain't got no hasn't got any can't really isn't any way out."

Garbled, nonetheless painfully realistic, this final utterance *replicated on the Time cover* represents extraordinary commitment by the magazine in overt publicity for both author and volume.

• • •

In fact, *Time*'s support did *not* prove predictive. Neither Harry Morgan nor this tale of his final days was understood as indicative or instructive regarding time present by reviewers, even as many were eager for Hemingway's anticipated serious return to contemporary issues in his new novel.

Numerous critical voices, such as Bernard DeVoto's in the *Saturday Review of Literature,* attacked the novel—strikingly in DeVoto's case, coming only after the critic's grim, even gross, opening salvo—a prejudicial sortie generalizing about Hemingway's previous fictional characters: "So far none of Ernest Hemingway's characters has had any more consciousness than a jaguar. They are physiological systems organized around abdomens, suprarenal glands, and genitals. They are sacs of basic instinct. Their cerebrums have highly developed motor areas but are elsewhere atrophied or vestigial. Their speech is rudimentary, they have no capacity for analytical or reflective thought, they have no beliefs no moral concepts, no ideas. Living on an instinctual level, they have no complexities of personality, emotion, or experience" (October 16, 1937, 8).

Despite the unwarranted (unprofessional?) tone here, Hemingway's much anticipated "return to the novel" found among professional reviewers, generally, a uniform disappointment. While less stunningly vicious than DeVoto, many critics drew only qualified or distinctly negative conclusions when quoting specific passages. J. Donald Adams, in the *New York Times* (October 17, 1937), while uniformly negative, assessed and critiqued in concluding judgments typical among other professionals. He concurred with contemporary naysayers (e.g., fellow Scribner authors John Peale Bishop, Wyndham Lewis) in detailing reservations touching Harry, the man, and, as harshly, Harry's creator:

> Since "*A Farewell to Arms*" . . . no mental growth whatever. . . . Essentially, this new novel is an empty book. . . . Harry was a big bruiser of a man, hard as they come, happily married by reason of strong physical attachment, the father of two girls. He owned a fast motor boat, which got him his living. Normally he took out fishing parties, but when he thought he could get away with it . . . ran liquor . . . smuggled Chinamen, and he met his end providing a getaway for a gang of hold-up men. Once, at least, he killed in cold blood just to make sure the job would come cleanly off. . . .
>
> There is nothing in Mr. Hemingway's story to indicate that Harry Morgan had ever tried to get his living by honest and lawful means. All he asked of a job was whether he could get away with it, with profit to himself. Society, so far as we have the story, owed him nothing. And he got nothing in the end, precisely what was coming to him. There is no tragedy; there is no ground for compassion.

Arguably, as *Time* certainly understood, a valid reading of the novel required *some* effort to sympathize with Harry's struggles and, no less, Hemingway's intentions in the events precipitating and contextualizing his character's last days. Regardless, most professional commentators demurred, finding little ground for understanding Harry—neither as a man nor as a "worthy" contemporary.

• • •

Harry Morgan—like Nick Adams, Jake Barnes, and Frederic Henry—*is* a man of his time. A working-class figure, Harry labors among realities. "Class consciousness" and socioeconomic concepts, as ideas, concern him not as he engages a gritty world: he witnesses murder in the streets; he is shot at; he is cheated out of a sizable payday for *honest* work, all in chapter 1.

Harry's "brutality" derives from the need to protect and provide for family. Faithful regarding his wife and daughters, he is otherwise shaped by the times—loner, mercenary, racist, murderer—an "outlaw figure" not unlike Robin Hood, Jessie James, Bonnie and Clyde. Harry's seagoing perils suggest seventeenth-century pirate Harry Morgan, whose name he shares.

Regardless, Harry is faithful to peers and subordinates: with Wesley, his Black crew member, and when his fishing vessel is successfully hired, with the indispensable "hand," the "*voodoo* nigger"; and on land, with fellow Conchs: Freddy, a bar owner; Captain Willie, a commercial boat owner; fellow worker (laborer) Albert—"no-nonsense" Harry respected by each.

Harry emerges a struggling "family man," his brusqueness "humanized" by loving, outsized wife, Marie, and their two teenage daughters. In a scene worthy of Dickens for stressing its broad domestic point, Harry embraces family: "That night I was sitting in the living room smoking a cigar and drinking a whiskey and water and listening to Gracie Allen on the radio. The girls had gone to the show and sitting there I felt sleepy and I felt good. There was somebody at the front door and Marie, my wife, got up from where she was sitting and went to it" (64).

These sentences capture an apt female-dominant family moment, Gracie Allen a superlative humanizing touch. Other positive parent-child relations develop, as do scenes presenting Harry and Marie as a "physically loving" married couple, in contrast to the overt sexual failures among the book's female "haves."

The emotional bond between Harry and Marie overshadows scenes dramatizing one-dimensional male "villains": that is, drunken, dehumanized World War I vets, abandoned "down-and-outers"; these then paired with soulless, loveless rich men on their yachts, characterized variously by their alcoholic, homosexual, guilt-ridden, shameful lives of tax cheating, serial infidelity, disease from various debaucheries. Visual and verbal snapshots freeze-frame this human detritus.

• • •

As in much Hemingway early fiction, from 1925 to 1933, *singular women* "voice" key perspectives, often balancing, uniformly intensifying, moral dereliction in males. Such centering characters include the rich, morally compromised Helene Bradley and Dorothy Hollis. The latter embodies an aware, not-entirely-vacuous "sexual playmate." Emptiness in these two women contrasts with the detailed emotional suffering of morally sensitive Helen Gordon. Her emotional verbal tour de force (the whole of chapter 21) catalogs details defining her marriage as consistently poisoned by a "socialist-writer" husband's infidelities—personal and religious.

Centered amid both social and economic human failures, Harry's Marie comes into focus. As characteristic in Hemingway's major fiction, women address and clarify the fundamental in human relations. Two female monologues highlight contrasts between the "haves" and "have-nots":

Dorothy Hollis's (a have) detailed account of her expensive, sexualized, sterile existence appears toward the novel's close. In bed alone—lonely but increasingly self-aware—Hollis reflects honestly: "Or they just get tired, I suppose. You can't blame them . . . and I can't help John's liver either or that he is drunk so much he isn't any good. He was good. He was marvellous. He was. He really was. And Eddie is. But now he's tight. I suppose I'll end up a bitch. Maybe I'm one now. Only her best friends would tell her. You don't read it in Winchell. That would be a good new thing for him to announce. Bitch-hood. Mrs. John Hollis canined into town from the coast" (244).

Marie's (a have-not) devastating catalog of things lost by Harry's death contrasts her with the decadent rich women and illuminates a deep love for "her man." Most painful now and into the future—as she herself articulates—the meaning of Harry's death for her and their two daughters: "Him, like he was, snotty and strong and quick, and like some kind of expensive animal. It would always get me just to watch him move. I was so lucky all that time to have him. . . . [And now?] You just go dead inside and everything is easy. You just get dead like most people are most of the time. . . . Well, I've got a good start then. . . . I'm way ahead of everybody now" (261).

Marie's embracing the need to go on despite despairing over her sense of lost purpose and self-worth reorients the novel's principal perspective and theme: "one man alone" becomes "one woman alone."

This powerful brief emphasizing the social import of the female perspective in Hemingway's single novel of the decade continues a point of view that is consequential across his major fiction.

It remained unnoted in reviews and among pundits and literary critics. The woman's role here became lost in uniform "socio/economic" readings, such emphases perhaps furthered by two contemporary "financial straits" narratives Hemingway had published earlier, then incorporated into this text: "One Trip Across" (*Cosmopolitan*, 1934) and "The Tradesman's Return" (*Esquire*, 1936).

Finally, "women" in *To Have and Have Not* were lost in critical debates centered on "function of literature" arguments. Masculine in perspective, these emphasized traditional male-female roles.

A final "black mark" in the contemporary critical history of the volume: it was the only novel by an American author banned from public sale and distribution in America during 1938—in Detroit and in Queens, New York. The rationale, generally: Harry lives with a former prostitute and runs black market contraband between Florida and Cuba. Such prejudicial readings were neatly typified in a primary venue by a major critical voice—that is, J. Donald Adams in the *New York Times*. His judgment of *To Have and Have Not* concluded as wholesale dismissal: "Mr. Hemingway's record as a creative writer would be stronger if it had never been published" (October 17, 1937).

Hemingway's issues with critics and official "censors" promulgating judgments such as a work should "never have been published" date back to the 1920s, specifically with *A Farewell to Arms* but also including, to a lesser degree, *The Sun Also Rises* and, among his stories, particularly, "Hills Like White Elephants." Censoring a Hemingway fictional text was *not new, nor was it over*, in 1937.

• • •

With or without regard to "censorable content," economic issues troubling late-1930s purchasing power could not be denied "in the book business." Scribner's Hemingway advertising presented its readership surprisingly hesitant, lackluster, even purely rote enthusiasm for his career short fiction collected in *The Fifth Column and the First Forty-Nine Stories* and published in October 1938.

Selling just 15,110 copies over four printings, the publisher marshaled little written or pictorial support for this collection. The volume was listed with as few as five other titles and with as many as twenty-one. What promotion did develop unfolded inexactly. Most problematic: a noticeable lack of consensus regarding whether the *stories* or the *play* should be the advertising focal point: the play "reads like a flash . . . the stories are just about the first [or finest? what does this mean exactly?] forty-nine stories of all time" (*NYTBR*, December 4, 1938). Read literally, taken seriously, neither blurb element makes precise nor even realistic sense. What is the reader to understand by the claim "of all time"?

• • •

Then, 1939 and . . . *Esquire, pace.*

Arnold Gingrich had made Hemingway *Esquire*'s preeminent monthly contributor, initially paying him twice the rate given other contributors, from the premier issue in October 1933 through August 1936 (the author missing just three months), then intermittently through 1939. A simple handshake at the outset produced thirty-one Hemingway texts: twenty-five essays between 1933 and 1936; six short stories between 1936 and 1939.

Among the most famous of his regular nonfiction essays and suggesting the range of subjects and details characterizing the whole: early (and soon infamous) "Defense of Dirty Words" (September 1934), in which Hemingway drew "heavy fire," especially from fellow professionals, for attacking the fictional "art" of recently deceased Ring Lardner; or at the other extreme, an essay attracting no special notice when published, "On the Blue Water" (April 1936), unmistakable later, however, for containing details shaping his Pulitzer Prize–winning *The Old Man and the Sea* (1952). That volume, Hemingway's only novel published in its entirety in a single magazine issue, appeared in *Life,* not *Esquire.*

Among Hemingway's six *Esquire* stories, "The Snows of Kilimanjaro" (August 1936) so impressed Gingrich that—as in the earlier "simple handshake" cementing their relationship in 1933—the editor responded with special recognition and support for both author and his work: in 1936, editor Gingrich convinced publisher David Smart to award Hemingway one thousand shares of stock (fifteen dollars per share) in recognition of his overall contributions to *Esquire.*

What did his editor see, understand, in "Snows" that made the story worth singular recognition and reward? Gingrich comprehended and appreciated Hemingway's literary genius as a man of and for his time—a conscientious, contemporary male writer and, no less critical, both craftsman and artist.

In "The Snows of Kilimanjaro," the fictional Harry is marred by serious personal faults, most severely his having corrupted or otherwise wasted his genuine talent as a writer primarily through mind-numbing relationships with rich women. These and other wastrel personal criticisms were widespread in this period, touching Hemingway, both man and writer. In "Snows," however—as Gingrich appreciated—the "last laugh" belongs to the writer in this masterpiece of that author's art.

That is, Harry is a wastrel. When honest, he acknowledges this truth and others of his failings. Dying, he understands his duty, responsibility, to write—but too late: now, only in his mind; here, only on his deathbed.

More important: Harry is a fiction. He only exists in this story that dramatizes his complicated "personal," "male-female," and "artistic" ruminations as he is dying—these the serious reflections of a "fallen man" honestly, accurately, assessing himself.

The man who wrote Harry's story—for all that Harry's problems seem to track his author's own—actually writes realistic, credible stories. Fictional Harry is *not* writing. Actual Hemingway *is* writing—fleshing out Harry's faults for *Esquire* and, not least in this artistic gem, for *Esquire*'s editor.

Gingrich understood. He believed that Hemingway had drafted, in "The Snows of Kilimanjaro," one of the era's finest stories, its singular artistry ranking it paramount among the short fiction. More important, because explicit to time present, Gingrich believed that the story successfully exploded contemporary critics' allegations of career-threatening personal excesses dominating Hemingway's own life—moreover, by 1936, seeming to center in a public, hypermasculine, misogynist persona.

While Gingrich's judgment is his own, that assessment is also the subject of the author's ruminations and judgments. In an unpublished text from this time, Hemingway, sensitive to contemporary personal criticism, identified what was crucial in his life as a writer. In so doing, he privately asserted what Gingrich, too, believed—that despite personal vagaries, "Ernest" was not "Harry":

> The ethics of writing are fairly simple but very confusing to the public. The fact that a man lies, is cruel, betrays his wife, gets drunk, betrays his friends, has this or that odd or ugly sexual habit does not mean that he is not as honest in his writing as any Sir Galahad. No matter what lies he tells in his life he is an honest writer as long as he does not lie or deceive his innermost self which writes. He may do cruel and wicked things but if his innermost self judges them

rather than makes excuses for them he is still all right. But once he lies to himself, inside himself, in the part with which he writes, once he defends an action in that inner self rather than understanding it without defense, but with all the remorse you may want, then he is a crooked writer, a faker, and from then on of no importance." (Scafella 15; item 754, JFK Library)

Albeit a merciless self-portrait, these words touch upon a concept fundamental in Hemingway's parents' English (here Victorian, especially Carlylean) heritage: the spiritual worth, even salvation, potential in unwavering commitment to one's *true work*—to be acted upon amid and despite imperfection. For Hemingway, life's meaning lay in the writing, his true work. His written words evidence "the spirit he worked in": they constitute what he "did," what he "became."

Hemingway was as aware as his editor of the negative personal press. It was abundant, overt, and varied as he ceased his monthly *Esquire* letters after August 1936.

• • •

Following his covering the war in Spain and, at home, after publication of *To Have and Have Not,* Hemingway's contact with Gingrich declined to a few brief wartime pieces for the editor's new, short-lived journalism outlet *Ken:* thirteen articles and the Spanish Civil War story "The Old Man at the Bridge," 1938–39. His relationship with Gingrich and *Esquire* in this period ceased after 1939.

Later an unrelated, potentially serious "misstep" briefly arose testing the Hemingway-*Esquire* relationship. In 1949, after the author's decade-long absence from the magazine and while Gingrich himself was away in Switzerland, *Esquire* reprinted "The Snows of Kilimanjaro" with the original text's belittling allusion to Scott Fitzgerald by name, as "Scott." As a matter of fact, *Scott* had been changed to *Julian* in all reprintings of "Snows" following the original publication. Ironically, at time present (1949), neither Gingrich nor Hemingway knew of this "inappropriate" reprinting—a one-time error effecting Hemingway's sole appearance in *Esquire* in the 1940s (and Fitzgerald by then deceased nearly a decade). This miscue produced no embarrassing results, as later clarified by Gingrich in a "Publisher's Page" column (September 1972, 6).

• • •

By decade's end, Hemingway's return to Key West had produced much personal stress and professional change: in 1940, divorce and remarriage; then his leaving Key West and moving to Cuba. On the upside were the sales and fanfare following publication of *For Whom the Bell Tolls* in October.

Then, unexpectedly amid these personal, multi-varied activities and events, came Scott Fitzgerald's unexpected death on December 21, 1940. "Friendship" between the two men, personal and professional, had waxed and waned. It had particularly diminished for Hemingway after Fitzgerald's confessional, failing writer's "Crack-Up" articles in *Esquire* in February, March, and April 1936. At the time, Hemingway openly disapproved of such a "public display" of a writer's creative issues. By the time of his death, Fitzgerald was not the writer's block "has-been" Hemingway and many others had envisioned in 1936. Regardless, on the *downside*, in 1940, his eight books still in print sold just seventy-two copies (Bryer xi), and unsold copies of the second printing of *The Great Gatsby* (1925) remained in Scribner's warehouse.

Nonetheless, at the time of his death, Fitzgerald had begun actually to effect an increasing upside. He was twelve months into publishing seventeen "Pat Hobby" Hollywood stories in *Esquire* (January 1940–May 1941). He was seventy thousand words into *The Last Tycoon*. (Scribner published *Tycoon* with *The Great Gatsby* and five short stories in October 1941.) Perkins had argued that, even incomplete, the in-progress manuscript "gave the lie" to Fitzgerald's despondent assessments of himself and his talent as expressed in 1936. The final *Tycoon* ad stressed Fitzgerald's having again anatomized American culture, here in its latest expressive form, the cinema. The ad appeared on Sunday, December 7, 1941—truly marking the end of an era.

Notable later: in 1960, Scribner established the paperback *Scribner Library.* Fittingly, for both the authors and their publisher, the first five of ten initial titles were Fitzgerald, *The Great Gatsby, Tender Is the Night;* Hemingway, *The Sun Also Rises, For Whom the Bell Tolls;* and Wolfe, *Look Homeward, Angel.*

• • •

By decade's turn, 1940, certain recent Hemingway personal acts had unfortunately mimicked his characters' own missteps, fictional reality threatening, even mirroring, actual personal suffering. Ironically, in 1936, socialite Jane Mason was pleased to be regarded as the "original" of Margot Macomber. Regrettable in his fiction now, Hemingway had unsympathetically portrayed Mason, actually the friend of both Ernest and Pauline, as the sybarite Helene Bradley in *To Have and Have Not.* Even more affecting at this time, because it was both negative and directly personal, Hemingway's marriage to Pauline ended, a result, in part, of his relationship, after 1936, with author, journalist, and fellow war correspondent Martha Gellhorn. Following marriage to Gellhorn in November 1940, the new Hemingway couple took up residence in the Finca Vigia outside Havana in the San Francisco de Paula region.

Amid such inordinate disruptions over several years, by fall 1940, Hemingway's professional prospects—as novelist—must have seemed uncertain at best, anxiety producing certainly. Actually, they simply captured the "truth" of the age-old adage: *It is always darkest just before dawn.*

• • •

By October 1940, Scribner might well have been uncertain or, at the very least, wary of Hemingway's continuing appeal as a novelist. To what degree might his recent negative personal, even publication, history prove "off-putting" to potential readers?

In fact, by the time he married Martha Gellhorn, Scribner appeared worried—not at all. Rather, it proved conspicuously confident regarding *its* author, *the* Ernest Hemingway. The first printing of *For Whom the Bell Tolls*—75,000 copies—more than doubled that for *A Farewell to Arms.* By the week in November that Ernest and Martha married, 310,000 copies of the novel were in print (including for the Book-of-the-Month Club).

Reviewers marveled: twenty excerpts the third week in the *New York Times Book Review;* seventeen in *Publishers Weekly.* Unprecedented advertising continued unfolding: a total of 503 ads, 105 in the *New York Times Book Review.* By May 1941, 565,000 copies (including Book-of-the-Month) were in print. Finally, seven printings, 693,486 copies in total, were published.

What was being sold?

> —*Understood immediately:* "In the four momentous days of this tense and dramatic story of an American, a young Spanish girl and their guerilla companions, there is a compressed lifetime of love and bravery." (*NYTBR,* October 20, 1940)
>
> —*Seven months later,* amid continuous approval by the general reader *and* nomination for the Pulitzer Prize, anticipated: "A book about all things we need to believe in today . . . 'courage and love and innocence and strength and decency and glory.'" (Dorothy Parker, review excerpt, *NYTBR,* May 11, 1941)

• • •

In October, shortly after its initial appearance—unexpected but not inconceivable, given a renowned author, a newsworthy personality, and not least, an increasingly literate reading public—*For Whom the Bell Tolls* garnered nomination support for the Pulitzer Prize in Literature in 1940.

The novel had been widely reviewed and generally applauded by major critical voices. Helpful for establishing that context, a recent, purely coincidental occurrence: In the *Atlantic*, July 1939, Edmund Wilson, in a lengthy, "career overview" piece, "Ernest Hemingway: Bourdon Gauge of Morale," had assessed and contextualized Hemingway's best work to date—for Wilson, residing in the early novels and stories.

Regarding the more recent work, Wilson had demurred, describing Hemingway as often appearing seriously sidetracked: exploiting "his personality for profit—soon, even turning out regular articles for well-paying and trashy magazines." Wilson's explicitly negative assessment described a Hemingway too much associated with *Esquire*. At his best, Wilson understood and affirmed, Hemingway was a serious, accomplished literary artist:

> The condition of life is pain; and the joys of the most innocent surface are somehow tied to its stifled pangs. The resolution of this discord in art made the beauty of Hemingway's stories. He had in the process tuned a marvelous prose. Out of the colloquial American speech, with its simple declarative sentences and its strings of Nordic monosyllables, he got effects of utmost subtlety [that related his work to] Ring Lardner, Sherwood Anderson, Gertrude Stein, using the American language for irony, lyric poetry, psychological insight . . . he now able to charge this naïve accent with a new complexity of emotion, a malaise. The wholesale shattering of human beings in which he has taken part has given the boy [a youthful midwesterner] a touch of panic.

Praising Hemingway's stories and novels of the 1920s, Wilson is significantly less sanguine regarding the fiction in the 1930s—including, currently, *To Have and Have Not*. Regardless, his generally approving critical voice takes up Hemingway's *For Whom the Bell Tolls* for the *New Republic* on October 28, 1940:

> This new novel of Hemingway will come as a relief to those who didn't like "Green Hills of Africa," "To Have and Have Not," and "The

> Fifth Column." The big game hunter, the waterside superman, the Hotel Florida Stalinist, with their constrained and fevered attitudes, have evaporated like the fantasies of alcohol. Hemingway the artist is with us again; and it is like having an old friend back. . . .
>
> [His] early work was, as it were, lyric; and "For Whom the Bell Tolls" is an effort toward something else, which requires a steady hand. The hero of this new novel . . . is a credible young man who is shown in his relation to other people . . . and these other people are for the most part given credible identities, too. . . .
>
> The author has begun to externalize the elements of a complex personality in human figures that have a more complete existence than those of his previous stories. That he should thus go back to his art, after a period of artistic demoralization, and give it a larger scope, that in an era of general perplexity and panic, he should dramatize the events of the immediate past in terms, not of partisan journalism, but of common human instincts that make men both fraternal and combative, is reassuring evidence of the soundness of our intellectual life.

Wilson says little explicitly about Hemingway's female characters, even about the active force in *For Whom the Bell Tolls* that is Pilar. He finds Maria's relationship with Robert Jordan not central to the novel's larger realities.

• • •

Moving female portraits *do* characterize Hemingway's novels and stories—from the beginning, 1925–33. And women, both as subject and theme, are again central at decade's end, 1937–40: in Hemingway's taking up the national economic depression in *To Have and Have Not;* also, now necessarily including broad, extra-literary implications exploring war and women in the contemporary moment—and within his most successful novel—the nearly nominated for the Pulitzer *For Whom the Bell Tolls.*

In his finest novels and stories of the 1920s and in *Winner Take*

*Nothing* (1933), then in his classic short stories, "The Snows of Kilimanjaro" and "The Short Happy Life of Francis Macomber" (1936), and, most recently, with Marie in *To Have and Have Not* (1937), Hemingway memorialized women: in his fullest vision, they prove essential to understanding and meaning; in their own right, many are characters both realistic and unforgettable.

Regarding the inordinately popular *For Whom the Bell Tolls*—as earlier, women prove essential in clarifying meaning, particularly as the reader encounters a young, sensitive, violated Maria and, even more impactful, developing the novel's contemporary political issues—middle-aged, overpowering, keenly sagacious Pilar.

• • •

At the point that *For Whom the Bell Tolls* appeared to be a Pulitzer nominee in 1940, few among the knowledgeable were surprised (although other distinguished writers were considered—a singular example, Richard Wright, for *Native Son*). Hemingway received unanimous support from the Selection Committee—excepting Columbia University (the award sponsor) president and ex-officio committee chair, Nicholas Murray Butler. Butler voted no to nominee Ernest Hemingway, rejecting all supportive arguments by the committee.

Then, and later, many believed that the conservative President Butler was angered by the book's anti-Fascist, anti-Franco perspectives. Butler's public statement—avoiding political, even any "contemporary moment" dimension to his decision—struck an altogether different note. He described the text as "obscene, vulgar and revolting." The president's conclusion regarding *For Whom the Bell Tolls* in words he forwarded to the committee: "The Trustees of Columbia University would never, under any circumstances, approve the awarding of the prize for the novel" (*New Yorker*, June 7, 1941, 9).

The Selection Committee chose not to recommend another title. "Case closed," excepting disappointment and frustration across efforts to understand.

This denial would prove to be the severest *authoritative* negative judgment—given the prestige of this award—assessed regarding any Hemingway work (or implicitly of its author). Unrelated but interesting at this juncture in 1941: the Pulitzer denial occurred at the proximate midpoint of Hemingway's publishing career: his initial fiction was "My Old Man" (1923); his concluding journalism will be "The Dangerous Summer" (1960).

• • •

Without regard to assessing or parsing the words and actions of Columbia's Butler, a truth underscored in this episode continues to be worth remarking on: Hemingway had a history pre-1941 with censors/censorship and the objectionable (not least from his parents and his publishers). Even a title-less, context-less overview of actual or potentially "censorable" material among his published texts is suggestive.

In the published texts, broadly, Hemingway saw as "dead" or seriously "weakened" in contemporary society values-laden, traditional, philosophical and/or religious ideas and their conventional repositories—community, domestic, legal, patriotic, political, military, religious. He believed that these individual or collective "authorities" had become enforcers of unexamined, arbitrary, false, or outmoded conventional belief systems.

Examples of these authorities avoiding specifically "male-female subjects" include acts and ideas—unprintable in his parents' time but present, often nuanced, throughout Hemingway's fiction: battlefield gore; coarse, blasphemous, obscene, or otherwise objectionable language; real persons depicted in libelous ways; racial, ethnic, or religious slurs; unpatriotic ideas, including acceptance of military desertion; a universe godless or malign.

Male-female relationships, of course, constitute a premier Hemingway subject, often presented in soul-searing complexities in which "good" and "bad" (evil?) compound beyond conventional moral grounds and shade into one another—in *stories:* "The Battler," "Hills Like White Elephants," "The Light of the World," "Mr.

and Mrs. Elliott," "A Simple Inquiry," "The Short Happy Life of Francis Macomber," "The Snows of Kilimanjaro," "A Very Short Story," "Up in Michigan"; and in novels up to this time: *The Sun Also Rises, A Farewell to Arms, To Have and Have Not, For Whom the Bell Tolls.*

Finally, touching the less abstract in both thought and deed are Hemingway's various presentations of subject matter uniformly understood as *objectionable* (even illegal)—in print, as well as in literal actions, regarding male-female relationships and purely sexual matters, ultimately to include (although not all these behaviors had yet appeared in his writing by 1940): "abortion, bestiality, bisexuality, buggery, cohabitation and unmarried pregnancy, divorce/remarriage, genital wounding, homosexuality, incest, interracial sex, masturbation, multiple-partnered sex, rape, self-mutilation, sex/gender role-playing, venereal disease."

• • •

All issues regarding the contemporary, the notable or censorable, even the prizeworthy, dimensions of *For Whom the Bell Tolls* in July 1941 were past history in every sense by early December 1941. Responding to direct military attacks on American lives and property, the United States declared war against Japan on December 8 and against Germany and Italy on December 11.

Neither Ernest nor Martha remained uninvolved for long.

# 7

Never think that war, no matter how necessary, nor how justified, is not a crime.

—*For Whom the Bell Tolls*

## War Writer

After April 1939, Hemingway lived with Martha Gellhorn at the Finca Vigia in Cuba. In September, they stayed as invited guests of the management at the new Sun Valley Lodge in Idaho, their Suite 206 overlooking the skating rink and, in the distance, the snow-capped mountains. In later years, these rooms, always Hemingway's when he was at the lodge, sourced storied details of parties and, not least, of their numerous famous attendees.

That fall, the couple were guests of the lodge as part of a four-page advertising "spread" in *Life* that also featured Gary Cooper, who would become a close friend, and wife Rocky. Published photographs emphasized grandeur: outdoors, hunting and fishing amid lakeside scenery and mountainous terrain; indoors, luxurious decor enriched by alcoholic beverages with exotic names, all details highlighting ambiance, encouraging social "pleasantries"—this lodge, the "place."

Here, at his typewriter, in the fall of 1939, Hemingway shaped personal wartime witness in Spain into the blockbuster narrative *For Whom the Bell Tolls*. (Chapter 13 even included reference to this western locale—specifically, to both Sun Valley and Missoula, Montana.) In the future, Hemingway would return regularly. This 1939 visit anticipated his divorce from Pauline on November 4, 1940, and, also that month, his return west to marry Martha—in Cheyenne, Wyoming, on November 21, 1940.

Inordinate popular response to *For Whom the Bell Tolls,* published October 21, 1940, prompted an offer from Paramount Studios of $100,000 for the movie rights. In a quieter vein, on December 28, Hemingway bought (Martha previously renting) the Finca Vigia for $12,500. "Right-hand man" Toby Bruce acted as his representative, minimizing "public" notice of the end to Hemingway's decade residing in Key West.

• • •

Restless amid the domestic realm, journalist Martha accepted an offer from *Collier's* to cover developing war activity in China. She traveled to Singapore with Ernest six months before the Pearl Harbor attack. Having returned to New York, Hemingway published eight pieces in spring 1941, datelined Hong Kong, Rangoon, and Manila, for Ralph Ingersoll, formerly an editor at *Fortune,* currently editor of *PM.* This ad-less New York newspaper, underwritten by department store magnate Marshall Field, offered opinion and commentary on current affairs. Beyond raw data and objective contemporary details, Hemingway's rhetorical shaping of content regarding both China's actions that he observed and the Chinese officials whom he interviewed are succinctly summarized by Robert O. Stephens: "As master journalist Hemingway played Chinese officials against British advisors to learn what each really thought of the other; he used his knowledge of Soviet military advisers gained in Spain to prompt Soviets in China to talk; his portraits of Chiang Kai-shek and other key people caught them in mid-motion while they made history" (*Hemingway's Nonfiction* 27–28).

• • •

In Cuba—from early June 1942, through fall and into April 1943—Hemingway took up wartime reality, designing and implementing what he termed his "Crook Factory," an operation using the *Pilar* to search for German submarines, U-boats actual threats along America's eastern shores. By this time, as documented in the press, their presence in Cuban waters also proved indisputable.

Jeffrey Meyers offers a succinct summary of briefly sanctioned FBI support for Hemingway's "military" action. Soon, however, despite the initial positive response, his plan first became strongly disapproved, then dissolved by express order of J. Edgar Hoover—that decision made following a secret 124-page FBI report on Hemingway. This history in brief:

> In October 1942 the local FBI agent told J. Edgar Hoover that the American Ambassador had granted Hemingway's request "to patrol certain areas where German submarine activity has been reported" and had given him scarce gasoline for this purpose. Hemingway thought that his boat, the *Pilar,* fully manned and heavily armed but disguised for fishing, would attract the attention of a German submarine. The sub would signal the *Pilar* to come alongside in order to requisition supplies and fresh water and food. As the sub approached Hemingway's men would machine-gun the crew on deck while a Spanish jai alai player would throw a small bomb into the conning tower. Fortunately, for both Hemingway and the Germans, he never actually encountered an enemy submarine. (juliawick, "Ernest Hemingway's WWII Spy Network"; see also Reynolds, *Final Years* 59–72)

Martha, absent on assignment for *Collier's* most of this period and despite being in the Caribbean area, never saw evidence of—nor fully understood—the explicit submarine threat. Even so, she strongly opposed and dismissed Hemingway's dangerous "search-and-destroy" U-boat enterprise.

• • •

On October 22, 1942, Crown Publishers released *Men at War: The Best War Stories of All Time.* Scribner had permitted Hemingway, who then recruited Perkins, to help produce and publicize this anthology, the author to provide an introductory foreword describing a thematically arranged collection of classic historical narratives and statements on war.

Eight subject groupings divided the texts: "WAR IS PART OF THE INTERCOURSE OF THE HUMAN RACE; WAR IS THE PROVINCE OF DANGER, AND THEREFORE COURAGE ABOVE ALL THINGS IS THE FIRST QUALITY OF A WARRIOR; WAR DEMANDS RESOLUTION, FIRMNESS, AND STAUNCHNESS . . . . The selections ranged from Joshua at Jericho and Livy on Horatius at the Bridge to Stephen Crane on Chancellorsville, George Dewey at "Manila Bay," and, not least, Hemingway's "Retreat from Caporetto" from *A Farewell to Arms.*

A quarter-century later, Robert O. Stephens, in *Hemingway's Nonfiction,* neatly summarized editorial intent with this historical spectrum of voices and visions. Mindful of "wartime present" (1942), Hemingway had organized the volume—its content and focus—for the contemporary reader, and especially for that reader of military age: "Hemingway's stance in the introduction was that of the father's generation talking to the sons now fighting another war. Indeed, he dedicated the book to his three sons, one of whom was already the age that Hemingway had been when he first went to war. The intent behind the introduction was pragmatic: to develop fortitude and moral endurance in his armed-service readers by convincing them that, whatever their agonies, other men throughout history had faced them and endured. He gained many non-military readers also and the book appeared on the best-seller list in November and December 1942" (28). Stephens emphasized Hemingway's thematic wartime focus.

Earlier, compelling because both of and in that wartime present, Carlos Baker, in the *Sewanee Review,* January 1943, explored Hemingway's purpose with these wide-ranging historical texts by assessing Hemingway's rhetoric. Baker focused on the power of the editor's craft, on Hemingway's shaping of intellectual understanding via emotional response: "A writer's job . . . is to tell the truth. His standard of fidelity to the truth should be so high that his invention, out of his experience, should produce a truer account than anything factual can be. For facts can be observed badly; but when a good writer is creating something, he has time and scope to make it an absolute truth." Hemingway's focus is upon that "something like unremitting conformity to the probable actual, the truth which is greater than the sum of its observed parts, the 'news that stays news' because it is true to both itself and to its constituents, which feed but do not compel it" (161–63).

Baker's formidable praise for the "Introduction" did not note a crucial personal truth touching the editor. This introductory essay was Hemingway's only "professional writing" over the previous three years—a troubling fact because, as Michael Reynolds later observed, that writing absence constituted the single "longest hiatus of his career" (*Final Years* 85).

This *Men at War* collection's "historical sweep" preceded Hemingway's contemporary wartime experience. That frontline exposure for *Collier's* began with D-Day, when he reported as a personal witness following the Normandy invasion and lasting through the breaking of the Siegfried line.

• • •

On July 14, 1943, the film version of *For Whom the Bell Tolls,* starring Gary Cooper and Ingrid Bergman and to be nominated for nine Academy Awards, premiered. Midmonth in Cuba, Hemingway and the *Pilar* concluded their aborted submarine patrol operations. Also significant for Hemingway, who deeply despised Mussolini when covering him for the *Toronto Star* was the news in September that "Il Duce" had surrendered.

Martha, in Europe by September 1943, took up her wartime coverage for *Collier's.* Alone at the Finca from October through December, a jealous, frustrated, peeved Hemingway drank overmuch and pouted about her role as reporter. Then, as 1944 began, a further, albeit unrelated, tweaking within their relationship: Martha's fifth novel, *Liana,* was published.

In April, Hemingway acted. He arranged for himself a role as frontline correspondent for *Collier's,* a deliberate move that effected his replacing Martha: the magazine allowed just one correspondent per family in combat zones. After upstaging her thus, he flew to Europe.

Angered but undeterred, Martha hustled travel from the United States to Europe by freighter, a vessel without passengers due to its raison d'être—to transport dynamite, always dangerous, and not least in wartime. Her trip, in a convoy, required nearly two weeks.

Soon, certainly by early May, Martha understood, acknowledged—could even describe when looking forward—that her marriage to Hemingway was over: "He is a good man, which is vitally important. He is, however, bad for me, sadly enough, or maybe wrong for me is the word; and I am wrong for him. . . . As far as I'm concerned it is all over, it will never work between us again" (letter to Hortense Flexner, ca. May 17, 1944, *Selected Letters of Martha Gellhorn* 163).

• • •

In London, May 22, 1944, Hemingway met Mary Welsh Monks, thirty-six years old and a reporter-researcher for *Time, Life,* and *Fortune.* Also fateful this week, he was in a nighttime automobile accident—May 25—producing a severe concussion and a head wound requiring fifty-seven stitches. Serious, debilitating headaches would continue as both immediate and long-term effects.

Undeterred, on D-Day, June 6, Hemingway was *Collier's* on-scene reporter aboard the *Dorothea M. Dix* and later aboard the infantry-landing vessel *Empire Anvil,* although it did not go ashore. With other reporters, he witnessed at a distance men (many in age still boys) struggling to get ashore and establish a beachhead position while under continuous shelling and blistering gunfire.

At the personal level regarding "getting the story" during these inarguably historical moments, Martha emerged victorious. She sneaked aboard a hospital ship at night disguised as a nurse, thereby managing to get ashore among stretcher-bearers at Omaha Beach, probably on June 7. Avoiding inevitable "official trouble" following this D-Day ruse—certainly making her the sole female journalist-novelist on this scene—Martha quickly moved on to cover developments in Italy.

In July, after finally arriving on the ground in Normandy a month after D-Day, Hemingway soon returned to England and to overt pursuit of Mary Welsh.

• • •

From July through November 1944, Hemingway produced six essays for *Collier's,* a journalism anchored in his personal perspectives. These ranged among on-scene details, both objective and heightened, and among titles suggesting subject content, locales, and scope: "Voyage to Victory" (Hemingway's first *Collier's* piece, July 22, an eyewitness D-Day account); "London Fights the Robots" (August 19); "Battle for Paris" (September 30); "How We Came to Paris" (October 7); "The GI and the General" (November 4); and "War in the Siegfried Line" (November 18).

Each text featured unique personal witness. Hemingway's initial coverage, a D-Day on-scene visual piece, "Voyage to Victory," notably minimalized artistic-literary tropes in favor of a data-driven journalism.

His coverage, faithful to physical action amid much fraught detail, unfolded as a matter-of-fact narrative, generally absent "imaginative," overtly "literary," shaping. Dawn presents a scene threatened by the sounds and visual disarray initiated by wide-ranging firepower. Action specific to Hemingway's opening scene unfolds objectively, save for a suggestive historical allusion: "No one remembers the date of the Battle of Shiloh [though it was a critical Civil War turning point]. But the day we took Fox Green Beach was the sixth of June, and the wind was blowing hard out of the northwest."

Hemingway's full opening masters the "effect" of "being there" through his presenting objective, historical detail. As a newsman, Hemingway did not go ashore under fire; his account appeared July 22, more than a month after the fact, his "details" presented to a well-informed audience.

In the immediate June 6, post–6:30 a.m. "time present" of his essay, none could have imagined, certainly not fully grasped, what was beginning: gathered all around—literally as *never before in history*—a volume and array of military land, sea, and air power being coordinated, and soon unleashed, by Allied forces. What could go wrong?

Hemingway's coverage unfolded almost entirely in objective detail, he shunning literary allusion or other shaping tropes, sufficiency developing in the simple matter-of-fact:

> As we moved in toward land in the gray early light, the 36-foot coffin-shaped steel boats took solid green sheets of water that fell on the helmeted heads of the troops packed shoulder to shoulder in the stiff, awkward, uncomfortable, lonely companionship of men going to battle. There were cases of TNT, with rubber-tube life preservers wrapped about them to float them in the surf, stacked forward in the steel well of the LCV(P) [Landing Craft Vehicle (Personnel)], and there were piles of bazookas and boxes of bazooka rockets encased in waterproof coverings that reminded you of the transparent raincoats college girls wear.
>
> All this equipment, too, had the rubber-tube life preservers strapped and tied on, and the men wore the same gray rubber tubes strapped under their armpits.
>
> As the boat rose to a sea, the green water turned white and came slamming in over the men, the guns and the cases of explosives. Ahead you could see the coast of France. The gray booms and derrick-forested bulks of the attack transports were behind now, and, over all the sea, boats were crawling forward toward France.
>
> As the LCV(P) rose to the crest of a wave, you saw the line of low, silhouetted cruisers and the two big battlewagons lying broadside

to the shore. You saw the heat-bright flashes of their guns and the brown smoke that pushed out against the wind and then blew away.

"What's your course, coxswain?" Lieutenant (jg [junior grade]) Robert Anderson of Roanoke, Virginia, shouted from the stern.

This painstakingly detailed opening unfolds realistically: "water that fell on the helmeted heads of the troops packed shoulder to shoulder in the stiff, awkward, uncomfortable, lonely companionship of men going to battle."

Just three literary images interrupt brief staccato paragraphs unfolding as *literal* moments, detail after detail. These images: "*coffin-shaped steel boats*" [amid] "*green sheets of water*" [are] "*crawling forward toward France*"; completing the opening movement: onboard "rockets encased in waterproof coverings reminded you of the *transparent raincoats college girls wear.*"

Moments and details unwind as in real time. The experiential threat to hundreds, perhaps thousands, of young men unfolds in realistic details—here in the opening and throughout the essay. The full opening illustrates, underscores, objective realism. Hemingway shapes just four brief visual tropes or images: "coffin-shaped boats" in "green sheets of water," "crawling forward toward France"; he then likens waterproof rocket coverings to "transparent raincoats college girls wear." Grotesque linking of "coffin-shaped" boats and rockets with the implicit youthful innocence of "college girls" is a powerful but rare technique amid otherwise matter-of-fact visuals.

Hemingway's closing words confirm the emphasis throughout on the literal, the bedrock experiential. He communicates with everyday directness some simple, albeit horrifying, truths. His is in no wise a classic stentorian wartime literary voice and narrative—such as in *The Iliad* or *The Aeneid*—and despite the historic proportions of the overall action here, in closing, he intones no Homeric exhortations, no Virgilian literary epithets, no Old Testament echoes: "There is much I have not written. You could write for a week and not give everyone credit for what he did on a front of 1,135 yards. Real war is never like paper war, nor do accounts of it read much the way it looks. But if you want to know how it was in an LCV(P) on D-Day when we took Fox Green beach and Easy Red beach on the sixth of June, 1944, then this is as near as I can come to it."

Herein, a grim reality requiring no rhetorical heightening. If any literary stylistic device underscores meaning across this powerful journalism, it is a simple, purposeful understatement.

• • •

"London Fights the Robots," the second of Hemingway's six reports from the front, records an altogether different voice—one employing life-energizing contemporary images. Again, Hemingway's language is not epic, his images not classical, his product not high art. From a British airfield, a wordsmith takes his reader through a pulsating few moments heightening appreciation of subject, feeling, meaning—a poetic shaping of reality *and* value beyond ordinary expression.

In 1962, renowned City College of New York historian-professor Louis L. Snyder described this Hemingway journalism (a few moments excerpted here) as "a masterpiece of war reporting":

> As the flare popped you would hear the dry bark of the starting cartridge and the rising scream of the motor, and these hungry big, long-legged birds would lurch, bounce, and scream off with the noise of two hundred circular saws hitting a mahogany log dead on the nose. They took off downwind, crosswind, any way the weather lay, and grabbed a piece of the sky and lurched up into it with the long, high legs folding up under them.
>
> You love a lot of things if you live around them, but there isn't any woman and there isn't any horse, nor any before nor any after, that is as lovely as a great airplane, and men who love them are faithful to them even though they leave them for others. A man has only one virginity to lose in fighters, and if it is a lovely plane he loses it to, there his heart will ever be. (August 19, 1944)

• • •

Previously, on July 24, in a consequential event that occurred in war-torn France, journalist Hemingway met Col. C. T. "Buck" Lanham, Commander, Fourth Division, Twenty-Second Regiment. As reporter, he soon attached himself to this commanding officer, and in short order, the two men became literally "friends for life."

Lanham came to view Hemingway as the "bravest man" he had known—although he also understood "bravado" in this figure to include the potential to decline into "jackassery." This coinage, Lanham's own, applied originally to a specific moment—an incident under fire in which Hemingway continued to eat while refusing to wear a steel helmet and to follow others into a cellar during direct shelling:

> The first "88" shells came through the wall of the place about three feet above our heads, I'd say. Of course, they might have exploded as they hit the wall, instead of going right through, and then they would have knocked everybody off in the place. It turned out—we later knocked them off—that they couldn't lower the gun. So Ernest may have felt that was why the shells went over our heads. Ernest was battle-wise. He was just smart as hell on the battlefield. He didn't normally stick his neck out in these ridiculous things he's widely credited with doing. He went a lot of jackass places. He went with me. He went in places he shouldn't have been, but by and large he knew what he was doing. He could have been killed in any of them, but he figured the odds were the other way. (Brian 179)

This description from a senior frontline officer in charge during a series of major conflicts was also echoed among various noncombat moments—for example, Hemingway as witnessed and *comprehended* during an active wartime period by young, nonprofessional frontline soldiers. In a particularly humanizing scene, this "warrior" Hemingway—as understood by such young men fighting in France—was captured in a particularly "relaxed" period described by artist-illustrator John Groth: "That morning he showed me war. We jeeped past men and machinery moving up. Not comfortably, for jeep seats are not wide, and Hemingway is. (And there were canteens of cognac on each hip.) When we reached pillboxes that had been captured the day before, he set up his canteens on the bank of a depression behind one of the boxes, making an impromptu bar. Infantry men stopped with him for a drink. They all knew him, but not as Ernest Hemingway the writer. They knew him as 'Pop.' He'd been with them in their drive across France. He'd been everywhere they had been. He didn't need any qualifications" (87).

While this latter scene and that earlier with Lanham are quite different, each describes a characteristic wartime Ernest Hemingway. Moreover, both center in a personality idiosyncratic and cavalier—as well understood today, albeit much less well comprehended or appreciated then, during actual wartime and in a frontline battle zone.

The scenes with Lanham and the youthful soldiers afford details sufficient for understanding that Hemingway well might be charged with violating military orders governing all war correspondents—for example, ignoring dicta forbidding a war correspondent from taking active part in the fighting. Charges that Hemingway had violated this explicit, in writing, Geneva Convention prohibition—that he did bear arms and that he did take active part in actual fighting by "commanding irregulars at Rambouillet"—were actually brought against him at a third Army Court of Inquiry in October 1944. The specific charges: "that Mr. Hemingway stripped off correspondent insignia and acted as a colonel, French Resistance troops; that he had a room with mines, grenades and war maps; that he directed resistance patrols, which action is believed to violate credential rights of the correspondents."

To the key question at his hearing—"Did you state to anyone at about this time, 'I am no longer a correspondent'"—he asserted that in Rambouillet, "I wasn't armed," and as to whether he had asserted "I am no longer a correspondent," he responded at some length: "I didn't make any such statement in a serious sense. I may have said, jokingly, 'I am now a hotel manager, the bouncer for this joint, the un-thanked billeting clerk, and general errand boy around the establishment,' but in the serious sense that I was not a correspondent it would be impossible for me to make such a statement since I am an accredited correspondent for *Collier's Weekly* and am so earning my living."

Thus, Hemingway appeared before General Patton's inspector general on October 6, 1944, at Nancy, France. In fairly short order—he testified only briefly—all charges were dropped (Brian, "Appendix A" 323–31).

With personal military issues "cleared up" by late October 1944, Hemingway necessarily, and no doubt with pleasure, turned his thoughts to his literary career. External encouragement was not wanting: A *Saturday Review of Literature* poll for "America's Leading Novelist" that appeared on August 5, 1944, found him that title figure by a two-to-one margin over his contemporaries (61). The following month, September 18, Malcolm Cowley's *Viking Portable Library: Hemingway* appeared, garnering high critical praise: In the *New Republic,* for example, Granville Hicks argued in his own voice and quoted published assessments by other professionals, all of them agreeing: "*For Whom the Bell Tolls* made it clear that Hemingway was the most disciplined craftsman of his generation" (524).

• • •

At this time regarding the personal: Hemingway, in Paris, learned that eldest son Jack had been taken a prisoner of war. Then, briefly in London, Hemingway and Martha initiated divorce proceedings, made final on December 21, 1945.

Hemingway and Mary were married in Havana, March 14, 1946. Soon thereafter, Jack emerged "all right," after having been a war prisoner for six months. The following year, a sincere, ever-growing relationship between Mary and Pauline deepened as seriously ill son Patrick recovered in Cuba—ministered to by both women. Peacetime normalcy returned—and with it, prosperity. Hemingway sold "The Killers" to Universal Studios and "The Short Happy Life of Francis Macomber" to Paramount.

• • •

Summer 1947 began a period of assessment and a new postwar world for Hemingway—on the literary scene and, no less, in personal relationships with and among contemporary players. On June 13, at the American Embassy in Havana, he was awarded the Bronze Star for his wartime actions. Almost immediately following, on June 17, 1947, Max Perkins died of pneumonia at home in Connecticut—a serious and affecting loss for Hemingway and for the larger contemporary American literary world as well.

In a letter to Charles Scribner, June 28, Hemingway wrote familiarly ("Dear Charlie") to reassure his publisher of his loyalty and to take stock, beginning with memories of and appreciation for Max: "We had a hell of a good time this last time in New York and wasn't it lucky it was that way instead of a lot of problems and arguments. Anyway he doesn't have to worry about Tom Wolfe's chickenshit estate anymore, or handle Louise's business, nor keep those women writers from building nests in his hat. . . . Max was my best and oldest friend at Scribner's and a great, great editor [who] never cut a paragraph of my stuff nor asked me to change one. . . . [Then, perhaps more to the point] Charles Scribners Sons are my publisher and I intend to publish with them for the rest of my life" (Baker, *Selected Letters* 621–22).

A further signpost of Hemingway's vision of how postwar assessments and transitions impacted him—beyond the "bonding" note to Charles Scribner—was an important "handshake" between Hemingway and William Faulkner. The latter, renowned for his experiments with narrative structure and prose style, had unwittingly slighted in print Hemingway's unwillingness—lack of "bravery"—with prose style experiments as compared with others among his contemporaries, especially Dos Passos and Wolfe (and although unmentioned, Faulkner himself). An infuriated Hemingway prevailed on Buck Lanham to send Faulkner an accounting of Hemingway's personal bravery (!).

Faulkner's immediate response more than cleared the air, as

Hemingway quickly noted on July 23, 1947: "I was sore and Buck was sore and we were instantly unsore the minute we knew the score." Certainly, Hemingway was sincere in writing to Faulkner: "You are a better writer than Fielding or any of those guys and you should know it and keep on writing. You have things written that come back to me better than any of them and I am not dopy, really. . . . You should always write your best against dead writers . . . [he lists Dostoevsky, Turgenev, Maupassant, Stendhal, Flaubert] and beat them one by one. Anyway, I am your Bro. if you want one that writes and I'd like us to keep in touch. . . . Excuse chickenshit letter. Have much regard for you. [Signed] *Ernest Hemingway*" (Baker, *Selected Letters* 623–25).

• • •

In this early postwar period, indeed well into the 1950s, many critics took issue with the contemporary literary scene broadly and, not least, with Hemingway, both man and artist. For some critics, worried concerns and judgments cast a wide net including, to one degree or another, *most* serious American literary voices at mid-century and, no less, aspiring new writers, each and all consciously facing a "brave new world."

Amid such intellectual-literary pulsations, *Time* magazine took up the contemporary "state of letters" (fiction predominating), part of which included "Hemingway in the Afternoon" (50, August 4, 1947, 80).

This piece constituted a particularly broad inquiry. Selected prominent contemporary fictionists—including Dos Passos, Faulkner, Marquand, Katherine Anne Porter, Saroyan, and Warren—were surveyed regarding their art and their perception of the state of "contemporary letters."

Regarding Hemingway, *Time* included, as an editorial note, Hemingway's specific request that both the magazine's questions and his answers be published, because, he said, "this has to do with my trade": "You can say that when you saw me I was unshaven, needed a haircut, was barefoot, wearing a pajama bottom and no top." Hemingway's effort at personal "protective" control of his participation is obvious, the seriousness of his reflections here is not as obvious.

The questions and Hemingway's responses:

> ***Which U.S. writers in your opinion are doing good work?***
>
> Writers my generation mostly dead except Dos Passos going very good with *Number One.* Robert Penn Warren writing very well. First rate books by new writers that have read are *All Thy Conquest,* Alfred Hayes—*Never Come Morning,* Nelson Algren—*The Big Sky,* A. B. Guthrie, Jr.—*The Assault,* Allen R. Matthews.
>
> ***Which once-prominent ones have slipped or failed to measure up to early promise?***
>
> Prefer not to answer this question. A writer has no more right to inform the public of the weaknesses and strengths of his fellow professionals than a doctor or a lawyer has.
>
> Writers should stick together like wolves or gypsies, and they are fools to attack each other to please the people who would exploit or destroy them. Naturally I know the weaknesses of my fellow professionals, but that information is not for sale nor for free.
>
> ***How much has the big money of slicks, Hollywood, radio, etc., taken writers away from serious personal themes?***
>
> Most whores usually find their vocations.
>
> ***Is a writer-Hollywood combination capable of doing good literary work?***
>
> So far hasn't. But Hollywood has proven can make good pictures from good stories honestly written.
>
> ***What is your own attitude toward writing for Hollywood?***
>
> Never done it.

*Do you detect any trends, or any new schools in recent U.S. writing? If so, what are they?*

Ask a professor.

*Has the "Hemingway influence" declined? If so, what kind of writing are we headed for?*

Hemingway influence only a certain clarification of the language which is now in the public domain.

• • •

Certainly, Hemingway was capable of serious, focused writing in this period. One needed to look no further than to the new Scribner edition of *A Farewell to Arms* (1948), featuring his sole "Introduction" for any one of his books. Therein, contextualizing *time present,* he alluded to global violence, spiritual desiccation, personal (and corporate) corruption. These personal reflections also touch in some detail his own art—he used contemporary moments to memorialize his earlier writing history.

He describes his mindset at the heart of *A Farewell to Arms* as equal parts intellectual and emotional—as felt at its creation (1929) and as felt now, when better understood, at the novel's republication almost twenty years later:

> So . . . this book was first published the day the market broke in 1929. The illustrated edition comes out this fall. Scott FitzGerald is dead, Tom Wolfe is dead, Jim Joyce is dead (he the fine companion unlike the official Joyce of his biographers, who asked me one time, when drunk, if I did not think his work was too suburban), John Bishop is dead, Max Perkins is dead. Plenty of characters that should be dead are dead too; hung upside down outside filling stations in Milano or hanged, well or badly, in over-bombed German towns. There are all the non-name men dead too; most of whom liked life very much.

> The title of this book is *A Farewell to Arms* and except for three years there has been war of some kind almost ever since it has been written. Some people used to say, why is this man so preoccupied and obsessed with war, and now, since 1933 perhaps it is clear why a writer should be interested in the constant, bullying, murderous, slovenly crime of war. . . . I believe that all the people who stand to profit by war and who help provoke it should be shot on the first day it starts by accredited representatives of the loyal citizens of their country who will fight it. ("Author's Introduction," 1948, ix)

For Hemingway in 1948, remembering the intellectual truths of this story proved no less important than remembering his merging emotional feeling with art:

> Making the country and the people and the things that happened I was happier than I had ever been. Each day I read the book through from the beginning to the point where I went on writing and each day I stopped when I was still going good and when I knew what would happen next.
>
> The fact that the book was a tragic one did not make me unhappy since I believed that life was a tragedy and knew it could have only one end. But finding you were able to make something up; to create truly enough so that it made you happy to read it; and to do this every day you worked was something that gave a greater pleasure than any I had ever known. Beside it nothing else mattered. ("Author's Introduction," 1948, vii–viii)

• • •

Hemingway's fiction centering in or around World War II concluded in the period 1949–50 with *Across the River and into the Trees*. Begun April 1949 and serialized, for eighty-five thousand dollars, in *Cosmopolitan*, February–June 1950, the Scribner volume appeared in September 1950.

Hemingway's critical reputation at decade's turn—when tied to contemporary reception of the new novel—proved almost uniformly negative. Some range of judgmental superlatives existed, of course, and an outlier at the positive extreme was novelist John O'Hara's (in)famous critical judgment praising Hemingway as the "greatest writer since Shakespeare"—O'Hara offering in those words, despite obvious and inevitable contemporary confusion, an *overall assessment* of Hemingway as author, not a heralding of Shakespearean "greatness" in that author as specific to this volume.

In fact, nearly uniform negative published critical response to the novel emerged among the most prominent of contemporary critics, including Alfred Kazin, Evelyn Waugh, Northrop Frye, Joseph Warren Beach. Many reservations about "man" and "work" explored in their reviews were identified and confirmed early by Morton Dauwen Zabel's lengthy assessments in the *Nation* (September 9, 1950), their "substance" abbreviated here:

> This is the novel . . . we've awaited for ten years, certainly with every hope that it would augur the renewal of a talent that has given us several of the memorable books of the century. Briefly, it doesn't. . . . The drama is almost static. The talk retaining only a few of its old living accents develops unbelievable prodigies of flatness, mawkishness, repetition, and dead wastes of words.
>
> The obvious truth is that this new novel is the poorest thing its author has ever done—poor with a feebleness of invention, a dullness of language and a self-parodying of style and theme even beyond *The Fifth Column* and *To Have and Have Not.* It gives no sign of the latent rigor that has permitted Hemingway, in tales like "The Undefeated," "Old Man at the Bridge," "Macomber," and "Kilimanjaro" to pull himself together after he had given every evidence of having gone to pieces, and to declare his old powers.
>
> A final sentiment closing the review: ". . . *Across the River and Into the Trees* (the title badly mars the fine rhythm of Stonewall Jackson's last words) is an occasion for little but exasperated depression." (Meyers, *Critical Heritage* 377)

• • •

Professional assessment of Hemingway's place among living American authors at the inception of a new decade began fully fleshed out with both emotion and detail, particularly in two broad magazine feature essays: from Malcolm Cowley, a prominent voice on the literary scene and editor of the *Viking Portable Hemingway,* 1944—"A Portrait of Mister Papa" (*Life,* January 10, 1949), his assessment here just prior to serialization of *Across the River and into the Trees;* then, fifteen months later, and appearing amid serialization of *Across the River,* Lillian Ross's *Profile:* "Portrait of Hemingway" in the *New Yorker* (May 13, 1950). Touching her quirky literary subject, she poses the question, "How Do You Like It Now, Gentlemen?"

Amid the flurry of varied activity in and about American letters during the transition to a new decade, the premier American literature capstone judgment / feature event for transition year 1949–50: William Faulkner awarded the Nobel Prize for Literature in 1949. At the award ceremony in Stockholm on December 10, 1950, notable among the powerful words of his "acceptance" speech, this contemporary literary figure's addressing the necessary role for American literature in the modern moment, *specifically for the writer.* He or she must leave "no room in [the writing] workshop for anything but the old verities and truths of the heart, the old universal truths lacking which any story is ephemeral and doomed—love and honor and pity and pride and compassion and sacrifice. . . . The poet's voice need not merely be the record of man, it can be one of the props, the pillars to help him endure and prevail."

8

# Midcentury Recognitions

Ernest Hemingway was America's war writer at midcentury. Regarding his recognition as "*the* American war *novelist*," a Shakespearean truth proves suggestive: "Uneasy lies the head that wears a crown." For Hemingway, largely negative critical assessments of *Across the River and into the Trees* (five-part serialization, 1950), despite its appearing for seven weeks on the *New York Times* Best Seller List, underscored successes by soon prominent war novelist contemporaries—Vance Bourjaily, James Jones, Norman Mailer, Irwin Shaw, Gore Vidal, and not least, ex-wife Martha Gellhorn, with *The Wine of Astonishment* (1948).

In reality, whether focused on the solitude required for the "artist" at his craft or on the drama and excitement of the "author" acting as public figure, at decade's turn, Hemingway dominated the contemporary American literary scene.

• • •

Serious journalist coverage of the author during the transition from the 1940s to the 1950s featured evaluative essays by prominent literary and cultural critics. These assessments developed in varied voices and venues. Positive for Hemingway, Malcolm Cowley's nine thousand-word "A Portrait of Mister Papa," including fifteen photos, appeared in *Life* on January 10, 1949. In a broad anecdotal style, critic and literary historian Cowley described Hemingway's wartime acts and locales: the *Pilar* seeking Q-boats, Hemingway at Rambouillet, his presence in fall 1944 with troops in the Hurtgen Forest, then in Paris. This essay in *Life*, the ideal outlet for such a piece—and it just one article among sixteen in the magazine on Hemingway's published work and on his other subjects and doings beginning in 1941—presented the author as a broad action figure: a "best-selling *novelist*," also a "major *writer*" and, not least, a popular persona—one both "colorful and photogenic."

Following Cowley's broad overview, Lillian Ross's May 1950 *New Yorker* "Profile"—"How Do You Like It Now, Gentlemen?"—unfolded as a narrower, genuinely idiosyncratic piece. Ross offered an assessment on balance positive but one, also, peculiarly mixed: undistilled "impressions" serve up varied, sometimes contradictory, conclusions. Hemingway's informal, spontaneous voices quoted here frequently lapse into pidgin English and ungrammatical or otherwise nonstandard phrasings. They dramatize him as never humble and not always serious or fully comprehensible—neither for Ross nor her readers. Then, also unexpectedly, a critical downside. Some reviewers of *Across the River and into the Trees* understood Ross's "Profile" as evidence of Hemingway's "disintegration—both as artist and as personality"—a few even citing her text to anchor prejudices of their own (Raeburn 130).

On an altogether different—nonliterary—level, in April 1951, sportsman Hemingway contributed a hunting article, "The Shot," to strictly male-focused *True: The Man's Magazine.* Throughout this decade, he encouraged "readings" of himself as *the* accomplished sportsman—for example, permitting *Argosy* to excerpt *Green Hills of Africa* in June 1954 and giving published interviews on hunting rifles to *GUNsport* in April 1958. A prime instance of this "popular take" on Hemingway as the American male sportsman—particularly as dramatized among an ever-growing number of contemporary men's magazines—is the twentieth-anniversary issue of the best-selling *True,* for February 1956. This edition heralded a "personality" captured photographically. Anticipating larger meanings, the article developed under a banner with a telling query: "Who the Hell Is Hemingway?"

The synthesizing imagery and argument in this celebratory anniversary issue distill its "full-frame Hemingway" as the hypermasculine ideal and, additionally for those so disposed, as misogynist: "His world was inhabited by 'beautiful dames' and 'rugged guys,' and his persona was without peer as a hunter, fisherman, drinker, and reporter of violence. He could 'tell the next guy to go to hell—and make it stick.' Therefore, he was a 'fitting symbol' for *True*'s anniversary issue because 'of all men, living or dead, Ernest Hemingway stands for much of what we, at *True,* admire. Hemingway represents a hairy-chested maleness, an irreverence for the conventional, a dislike of the traditional. He is, truly, a rogue male'" (Raeburn 152).

By the time this piece appeared in 1956, "rogue male" former war correspondent and renowned contemporary sportsman, Hemingway, while hunting in East Africa during January 1954, had survived, quite publicly given the follow-up press coverage, two small-plane crashes over two days in the Murchison Falls area of Uganda. In each mishap, despite burns and semi-serious injuries, Hemingway had retained focus, and exerting extraordinary physical effort, he had helped rescue himself and wife Mary from life-threatening realities. These actions, enhanced and summarized variously, appeared in both news and sports outlets worldwide. *Look* magazine printed his personal retelling, in April–May 1954, as "The Christmas Gift."

• • •

Returning to the earlier 1952 as time present and to serious, popular writer Hemingway, a "night-into-day" career development soon followed, mitigating the widespread negative assessments blemishing *Across the River and into the Trees.* Future prospects soon brightened dramatically for Hemingway, man and author, among the more representative reading public.

Even so, well into summer in 1952, a period immediately preceding *extraordinary* literary success(es), including numerous professional recognitions, Hemingway seemed without "prospects." His interactions with and among professional critics, fellow fictionists, and journalist commentators had become complicated, often strained, whether specific to his art, to his person, or to both. A case in point: William Faulkner's recent Nobel Prize, in 1949. That recognition and follow-up accolades aggravated his singularly competitive contemporary—Ernest Hemingway.

• • •

At this time—perhaps unnoted by Hemingway and unimportant for him in 1952 regarding his perceived "nemesis" Faulkner—a new reality developed at *Esquire*. Founding editor Arnold Gingrich, who had retired in 1945, returned as publisher. The significance of his appointment for Hemingway was not immediately consequential; over the long term, post-1961, it would be profound.

Expressing a singular voice nuanced variously, Hemingway's original work throughout *Esquire*'s "golden era," 1933–39, had featured his various personas from newsman to *litterateur*—he was then writing in many modes and from multiple perspectives as reporter and journalist, as essay writer, as fiction author (six short stories), as *the international sportsman*. From wide-ranging viewpoints, in words outspoken and effecting tones and perspectives unmistakable, Ernest Hemingway had emerged as a unique contemporary figure in America—the literary public man.

Regarding *Esquire* in 1952, that earlier Hemingway had moved, was moving, on—dramatically. His path soon included a Pulitzer (1953) and, in March 1954, the Award of Merit from the American Academy of Arts and Letters. Most important in 1954, his voice and persona became acclaimed across the international literary scene—he was named a Nobel laureate. At first, even prior to his receiving these recognitions, Gingrich as editor had approached him cautiously, envisioning "author" Hemingway as a potential *Esquire* "subject" but not a "contributor." Then, following this two-year period of major national-international accolades, 1952–54, any formal relationship between Gingrich and *Esquire* and the contemporary litterateur Hemingway had, for the time, effectively ceased.

• • •

Returning to the earlier time present, September 1952, *The Old Man and the Sea* appears in its entirety in a single issue of *Life* magazine, and as the saying goes, "the rest is history."

Publication in *Life,* Hemingway's favorite mass-market magazine, yielded an extraordinary response. First-week sales exceeded five million. The author "appears" and his text unfolds amid impressive visuals: a black-and-white photograph of Hemingway's head and shoulders fills the magazine's cover; inside, the complete text, approximately twenty-seven thousand words, and more: throughout, twenty action drawings appear atop, in the middle, at the bottom, of their appropriate (action) pages.

*Professional* acclaim for *The Old Man and the Sea* would lead to Hemingway's being awarded the Pulitzer for fiction in 1953, that critical praise completing groundwork for—the following year—his crowning career accolade, the Nobel. Such popular renown, of course, prompted Hollywood to think "silver screen." A half-decade later, the novel unfolded as a celluloid success: a film benefiting during its creation from Hemingway's deep-sea fishing expertise; a movie starring the author's good friend and noted actor, the inimitable Spencer Tracy.

• • •

Hemingway's principal publication in his last decade—*The Old Man and the Sea*—did not occur in a vacuum. In a *Life* magazine piece for August 25, 1952, the week before publication, the author, in a stentorian, self-promoting voice and tone, alluded to his having yet to be honored with the Nobel Prize. "Mentioning" this fact was certainly staking out a personal claim to that honor, one he underscored in the work forthcoming the following week—*The Old Man and the Sea,* published in toto in *Life,* on September 1, 1952: "I'm very excited about *The Old Man and the Sea* and that it is coming out in *LIFE* so that many people will read it who could not afford to buy it. [At twenty cents per copy, *Life*'s five-million-copies 'run' sold out within two days; this premier edition, for which *Life* paid the author twenty-one thousand dollars, remained on the *New York Times* Best Seller List for twenty-six weeks.] That makes me much happier than to have a Nobel Prize. To have you guys being so careful and good about it and so thoughtful is better than any kind of prize."

While much in those words might make a sensitive reader wince, as Hemingway goes on, author and "persona" appear somewhat more attractive, more humble, perhaps even more honest—perhaps:

> Whatever I learned is in the story but I hope it reads simply and straight and all the things that are in it do not show but only are with you after you have read it. . . .
>
> I had wanted to write it for more than 15 years and I never did it because I did not think I could. . . . Now I have to try to write something better. That is sort of rough. But I had good luck with this all the way and maybe I will have luck again. . . .
>
> Don't you think it is a strange damn story that it should affect all of us (me especially) the way it does? I have read it now over 200 times and everytime it does something to me. It's as though I had gotten finally what I had been working for all my life. (Quoted in Bruccoli, *Hemingway and the Mechanism of Fame* 121)

• • •

Popular sales numbers for the novel continued growing, disregarding the sometimes—albeit less frequent here than in the recent past—disputatious judgments among formal reviewers. An undeniable "blockbuster" popularity developed for the novel among the general reading public. Professional voices, while collectively approving, not unexpectedly ranged in their levels of enthusiasm. Both readerships embraced character and narrative presentation when compared to the previous *Across the River and into the Trees*, especially in the "touching" human emotions inhering in Santiago amid his multiple plights. Even so, no single emphasis nor judgment regarding *The Old Man and the Sea* proved universal.

A representative positive review, matter-of-factly attentive to both art and theme, is that by literary scholar R. W. B. Lewis for the *Hudson Review* (6 [Spring 1953]: 146–48):

> It is the ultimate sizing up of experience that interests us. And where, at the end of *To Have and Have Not* (1937), the dying Harry Morgan concluded that, "A man alone doesn't have a bloody chance," here the old man awesomely alone reflects in all humility that "Man is not made for defeat. . . . A man can be destroyed but not defeated." This is the sign of *virtu* prepared to survive any calamity; even the appalling *fortuna* represented by the sharks, who devour the greatest catch—an eighteen-foot marlin—the old man has ever dreamed of. . . . Now, with this curiously peaceful account of the old man's splendid failure, Hemingway returns to the role of the perceiver; and what he perceives is once again the stimulating and fatal relation between integrity of character and the churning abundance of experience. . . . The old man's old man is realised in prose that honors them both.

Typical among the positive newspaper reviews, Robert Gorham Davis in the *New York Times*, September 7, 1952: "In *The Old Man and the Sea*, Hemingway has like the young man in 'Big Two-Hearted River' got back to something good and true in himself that has always been there. And with it are new indications of humility and maturity and a deeper sense of being at home in life which promise well for the novel. . . . Hemingway [is] a great writer with the strength and craft and courage to go far out and perhaps even far down for the truly big ones."

Philip Rahv in *Commentary* offered a representative downbeat: "The meaning of *The Old Man and the Sea* is sought in its profound symbolism. It may be that the symbolism is really there, though I for one have been unable to locate it. . . . Hemingway's big marlin is no Moby Dick, and his fisherman is not Captain Ahab nor was meant to be."

• • •

Earlier, on June 27, 1952, Hemingway had mentioned both Faulkner and the Nobel Prize in a letter to critic Harvey Breit. Faulkner had turned down Breit's invitation to review *The Old Man and the Sea,* having seen nothing of the unpublished text at the time. Becoming aware of this interaction, and hesitancy, Hemingway, piqued, "unloaded" on Faulkner to Breit:

> He made a speech [accepting the Nobel Prize], very good. I knew he could never, now, or ever again write up to his speech. I also knew I could write a book better and straighter than his speech and without tricks nor rhetoric. . . . You see what happens with Bill Faulkner is that as long as I am alive he has to drink to feel good about having the Nobel prize. He does not realize that I have no respect for that institution and was truly happy for him when he got it. I cabled him how pleased I was truly and he would not answer. . . .
>
> I wish him luck and he needs it because he has the one great and un-curable defect; you can't re-read him. When you re-read him you are conscious all the time of how he fooled you the first time. In truly good writing no matter how many times you read it you do not know how it is done. That is because there is a mystery in all great writing and that mystery does not dis-sect out. (Baker, *Selected Letters* 770)

This exchange with Breit occurred just weeks before Hemingway publicly mentioned the Nobel (albeit not Faulkner) in *Life* magazine on August 25, the week preceding publication of *The Old Man and the Sea.* The somewhat "forced" context for his mention of the prize was his claiming to be pleased regarding *Life* as an inexpensive venue: "Many people will read it who could not afford to buy it. . . . That makes me much happier than to have a Nobel Prize."

Clearly Faulkner, and Faulkner's Nobel Prize, aroused Hemingway's competitive sense of self, his own achievements, and not least, his "rank" or "station" among his immediate contemporaries.

Noteworthy in this context, Faulkner, after reading *The Old Man and the Sea,* did publicly record his reaction and assessment regarding its author, the work, and his sense of posterity for them both:

> His best. Time may show it to be the best single piece of any of us. I mean his and my contemporaries. This time, he discovered God, a Creator. Until now, his men and women had made themselves, shaped themselves out of their own clay; their victories and defeats were at the hands of each other, just to prove to themselves or one another how tough they could be. But this time, he wrote about pity: about something somewhere that made them all: the old man who had to catch the fish and then lose it, the fish that had to be caught and then lost, the sharks that had to rob the old man of his fish; made them all and loved them all and pitied them all. It's all right. Praise God that whatever made and loves and pities Hemingway and me kept him from touching it any further.(*Shenandoah* 3 [Fall 1952]: 55)

• • •

Central in *The Old Man and the Sea,* as throughout Hemingway's major stories and novels, is the sympathetic portrayal of the "female"—as a specific character, as a concept. Here the featured woman shared an enduring, long-lived relationship with Santiago—his deceased wife, whose presence now survives in a treasured, fading, photograph. Santiago's continuing attachment to his beloved centers and humanizes his world, he a man of mental toughness and one possessed of both courage and self-discipline. Although she is absent, her image still moves and inspires both the fisherman and his loyal young acolyte, Manolin (this ministrant as close to a son as Santiago has known).

Given the at-sea plot of this narrative, "meaning" centers primarily on the aged fisherman, his memories, and his broad natural world, here including the imagined lion cubs on the beach and, of course, in the deep-sea kingdom, the magnificent marlin—*the* catch. This old man's love of *la mar,* for even the most dangerous of her multivarious life forms, remains unforgettable *and* "female"! Santiago consciously resists growing male sentiment at this time—literally an organized movement to "masculinize" the sea and its multidimensional meanings, real and imagined, by changing the linguistic descriptor *la mar* to *el mar.*

Santiago is a man plagued by "bad luck": earlier, eighty-seven days without a fish; now, in the novel's contemporary action, eighty-four days. When faced with serious physical hardships, Santiago reflects upon the hero of his imagination—professional baseball star (perhaps the most renowned name in contemporary America's "national pastime"), New York Yankees all-around "phenom" Joe DiMaggio—aka "The Yankee Clipper."

DiMaggio, son of a commercial fisherman with a large family—like fisherman Santiago—suffered on and off from a variety of bad luck, even career-threatening injuries. Not least among these in 1949, an especially challenging—as reported on in detail by the sports press—recurring bone spur. DiMaggio's playing through various chronic and painful physical trials especially impressed Santiago, who reflects in his own hour of crisis on his hero's personal strengths: "I must have confidence, and I must be worthy of the Great DiMaggio who does all things perfectly even with the pain of the bone spur in his heel" (*Old Man* 68).

Of course, Santiago and this "Great DiMaggio" are both fictional constructs—Santiago by Hemingway; DiMaggio by Hemingway and in the mythmaking bylines and lore of the New York sports press. Comparing both characters, DiMaggio biographer Jack B. Moore observes astutely: "Santiago's combat is juxtaposed with the distant DiMaggio's. And it is the real human, DiMaggio, who comes to seem unreal, or possibly diminished, as though seen through a wrong-ended telescope. His exploits on the sporting field seem child's play next to Santiago's deadly adventure" (143).

Put another way: Santiago's belief in DiMaggio's greatness, however exaggerated, does not mar *his* own heroism and sensibilities. The reverse, however, is telling. The fisherman's *humility* demonstrates mental focus and both expertise and physical strength, making Santiago heroic, even iconic. The actual man, DiMaggio, is "a game-day hitter"; his greatness exists in a popular *sport* as defined and heightened by sportswriters' prose registering a wide variety of vested interests. This flesh-and-blood DiMaggio is necessarily diminished by simple comparison. Elderly Santiago, one of the least masculine, most serene, among Hemingway's protagonists, is indisputably among his finest male "heroes."

Fittingly, at this juncture, Hemingway's festering concern regarding "official judgments" and "in-print assessments" of his work (vs. Faulkner's and others') dramatically eased. In May 1953, Ernest Hemingway was awarded the Pulitzer Prize in fiction for *The Old Man and the Sea.*

• • •

Early in what became *the* banner year—1954—a minor "sidebar" reference exemplified the breadth of the "ordinary reader's" level of awareness of Hemingway as icon: biweekly *Look* magazine's "Photoquiz" section for February 23 reflected the "general reader's" recognition of notable individuals in the current year. The reader's task with the magazine's "quiz" was to identify famous contemporaries by a trademark characteristic. That feature for Hemingway was his beard. The dramatic, albeit purely coincidental, point established in this edition of the quiz: Hemingway's comparable renown among his *prestigious* contemporaries. Save for one, the fifteen "Photoquiz" photographs captured mainly political or show business personalities—"Ernest Hemingway" being the exception. *Look* editors and readers ranked the author among notable male contemporaries, including Charlie Chaplin, Cary Grant, President Eisenhower, and Marlon Brando (Raeburn 1).

• • •

Essentially nonstop following the Pulitzer, Ernest Hemingway enjoyed major professional awards for career distinguished achievement: the American Academy of Arts and Letters Award of Merit Medal, March 1954; Cuba's highest civilian award, the Order of Carlos Manuel de Cespedes, July 1954; and in October 1954, for him the most coveted among all formal distinctions, the highest international honor: the Nobel Prize for Literature—Hemingway just the fifth American to receive this high honor.

For Hemingway, epochal 1954 had begun inauspiciously with the drama recorded worldwide in January, when he and Mary narrowly avoided serious catastrophe in the two plane crashes in Africa. Indeed, nearly a year later, still troubled with residual pain from incomplete recovery from those injuries, the new laureate cited "health issues" as grounds for not attending the Nobel Prize Award Ceremony and Banquet in Stockholm on December 10, 1954.

• • •

Contextualizing the Nobel Award at the ceremony was the moving, finely nuanced "Presentation Speech" by Swedish Academy permanent secretary Anders Österling—in part:

> Hemingway's significance as one of this epoch's great molders of style is apparent in both American and European narrative art over the past twenty-five years, chiefly in the vivid dialogue and the verbal thrust and parry, in which he has set a standard as easy to imitate as it is difficult to attain. With masterly skill he reproduces all the

nuances of the spoken word, as well as those pauses in which thought stands still and the nervous mechanism is thrown out of gear. It may sometimes sound like small talk, but it is not trivial when one gets to know his method. He prefers to leave the work of psychological reflection to his readers, and this freedom is of great benefit to him in spontaneous observation.

Moreover, one may trace a distinctive linking thread—let us say a symbolic warp reaching back a hundred years in the loom of time—between Hemingway's latest work, *The Old Man and the Sea,* and one of the classic creations of American literature, Herman Melville's novel *Moby Dick,* the white whale who is pursued in blind rage by his enemy, the monomaniac sea captain. Neither Melville nor Hemingway wanted to create an allegory; the salt ocean depths with all their monsters are sufficiently rewarding as a poetic element. But with different means, those of romanticism and of realism, they both attain the same theme—a man's capacity of endurance and, if need be, of at least daring the impossible: "A man can be destroyed but not defeated." ("Nobel Prize," Nobelprize.org, Nobel Media AB 2013)

Absent from the evening's ceremony and gala moments for health reasons, Hemingway had his brief prepared remarks delivered by John C. Cabot, United States ambassador to Sweden:

Writing, at its best, is a lonely life. Organizations for writers palliate the writer's loneliness but I doubt if they improve his writing. He grows in public stature as he sheds his loneliness and often his work deteriorates. For he does his work alone and if he is a good enough writer he must face eternity, or the lack of it, each day.

For a true writer each book should be a new beginning where he tries again for something that is beyond attainment. He should always try for something that has never been done or that others have tried and failed. Then sometimes, with great luck, he will succeed.

How simple the writing would be if it were only necessary to write in another way what has been well written. It is because we

> have had such great writers in the past that a writer is driven far out past where he can go, out to where no one can help him.
>
> I have spoken too long for a writer. A writer should write what he has to say and not speak it. Again I thank you.

The powerful allusive linking of Santiago and Ahab in the third paragraph is genuine, sincere. Hemingway could not have known writing it how these words, the broad allusion in these sentiments, would also key Secretary Österling's own praising words.

• • •

Hemingway's appearances in *periodicals* continued throughout the 1950s in an inordinate variety of texts that only increased following his major awards. Early on, he had serialized *Across the River and into the Trees* in *Cosmopolitan* (1950) and published *The Old Man and the Sea* in a single issue of *Life* (September 1952). Later he "published in" and "was published about" across multiple broad outlets: *Holiday, Life, Look,* the *New York Herald Tribune Book Review,* the *New York Times Book Review, Time, Sports Illustrated.* He appeared routinely as a subject in syndicated columns, particularly by Leonard Lyons and Earl Wilson in the *New York Post;* in Cuba, he occasionally sat for magazine interviews. *Field and Stream* reprinted "Big Two-Hearted River" (May 1954), and his last published short stories—"Get a Seeing-Eyed Dog" and "A Man of the World"—appeared in the *Atlantic* (December 1957).

• • •

Important amid this flurry of newspaper and magazine publishing activity in the late 1950s, Arnold Gingrich took up a renewed interest in now Nobel laureate Hemingway in 1958—an interest initially centering in the editor's plans for *The Armchair Esquire,* a collection drawn from the magazine's first twenty-five years.

Gingrich selected for inclusion in this commemorative volume the last three of Hemingway's six *Esquire* stories: set in Madrid (originally published November–December 1938–February 1939), they memorialize the Spanish Civil War via their setting in famed Chicote's Bar. Hemingway insisted on rewriting two of the three stories, even briefly initiating a lawsuit to halt publication. The result: from among "The Denunciation," "The Butterfly and the Tank," and "Night Before Battle," only "The Butterfly and the Tank" appeared in the *Armchair* collection published in 1958.

This unfortunate flap ended for the "present" any positive personal element in this author-editor relationship. Unexpectedly, within three years, Hemingway was dead.

Eight years later, in a lighthearted memorial gesture, Gingrich "erased" that earlier unpleasantness marring their relationship at its end, bringing forward a humorous retelling of Hemingway's lawsuit to halt republication in the *Armchair* volume. The editor's recapitulation emphasized a detailed contemporary *Wall Street Journal* parody of this author-editor-publisher brouhaha—"The Old Man and the Fee" (1958). Focused on Hemingway's lawsuit, the *Journal*'s "news coverage" included specific allusion to seven of the author's book titles: "The writer has served with honor in many wars and he does not care what people think about his politics. [He] wants to revise . . . to protect his reprint rights . . . a mistake [that] reflects badly on his courage. What a way to be wounded! . . . The publisher wondered if he was to have or have not. But the author did not bid farewell to the *Armchair Esquire.* One Spanish war story will be printed in the book by a magazine not noted for men without women. . . . The publicity is not too bad. The people now know the book and many will buy it. Do not believe the winner takes nothing. When you hear the bookstore cash registers ring, don't ask for whom the bell tolls. Just know that the sum also rises" (reprinted in "Scott, Ernest, and Whoever," *Esquire,* December 1966, 186–89, 322–25).

This author-editor relationship would achieve fruition, its full ongoing reality, only in the following decade—then centering in important initial posthumous assessments in *Esquire* of Ernest

Hemingway, WRITER. Gingrich would once again assert, explore, adjust, and print materials and voices assessing Hemingway, man and writer—these evaluations appearing in the magazine throughout the 1960s, then well into the 1970s.

• • •

Hemingway's final journalism was published serially, he returning to longtime favorite subject and theme *la corrida:* "The Dangerous Summer," in three installments for *Life* in September 1960.

• • •

A public personality, Ernest Hemingway enjoyed consistent international renown. A private figure, he engaged real-world issues as a professional writer *at his work.* He was, or had been, journalist, war correspondent, litterateur, aesthetician, media darling, world traveler, yachtsman, big-game hunter, and fisherman (regarding the latter, he was briefly a record holder at sea).

Professional writer Hemingway, at work throughout his last decade, left behind at his death a novel fragment, "The Last Good Country"—returning in this narrative to early Michigan lake country materials and his inimitable youth, "a boy for all times," Nick Adams. Much more among the manuscripts incomplete at his death would be carved out by later editors, these texts emerging posthumously—edited, titled, and published by other hands.

• • •

Firsthand experiential knowledge and a focused professionalism anchored Hemingway's at times outsized personas—not least over his last decade: as teacher, husband, parent, patriot, collector (art, books, music), oenophile, sportsman (and naturalist), benefactor, and, throughout, friend of the famous. Celebrities, male and female, were guests at the Finca—more or less continuously.

Among these early, a special case: from Italy, regarding the nobility—and causing friction between Ernest and Mary—twenty-year-old Adriana Ivancich (his muse for Renata in *Across the River and into the Trees*) and her mother. More positively were famed "professionals": from the movies, Ava Gardner, who particularly enjoyed private nude swimming in Hemingway's pool, and especially, Gary Cooper, and both Spencer Tracy and Katharine Hepburn; also, and, not unexpectedly, given his knowledge of the expertise grounding their profession, prizefighters Rocky Marciano and Gene Tunney.

Continual stress at the Finca between Hemingway and Mary, his excessive alcohol consumption, and early signs of both mental and physical decline produced pressure for change. Stress was a factor throughout this decade; examples anchored wholly in the domestic realm had prompted alarm and action as early as 1951: Hemingway's mother, Grace, died in Memphis in June, and he did not attend her services; then, in October, ex-wife Pauline died of fatal hypertension following an emotionally angry phone conversation with Hemingway related to son Gregory's public behavior. Two years later, a return to Africa for a safari, in September 1953, ended with the near-catastrophic plane crashes in January 1954.

• • •

Desiring to escape the inveterate chaotic life at the Finca—politics also a major factor—Ernest and Mary moved to Ketchum, Idaho, in 1959. He had enjoyed hunting, fishing, and the area's compelling terrain and beauty since the 1930s, and they both had developed these feelings in regular visits after their marriage in 1946.

• • •

In the specific contemporary period—winter 1960–spring 1961—Ernest would spend nearly seven months at the Mayo Clinic in Rochester, Minnesota, being treated for depression. He experienced a program there that unfolded continuously with unorthodox medical (and social) dimensions—extraordinary in both their positive and negative long-term effects: "The doctors had locked him in the psych ward but allowed him to roam about town; diagnosed him as suicidal yet took him trapshooting; acknowledged his alcoholism then allowed him to drink. Even by the standards of the day, the treatment and protocol appear questionable. At times, the doctors behaved toward him more as a friend than a patient. Such was the power of Hemingway's charisma, which could intoxicate those in his orbit" (Rosengren 4).

This Ernest Hemingway under treatment had suffered roughly a dozen concussions over his life. Now at sixty-one, he had become increasingly paranoid, deluded, and depressed—even, at times, attracted to, willingly speaking of, his own suicide. Further, he was haunted by memory loss, this latter condition decidedly hurtful to his writing. Among his treatments at Mayo, the most severe—electroconvulsive therapy, triggering brief seizures—Hemingway underwent fifteen times.

Among the results: invited, he was unable to attend the Kennedy inauguration in January 1961, and in April, he wrote his publisher conceding an inability to write further on his Paris memoir; in June, A. E. Hotchner asked—"Papa, why do you want to kill yourself?" The answer, having been pondered now for some time—because he could no longer write: "Hotch, if I can't exist on my own terms, then existence is impossible" (Rosengren 23).

• • •

Today more conclusive data exists. Andrew Farah, chief of psychiatry, the University of North Carolina Healthcare System, believes that Hemingway suffered from chronic traumatic encephalopathy and early stages of dementia. More to the point, "Hemingway received state-of-the-art psychiatric treatment in 1960 and 1961, but for the *wrong* illness" (Rosengren 18).

• • •

Ultimately, such discussion and search for "answers" becomes purely academic. Regarding Hemingway's last twenty-four hours at home in Ketcham, on July 1–2, 1961, the details, as memorialized in Mary's retelling, remain: "While they got ready for bed, she sang an Italian folk song and her husband joined in from his bedroom, then in a 'warm and friendly' voice, said his last words to her, 'Good night, my kitten.'"

What do we know? Little more than that the profound aspirational reality and personal truth he had communicated to her years earlier in the poem "To Mary in London" (May 1944) continued as a driving force:

> I, loving only the word
> Trying to make with a phrase and a sentence
> Something no bomber can reach
> Something to stand when all of us are gone
> And long after.

Rosengren posits simply: "Perhaps he had finally found peace in his resolve [to kill himself]. Or perhaps she created this version later. In either case, she would maintain for the next five years that his self-inflicted death [by shotgun] early the following morning had been an accident" (24).

## Coda

> Ernest Hemingway was the embodiment of America's promise: the young boy from Oak Park who set out to be the best writer of his time. With pluck and luck, talent and wit, hard work and hard living, he did just that. In the process he told us that pursuit was happiness, that man alone was no fucking good, and that any story followed far enough would end badly. Before he burned out, he lived constantly out on the edge of the American experience. In the process he fathered sons, wrote books, influenced friends, and won every prize

available to a writer. He remodeled American short fiction, changed the way characters speak, confronted the moral strictures confining the writer, and left behind a shelf of books telling us how we were in the first half of this century. His is a classic American Story: the young man who transforms himself following his ambition, succeeds beyond his dreams, and finally burns out trying to be true to the person he has become. His imagination, which created "Big Two-Hearted River," also created his paranoia. His ambition, intensity, creative drive, sense of duty, belief in hard work, and faith in the strenuous life carried him to the pinnacle of his profession, provided him wide recognition and considerable wealth, before destroying him when he could no longer meet their demands. It is an old story, older than written words, a story the ancient Greeks would have recognized. (Reynolds, *Hemingway: The Final Years* 360)

9

There are people about whom anything new is news. Ernest Hemingway dead is still far more newsworthy than almost any writer you can think of who is still living.

—**Arnold Gingrich, *Esquire,* June 1967**

# The First Posthumous Decade

## HEMINGWAY'S LITERARY REPUTATION AND *ESQUIRE*

### Who Was Ernest Hemingway, Author—Posthumously?

By the 1950s, despite serious health issues, Ernest Hemingway exemplified the *complete* man of letters: sportsman, insider, teacher, connoisseur, celebrity, journalist, literary artist, even oft-dissed "public man"—his worst in-print characterizations derived from the pulps: variations on the "hypermasculine misogynist" meme.

*Journalist* Hemingway coexisted with the Pulitzer and Nobel *artist.* The *literary* figure assumed dominance toward the end of his life, Hemingway shaping his lived experience in the latter period primarily into fiction, albeit drafting some material as autobiographical nonfiction-memoir. Among mainstream print media—intellectual periodicals, weekly magazines, daily newspapers—both scholarly and journalist postmortem assessments tended to emphasize Hemingway as *fictionist,* somewhat undervaluing the range and variety characterizing his texts. In these latter volumes, in fact, he crafted both fiction and nonfiction. (A sustained example of the former: work centering on his earliest major character—Nick Adams—in the extended, incomplete narrative "The Last Good Country," 1952–58.)

Regardless of mode, even when mixing modes, Hemingway's personal perspectives shaped meanings across genres. These latter narratives appeared posthumously over four decades: *A Moveable Feast* (1964); *Islands in the Stream* (1970); *The Nick Adams Stories* (1972); *The Dangerous Summer* (1985); *The Garden of Eden* (1986); and *True at First Light* (1999); *Under Kilimanjaro* (2005).

## Who Was Ernest Hemingway, Author—Posthumously, in *Esquire*, 1961–1973?

Hemingway's manifold *Esquire* "presences," 1933–58, have been broadly commented upon over time. In print and among sites ranging from publishers' editorial offices to professors' college classrooms, this history, these data, have furthered "Hemingway" assessments both literary-cultural and biographical. Of interest in this context, later commentators taking up "Hemingway *and Esquire*" have generally ignored two pieces of "Hemingway *in Esquire*"—chronologically important because they appeared at the close of the 1950s, the author's final complete decade and the years of his broadest literary recognitions and awards.

Journalist Eric Sevareid's substantial "Mano-a-Mano" for *Esquire* (November 1959) tracked the summer bullfight season in Spain, May–September, the subject of Hemingway's final published journalism. Sevareid focused on the Pulitzer and Nobel–awarded Hemingway's active involvement with two premier Spanish matadors, brothers-in-law Antonio Ordóñez and Luis Miguel Dominguín, both well-known to the American aficionado.

Sevareid's analysis for *Esquire* to a degree "pre-empted" Hemingway's own descriptive accounts, these soon following and, unsurprisingly, shaped for *Life* magazine. Hemingway had promised personal coverage of that summer's bullfight competitions featuring Ordóñez and Dominguín to the magazine at ten thousand words.

Begun in October 1959, his narratives, after much anguishing over and editorial downsizing, unfolded in three installments as "The Dangerous Summer" (*Life,* September 1960).

The import of *Esquire*'s coverage? Presence and firsthand reporting of these taurine events: they the subject action of Hemingway's final journalism; they the last original texts published in his lifetime.

Further, quite fortuitously, a second description and assessment for *Esquire* of the more broadly known Hemingway in his final period. Carson McCullers, in "The Flowering Dream: Notes on Writing" (December 1959), produces a more typical piece, characterizing and critiquing the author. In this final month of his last complete decade, fictionist McCullers declares Hemingway "the most cosmopolitan of all American writers" (163).

After his death in July 1961, Hemingway's varied presences in *Esquire* became fewer—only briefly. Motivating publisher Gingrich, issues of content and focus. Even deceased, "Hemingway" constituted a desirable subject: one to be neither overrated nor undervalued, certainly, but also one not to be overlooked nor ignored.

Thus, going forward—from Hemingway's death in 1961 until Arnold Gingrich's retirement in 1973, *Esquire,* alone among American periodicals, continually published wide-ranging, assessing commentaries on the author—the man, his work.

• • •

These *Esquire* pieces emphasized both the journalism and the fiction—then, not least, the intersection of these genres in Hemingway's *personalized* nonfiction. As earlier in *Death in the Afternoon* and *Green Hills of Africa,* so now, during this later period, in the first among his posthumous volumes—*A Moveable Feast,* 1964. (Ironically, this apologia, and elegy of sorts, appears in the centennial year of the most renowned spiritual autobiography in modern English—British cardinal John Henry Newman's *Apologia pro Vita Sua.*)

Continuing much unacknowledged and underappreciated even today are Hemingway's varied, often dramatic, posthumous "presences" in *Esquire* recorded during Gingrich's later years. As he had done three decades earlier, editor, and now publisher and senior vice president, Gingrich took up the "posthumous writer" in toto—as author, celebrity, complex public figure. After July 1961: Hemingway, an ongoing subject in reprintings; then, more consequentially, Hemingway, in new, evaluative assessments by biographers and literary critics and, not least, by fellow fiction writers.

• • •

Arnold Gingrich fully appreciated the personal, albeit disparate, voices Hemingway had cultivated in the magazine. The author now deceased, his journalist editor determined to "re-present" him. Gingrich would do so over *sixty times in thirty-four magazine issues* from 1961 through 1973, concluding with Hemingway's multi-varied appearances in the singular, even spectacular, *Esquire* fortieth anniversary "special issue" in October 1973.

During the first posthumous decade and well into the 1970s, *Esquire*'s editor posed questions to the magazine's readership touching Hemingway's multifaceted personality: that is, he emphasizing the "literary figure" without ignoring the "public person." Gingrich then printed reader responses, especially taking up various versions of both question and query: "Who was Ernest Hemingway?"—artist, celebrity, cultural icon—and also the reality, Hemingway described here among no shortage of colorful negative epithets.

Unsurprisingly, "voices," in multiples across many contemporary magazine and journal outlets, effected extensive give-and-take commentary on Hemingway's life and work (both his journalism and the fiction) during the first decade following his death.

Gingrich began *Esquire*'s posthumous portraits with his own, "E.H.: A Coda from the Maestro," in October 1961. The editor initiated his evaluative judgments by quoting Hemingway's expressing key personal ideas in *Esquire* from 1933 to 1936. Powerful among these tenets: "Any good man would rather take chances any day with his life than with his livelihood and that is the main point about professionals that amateurs seem never to appreciate."

An authoritative professional, Hemingway was also fully "human," as sensitive, attentive readers understood. This "character" was powerfully suggested by Arnold Samuelson, the young man nicknamed the "maestro," a violinist from Minnesota who had worked for Hemingway over a year in exchange for writing instruction. At the author's death, protégé Samuelson offered, in effect, a brief eulogy, which Gingrich recorded in "E.H.": "Ernest lived as long as he could. His last act was the most deliberate of his life. He had never written about his own suffering. He did it all without words in the language any man can understand" (8).

Roughly half of Hemingway's posthumous "appearances" in *Esquire* unfolded as article-length critical assessments of "the man" and "his art": anecdotes shaping analyses of his character; reprintings of his *Esquire* writings; full-length critical essays by various professionals placing him within the broader contemporary cultural milieu. Readers' responses to this emerging and ever-enlarging controversial figure (despite or because that personality had now been silenced) enlivened the magazine's monthly "Sound and Fury" letters section—as in the "days of old," when Hemingway also appeared regularly in the magazine on the "Publisher's Page" and in the "Editor's Notes."

• • •

In his youth, Gingrich had "idolized" Scott Fitzgerald, a predisposition he had developed further as *Esquire* editor. Between February 1934 and July 1941, *Esquire* published forty-five Fitzgerald pieces, and in 1962, Gingrich edited a volume of Fitzgerald's seventeen "Pat Hobby" stories for Scribner. Comparison of the editor's dealing with Hemingway and with Fitzgerald is both inevitable and complicated, but, finally, too, a testament to Gingrich's efforts to be "fair."

Respected historian and biographer Andrew Turnbull published his authoritative biography *Scott Fitzgerald* in 1962. Gingrich asked Turnbull to describe and assess the relationship between the two literary figures. Highlights include:

> Fitzgerald's attitude toward Hemingway was resignation tinged with jealousy. . . . Hemingway's attitude toward Fitzgerald was a mixture of condescension and scorn. People . . . remember his saying that Fitzgerald was a "rummy," that he was "washed up," that he had "gone social" and hung around with the rich. "The Crack-Up" merely confirmed this view. On reading the first installment Hemingway wrote Perkins that it was so miserable—this whining in public. A writer could be a coward, but at least he should be a writer. Fitzgerald had gone from youth to senility without manhood in between. . . . And Hemingway, for all his condescension, sent Fitzgerald a copy of *For Whom the Bell Tolls* inscribed: "To Scott with affection and esteem." "It's a fine novel, better than anyone else writing could do," Fitzgerald wrote back, and signed himself, "With old affection." (*Esquire*, March 1962, 121–23)

As editor, Gingrich presented Hemingway variously. In October 1970, he excerpted in *Esquire* the author's first posthumously published fiction, the novel *Islands in the Stream* (thirty-four thousand words). Moreover, for *Esquire*'s fortieth anniversary in 1973, he reprinted two Hemingway pieces from 1936, one journalism, one fiction: "On the Blue Water" (with central details prefiguring *The Old Man and the Sea*) and arguably his finest short story, "The Snows of Kilimanjaro." In the same issue he reprinted Scott Fitzgerald's "Pasting It Together," one of his three very personal "Crack Up" essays from the mid-1930s.

*Esquire* achieved much with its detailed, effectively continuous Hemingway homage between 1961 and 1973. Ultimately, Gingrich published in the magazine the broadest professional commentary on the author's life and work found in any periodical the first posthumous "decade" (actually over twelve years): sixty pieces, concluding in October 1973 with the singular celebratory volume publication *Esquire: The Best of Forty Years*—at 564 pages (369 content, absent advertisements), in its time the largest ever single issue of an American magazine.

The cover of this fortieth anniversary edition consisted of in-color, numbered (for name identification), pictorial images of thirty-nine contributing writers from the magazine's much larger cast of famous contributors (here, each and all, standing, drinks in hand). Authors throughout the magazine's four-decade history memorialized here range from#1 John Kenneth Galbraith to #39 Laurence Stallings. For this "anniversary" gathering, a special sticker singles out fifteen literary figures (including Dreiser, Fitzgerald, Hemingway, Nabokov, Steinbeck, Updike, Wolfe) from those standing side by side and effecting a color photomontage filling the cover, both front and back sides.

Notable to the eye in passing, *Esquire*'s principal figure, as founding editor, Arnold Gingrich is #35. (Standing near the editor—and of the same slight physical stature—Truman Capote, #23). Telling among these famed figures, if not exactly clear *how* meaningful: just two women appear—#3 Nora Ephron and #20 Dorothy Parker. Similarly, there are only two persons of color—#15 James Baldwin and #29 Ralph Ellison. Among these contemporary "*Esquire* writers" / "writers in *Esquire*" are voices—most renowned, some becoming so, "movers and shakers" —and in this "historical" moment, regarding Hemingway specifically: some now his "peers"; some later to become his "heirs."

Missing from these widely recognized, genuinely varied writers and personalities, Jesse Stuart, *Esquire*'s "champion" contributor, author of fifty-eight pieces from 1938 to the mid-1950s. An especial favorite of editor Gingrich, this "regionalist" storyteller is understandably, to use Gingrich's own words, "out of synch" with the "New Fiction" emphasis of the present and, thus, absent here (10).

Publication of this singular "volume-length" edition of the magazine proved not to be an explicitly literary event. It did produce and ground a historical overview of the *Esquire* years, appropriately featuring, among much else, Hemingway's various presences, his words scattered among texts by numerous other well-known contemporaries. Among these collective figures, underscored throughout, an explicit historical dimension: their interactions, their art, their personalities, their varied and personal *public* vicissitudes—a record of successes and stumblings regarding contemporary and ongoing social-political-historical issues.

Regardless, the volume justly centered in *Esquire*'s history and its continuous commitment to publishing fine writing from a cast of broadly varied literati, each reflecting the magazine's conscious commitment to introducing *new* ideas from disparate, contemporary voices.

A snapshot of "voices" and "issues" across this volume's contents:

- "My Generation" by Scott Fitzgerald
- "Scott, Ernest and Whoever" by Arnold Gingrich
- "The Snows of Kilimanjaro" by Ernest Hemingway
- "The Trial of Arthur Miller" by John Steinbeck
- "The Death of James Dean" by John Dos Passos
- "Kennedy without Tears" by Tom Wicker, by special request following his assassination coverage
- "A Few Words about Breasts" by Nora Ephron
- "The Eighty-Yard Run" by Irwin Shaw
- "The Illustrated Man" by Ray Bradbury
- *Breakfast at Tiffany's* by Truman Capote

Other major contemporary writers appearing in this *Esquire* birthday volume included Saul Bellow, Ralph Ellison, William Faulkner, Graham Greene, Dorothy Parker, Philip Roth, John Updike, Orson Welles.

• • •

Notable, also, this anniversary *Esquire* volume in 1973 illustrated Gingrich's commitment to both independence and quality for the magazine, apparent over the years and epitomized earlier in the editor's recalling in 1966—then halfway between Hemingway's death in 1961 and the celebratory "Best of Forty Years" volume of the present, 1973—a long-past, telling event and a history that strengthened, thus assured early on, the magazine's future.

This historical moment proved emblematic of Gingrich's thinking. It identifies in his own words the occasion when and where, as editor and publisher, he came to understand the meaning—particularly for himself—of the *right*, the *just*, the *sacrosanct*. His commitment enacted and powerfully recorded here—in the magazine and for the record—developed initially through H. L. Mencken's testimony in federal court two decades previously. Mencken had formally defended *Esquire*'s breadth and content quality, against charges of "obscenity," and the magazine's right, under law, to exist and to enjoy unfettered "distribution via the U.S. Mail" (the issue then at hand—in the 1940s).

Gingrich, much later, remarked upon these truths: "Ever since Henry Mencken testified for us in the Post Office case, over twenty-three years ago, to the effect that *Esquire* had printed virtually every author of significance in this century 'headed by Dreiser,' the list of well-known literary figures who have contributed to these pages has been growing steadily, to the point where now it would be much easier and quicker to make up a list of the famous writers of our time who have not appeared in our pages than to attempt to enumerate all those who have" ("Publisher's Page," *Esquire*, December 1966, 8).

Immediately following this statement in the original magazine article, Gingrich named—in columns, literally printed in alphabetical order—a complete list of authors who had published in *Esquire* to that mid-1960s date—a cast in the hundreds already, eventually to include, on Gingrich's watch, sixteen Nobel laureates.

• • •

As publisher, in 1952 and in 1958, Arnold Gingrich had experienced brief, unsuccessful forays regarding "Hemingway and *Esquire.*" Then, post-1961, following the author's death, he seized upon a critical (opportune) period at the magazine regarding Hemingway's posthumous reputation—and no less, a plan for a second reunion of author and magazine. This latter action, developing quickly, eventuated in Gingrich's personal—designed in significant detail—plan to memorialize "Ernest Hemingway in *Esquire.*" In accord with an outline shaped solely by Gingrich, "Hemingway" was taken up in the magazine and formally presented as the literary, historical, biographical, "*name* artist" of his generation: major American literary figure; master of the creative imagination; contemporary cultural icon—and not least, he, now and into the foreseeable future, recovered, assessed, as *the Esquire* literary personality.

In *Esquire,* for more than a decade—through the 1960s and well into the 1970s—Gingrich, empowered as editor, publisher, and senior vice president, designed and effected his own "master plan": to recover and "reclaim" a major figure popularly associated with the magazine from its inception and across numerous unique, even halcyon, "touchstone" moments from those earliest days.

Gingrich's idea as implemented: to *republish* original Hemingway materials from *Esquire*'s "golden years," 1933–39; to *reprint* 1930s professional literary, critical, journalist voices from *Esquire*'s pages reacting to, and interacting with, that earlier Hemingway. Pieces such as these had laid the groundwork in those early days for what became Gingrich's contemporary purposeful "posthumous Hemingway" plan; that creative enterprise with a specific purpose; and to *publish* across the present (i.e., post-1961) journalism-literature "scene," a continuous (in fact, lasting well into the 1970s) *professional* assessment of Hemingway's "life and writing" tailored to an educated audience and expressed by both contemporary literary figures and professional critics.

These 1960s *Esquire* "voices" collectively effected—over more than that decade—the *most extensive* published commentary on Hemingway's life and work, both the journalism and the fiction, to be found in any American periodical in the early years following the author's death.

Gingrich's achievement exceeded expectations. Hemingway (biographical) or some version of him as author (formal criticism) appeared in sixty pieces across thirty-four issues over the period 1961–73. Gingrich's publishing plan—to focus on the historical "Hemingway in *Esquire*" as subject matter—unfolded as the editor envisioned. Results exceeded all expectations—in multifaceted "dimensions" and across numerous "fronts."

In the magazine, thus *on the record,* contemporary authors-critics-biographers-literary historians took up "Ernest Hemingway." Following Gingrich's formal invitations, these various, respected, midcentury "moderns" accepted and agreed to write about and explicitly assess (free of external restrictions touching their expression) "Hemingway and ______." The range of emotion and substance can be suggested by noting early brief (Mailer's, even visceral) responses from two prominent literary voices. Norman Mailer wrote: "Ernest, so proud of his reputation. So fierce about it. His death was awful. Say it. It was the most difficult death in America since Roosevelt. One has still not recovered from Hemingway's death. One may never" (*Esquire,* November 1962, 134); and Gay Talese, in context, contrasted Paris in the 1920s with Paris in the 1950s: "Once there was Ernest and Scott and Gertrude, and the wine flowed and the talk was good. But now there is Doc and Jimmy and George and Patsy, and the Scotch is light and gossip is gossip" (*Esquire,* July 1963, 44).

Unsurprisingly, even in death, the "perceived to be un/anti-intellectual" Hemingway produced powerful, sometimes extreme, responses. British socialist-satirist Malcolm Muggeridge's anti-Hemingway rant literally stings: "Hemingway destroyed himself as our world is destroying itself, by excessive indulgence in fantasy and self-delusion; by coming to believe in the ravings of his own ego as it strove with increasing hysteria to maintain itself against the ravages of flagging appetites, tired vanity, and the flesh's weariness. The gunshot only completed the job. It was an act of final surrender, the ultimate succumbing to an irremediable hangover" (*Esquire,* June 1966, 34).

Additional "prominent commentator" voices included a broad intellectual spectrum: Jerome Beatty, Matthew Bruccoli, Malcolm Cowley, Carson McCullers, George Plimpton, William Styron, Edmund Wilson.

As planned, these figures' comments, positive and negative, produced *for Esquire* original, substantive pieces on "author and Nobel Laureate" Hemingway. They included personal details—emphasizing the writer both as public artist and as private person. Their texts fulfilled the editor's design to publish both personal and professional moments/judgments touching the author—the "individual" formally recalled, remembered, even "re-shaped" into literary images underpinning contemporary professional critical judgments.

Hemingway emerges as the conscientious award-winning writer: literary artist (Pulitzer, Nobel); sophisticated sportsman (master of the African savanna, authority on Spanish taurine culture, record-holding, deep-sea angler); he, indisputably, an accomplished "man of the world."

Gingrich's collected speakers were themselves prominent literati. Their *Esquire* texts, generally article length, unfolded periodically, but consistently, in the magazine's monthly issues *over more than a decade.*

Important, indeed critical, for "effect" and also for "truth," these assessments appeared side by side in the magazine with reprintings from and among Hemingway's own *and* other voices from 1930s *Esquire* pieces. These texts, reprinted from the earlier halcyon days, as Gingrich had hoped, contextualized Hemingway alone and, not least, he among renowned literary contemporaries from that bygone era, they, each and all, *Esquire* contributors "in the beginning": Sherwood Anderson, Erskine Caldwell, Morley Callaghan, Willa Cather, John Dos Passos, Scott Fitzgerald, Ring Lardner, Sinclair Lewis, Thomas Wolfe, as well as extraliterary personalities as diverse as Clarence Darrow and Havelock Ellis.

• • •

Turnbull and Gingrich focused on the man, Ernest Hemingway. Taking on numerous critics offering severely negative criticism of the author—for example, Vance Bourjaily, Stanley Edgar Hyman, Leslie Fiedler, Dwight MacDonald—longtime Hemingway appraiser and literary critic–historian Malcolm Cowley took up and again, as he had done often earlier, persuasively explained Hemingway's "role," his "fit," in the contemporary moment amid the current intellectual "environment" or "scene":

> Hemingway's real subject is the barriers that can be erected against death and loneliness and the void. . . . The discipline of one's calling and the further discipline required of every human being if he is to live as a man, not collapse into a jelly of emotions, is the strongest of those barriers. . . . Landscape, the weather, fishing and hunting, eating and drinking, talking around the fire and making love: those are the wonderful things in Hemingway. The ideas are interesting too, even though merely implied, for he was always more of an intellectual than he pretended to be. . . . With the necessary subtractions made, Hemingway's work as a whole is so clearly permanent, that, even if his reputation were destroyed for the moment, and the work buried, it would be exhumed after a hundred years, as Melville's was. ("Papa and the Parricides," *Esquire,* June 1967, 103)

Hemingway's *Esquire* canon embodies a scope and candor not found elsewhere among his writings. The essays, collectively, offer broad-canvas explorations of his major interests from big-game sport to authorship, and they emphasize the role and responsibilities of the artist. He presents himself as a literary, intellectual, and sophisticated man of the world. His persona is no longer the oft-exaggerated creation found in certain writing from his formative period—Kansas City, Milan, Toronto, Paris. His voice is authentic, even down to frequent, humorous self-mockery. In *Esquire,* free to write whatever he wants, from wherever he might be, he writes sometimes quite broadly, speaking as the quintessential man of action enmeshed in, surrounded by, the natural world.

Among his twenty-five "letters" from 1933 to 1936, twelve involve deep-sea fishing, especially for marlin. His scientific interests touch this sport no less than in the obvious appeal of competition. Most important, finally: the role of this sports activity and his twelve *Esquire* essays in Hemingway's biography and, not least, in his literary canon.

The import of the *Esquire* essays—twenty-five in all—inheres in their centrality in Hemingway's activities throughout the 1930s, including their position vis-à-vis *Death in the Afternoon* and *Green Hills of Africa,* in which, too, his writing is partly autobiographical. In the *Esquire* letters, more than elsewhere in this period, Hemingway willingly chances talking about himself. In doing so, his singular purpose *as an artist* is to explain and justify his actions and writing. Thus, not infrequently, he "takes up" his critics—referring generally to recent published critiques, occasionally even taking on a detractor by name.

In *Esquire,* free to write whatever he wants, from wherever he might be—this matter shaped and adapted as he sees fit—Hemingway writes in an authentic voice as the quintessential man of action enmeshed in, surrounded by, the natural world. As in *Green Hills of Africa,* specifically, *Esquire* presents the first-person Hemingway voice occasionally taking on critics—of both his lifestyle and writing. Increasingly, the Left, for example, presses for explanation of the place and purpose of his texts "explicating" bullfights and "justifying" safaris amid a national depression.

Most important, albeit not widely appreciated at first, each *Esquire* essay is informational and instructional—Hemingway's voice consistently that of teacher, even magister. When he talks about marlin, he offers all manner of details learned or experienced by him firsthand—that is, the history of the species; his belief that marlin are all, finally, the same fish; that their different colorations don't matter; that when old, they are all females. These letters reveal intellectual import and understanding from personal lived experience. Similarly, his readers (principally male adults of some wealth) should develop their leisure into something intellectually worthwhile—something capable of being shared: that is, rewarding because an idea and action shaping meaningful leisure activity.

These essays are not devoted exclusively to fishing or big-game pursuit in Africa. Politically knowledgeable and astute, fearing the next war, Hemingway writes from Paris, from Spain, and about Italy. Since his early *Toronto Star* days, he has witnessed the developing political and economic stresses across Europe.

By 1936, *Esquire* is selling between 500,000 and 700,000 copies monthly. Hemingway has an enormous audience for his ideas. Defense of himself in the 1930s reaches a kind of epic moment in these letters via consistency. He is consistent in the vision of his art; on the weaknesses of his critics; and on putting himself forth as an insider who knows how to get things done.

Hemingway had shared the stage—for twice the fee—with Erskine Caldwell, Clarence Darrow, John Dos Passos, Theodore Dreiser, Scott Fitzgerald, Dashiell Hammett, Langston Hughes, Aldous Huxley, D. H. Lawrence, Ezra Pound. Moreover, his writing for the magazine had actually reduced criticism regarding the "sexual" dimensions of the publication, particularly in its cartoons and photospreads featuring the "Petty Girl."

Periodically, Gingrich took up glib, "holier-than-thou" attacks from readers and "concerned" citizens. In the preface to the *Armchair Esquire* volume, which collects twenty-nine essays from the magazine's first twenty-five years, readers find texts by Bellow, Fitzgerald, Hemingway, Lawrence, Mailer, Mann, Salinger. The collection concludes with an appendix, "Check-list of Contributions of Literary Import to *Esquire,* 1933–1958"— *twenty-two double-column pages.* Gingrich observes: "The sad truth that brains wear better than beauty was never more evident than in looking back over old issues: the pictures . . . reflections of the passing moment, the fads and foibles and the fleeting fancies of the stage and screen, whereas the words . . . concerned, in major part, the verities that are eternal" (17–18).

And a (perhaps the) final overview judgment of Ernest Hemingway—in the eyes of his longtime observer and sometime employer.

• • •

Editor Gingrich's heart and mind regarding artist Hemingway center in the achievement of idea and expression in a story such as "On the Blue Water," *Esquire,* April 1936. *Esquire*'s portraits, not least this one, express, embody, the creative literary imagination of this talented novelist and journalist. This feature story expresses and explores the exhilaration of marlin fishing in the Gulf. Moreover, at its center, it contains the germ of the *Old Man and the Sea.*

Ernest Hemingway—an artist with a singular creative imagination and also a dedicated professional writer and Nobel laureate—changed the matter and manner of modern American narrative. By Gingrich's choice and with his assistance, Hemingway dominated *Esquire*'s early years, appeared as a principal in the middle period, and then returned, in the end, as a major focus. He shared space in the magazine with notable contemporary writers—James Baldwin, John Barth, Ray Bradbury, Saul Bellow, Truman Capote, Philip Roth, J. D. Salinger—and their finest work, for example, Bradbury's *Illustrated Man* (1950) and Capote's *Breakfast at Tiffany's* (1958). After the fact, editor Gingrich explicitly judged and averred:

> As a short story writer, Hemingway was remarkably consistent. As a novelist, he was an in-and-outer. His big book, as his work now stands and must stand, is *For Whom the Bell Tolls.* His best book is still his first one, *The Sun Also Rises* because it is his most perfectly realized. . . .
>
> What is left? Some of the best writing, in the non-fiction books: *A Moveable Feast, Death in the Afternoon,* always terribly underrated because it was about bullfighting, and *Green Hills of Africa,* given similar short shrift because it had to do with big-game hunting on safari. That Hemingway could still write on the master virtuoso level

is proved by *A Moveable Feast*. (*Esquire*, "Publisher's Page," October 1970, 6, 12)

Noteworthy in these words: Gingrich's assessment ignores "Hemingway and/in *Esquire*." Ever the professional, the editor avoided commenting on the part of Hemingway's achievement that had passed through his own hands.

(Unsurprisingly, in 1968, because so clearly appropriate, *Esquire* editor Arnold Gingrich was presented the Henry Johnson Fisher Award, the highest recognition accorded by the Magazine Publishers' Association).

Unquestionably, Hemingway's *Esquire* canon exhibits and justifies a lifestyle and a career. It does so through the multiple voices of a complexly nuanced persona often very close to the "real" Ernest Hemingway. This key public testament appears in the decade of the author's greatest productivity, deepest personal growth, and widest range of self-expression.

Born in 1899 into a world of horsedrawn buggies, ragtime, and old growth forests, a world without airplanes, television, or women's suffrage, Hemingway committed suicide in 1961, the year the Berlin Wall was built, the Bay of Pigs debacle took place, the first intercontinental ballistic missile was launched, and Pete Seeger composed "Where Have All the Flowers Gone?"

**—Susan F. Beegel, "Conclusion: The Critical Reputation of Ernest Hemingway"**

# Afterword

Through the Roaring Twenties, the Depression, World War II, and the 1950s, Americans read Ernest Hemingway. Continuing today across his written words—those published, those in private correspondence, those memorialized by others tracking his intellectual-emotional progress—more than six decades after his death, Hemingway maintains a prominent presence in cultural debates describing twentieth-century America.

A witness to the wars, revolutions, and other volatile instabilities of his time, Hemingway investigated many issues: domestic, legal, patriotic, political, military, religious, and those related to community. The domestic he explored in extraordinary breadth, particularly across his seventeen "Nick Adams" stories. Among the most important subjects therein: male-female relationships. Hemingway expressed a pronounced understanding and sympathy—still today insufficiently appreciated—for his major women characters.

Regardless of which years were formative for a particular reader—the war-revolutionary decade of the teens; the grimly conservative or wildly hedonist drift of the 1920s; the decade of Depression; World War II; the Cold War era, concluding for Hemingway with the Cuban Revolution in 1959—many Hemingway readers certainly felt the WASP system of their heritage slipping away. They found themselves spiritual wanderers, as in Matthew Arnold's words, "between two worlds, / One dead, the other powerless to be born."

Earlier, experiencing this existential crisis, Jake, in *The Sun Also Rises* (1926), formulated the central Hemingway question (felt by many sensitive readers today, every bit as much as throughout the first six decades of the twentieth century): *How does one discover in a world of discredited or otherwise destabilized values and traditions the way to live now?*

Without taking up that query per se, *Esquire* founding editor Arnold Gingrich had suggested in the late 1930s that a valuable addressing of such issues could be found throughout the writings of his prized author (ironically, even as Gingrich himself understood that Hemingway was then moving away from the magazine): "His influence on other writers has been wide but . . . the temptation has always been to copy the mannerism without succeeding in duplicating the method. And the Hemingway method is to the Hemingway style what the submerged seven-eighths is to the iceberg's exposed eighth. For like Cézanne, Hemingway not only worked out a new way of setting things down, but, far more important, he worked out a new way of looking at things before setting them down" ("Reviving Salutes to the Living," *Esquire*, February 1937, 28).

# *ESQUIRE* BIBLIOGRAPHY


Hemingway, Ernest. "Marlin Off the Morro. A Cuban Letter." 1 (Fall 1933), 8–9, 39, 97.

———. "The Friend of Spain. A Spanish Letter." 1 (January 1934), 26, 136.

———. "A Paris Letter." 1 (February 1934), 22, 156.

———. "a.d. in Africa. A Tanganyika Letter." 1 (April 1934), 19, 146.

———. "Shootism Versus Sport. The Second Tanganyika Letter." 2 (June 1934), 19, 150.

———. "Notes on Dangerous Game. The Third Tanganyika Letter." 2 (July 1934), 19, 94.

———. "Out in the Stream. A Cuban Letter." 2 (August 1934), 19, 156, 158.

———. "Defense of Dirty Words. A Cuban Letter." 2 (September 1934), 19, 158B, 158D.

———. "Genio After Josie. A Havana Letter." 2 (October 1934), 21–22.

———. "Old Newsman Writes." 2 (December 1934), 25–26.

———. "Notes on Life and Letters. Or a Manuscript Found in a Bottle." 3 (January 1935), 21, 159.

———. "Remembering Shooting-Flying. A Key West Letter." 3 (February 1935), 21, 152.

———. "Facing a Bitter World. A Portfolio of Etchings by Luis Quintanilla." 3 (February 1935), 26–27.

———. "Sailfish Off Mombasa. A Key West Letter." 3 (March 1935), 21, 156.

———. "The Sights of Whitehead Street. A Key West Letter." 3 (April 1935), 25, 156.

———. "a.d. Southern Style. A Key West Letter." 3 (May 1935), 25, 156.

———. "On Being Shot Again. A Gulf Stream Letter." 3 (June 1935), 25, 156–57.

———. "The President Vanquishes. A Bimini Letter." 4 (July 1935), 23, 167.

———. "He Who Gets Slap Happy. A Bimini Letter." 4 (August 1935), 19, 182.

———. "Notes on the Next War." 4 (September 1935), 19, 156.
———. "Monologue to the Maestro. A High Seas Letter." 4 (October 1935), 21, 174A–B.
———. "The Malady of Power. A Second Serious Letter." 4 (November 1935), 31, 198–99.
———. "Million Dollar Fright. A New York Letter." 4 (December 1935), 35, 190B.
———. "Wings Always Over Africa. An Ornithological Letter." 5 (January 1936), 31, 174–75.
———. "The Tradesman's Return." 5 (February 1936), 27, 193–96.
———. "On the Blue Water. A Gulf Stream Letter." 5 (April 1936), 31, 184–85.
———. "There She Breaches! Or Moby Dick Off the Morro." 5 (May 1936), 35, 203–5.
———. "Gattorno: Program Note." 5 (May 1936), 111, 141.
———. "The Horns of the Bull." 5 (June 1936), 31, 190–93.
———. "The Snows of Kilimanjaro." 6 (August 1936), 27, 194–201.
———. "The Denunciation." 10 (November 1938), 39, 111–14.
———. "The Butterfly and the Tank." 10 (December 1938), 51, 186, 188, 190.
———. "Night Before Battle." 11 (February 1939), 27–29, 91–92, 95, 97.

• • •

Hemingway was written about in *Esquire* from the magazine's initial publication (October 1933) to his death (July 1961).

**"Backstage with *Esquire*"**

Gingrich, Arnold. *Esquire,* Fall 1933, 7.
———. *Esquire,* January 1934, 16.
———. *Esquire,* February 1934, 16.
———. *Esquire,* March 1934, 16.
———. *Esquire,* April 1934, 16.
———. *Esquire,* July 1934, 16.
———. *Esquire,* September 1934, 14D.
———. *Esquire,* October 1934, 18B.
———. *Esquire,* November 1934, 22.
———. *Esquire,* December 1934, 18.
———.*Esquire,* February 1935, 14.
———. *Esquire,* March 1935, 18.
———. *Esquire,* May 1935, 22B.
———. *Esquire,* June 1935, 22.
———. *Esquire,* August 1935, 12.
———. *Esquire,* September 1935, 14.

———. *Esquire,* June 1936, 28.
———. *Esquire,* November 1936, 42B.

**Editorial Comment**

Gingrich, Arnold. "As for the Use of Dirty Words." *Esquire,* September 1934, 11.
———. "A Thought on Propaganda." *Esquire,* November 1935, 5.
———. "Autobiography of a Two Year Old." *Esquire,* December 1935, 5.
———. "Death in the Afternoon Cocktail." *Esquire,* December 1935, 55.
———. "Reviving the Practice of Salutes to the Living." *Esquire,* February 1937, 5, 28.
———. "A Farewell to the Lead-off Man." *Esquire,* June 1937, 5.
———. "About 'For Whom the Bell Tolls.'" *Esquire,* December 1940, 5.
———. "From Billy Phelps to Battered Britain." *Esquire,* February 1941, 6.
———. "All about Graffis the Artist, Editor, Anthologist, and Grocery-Buyer." *Esquire,* May 1945, 6.

**Articles**

Salpeter, Harry. "Rabelais in a Smock." *Esquire,* July 1936, 101, 118, 121–22.
Phelps, William Lyon. "*Esquire*'s Five-Minute Shelf" column. Review of *For Whom the Bell Tolls. Esquire,* February 1941, 76, 135.
Gingrich, Arnold. "Publisher's Page." *Esquire.* February 1958, 10.
Sevareid, Eric. "Mano a Mano." *Esquire,* November 1959, 40–44.
McCullers, Carson. "The Flowering Dream." *Esquire,* December 1959, 162–64.
Cohen, Lester. ". . . And the Sinner: Horace Liveright." *Esquire,* December 1960, 107–8.
Stern, Edith. "Papa's Flops." *Esquire,* February 1961, 22.

**"The Sound and the Fury"**

Matthew, E. W. "A Feast on Rian's Poison." *Esquire,* May 1934, 12.
Vela, J. G. "P-173 Must Be in Jail." *Esquire,* May 1934, 12.
Smith, McKelden. "No Credit to Oscar Wilde?" *Esquire,* September 1934, 14B.
Smith, Edmund E. "Anything for the Locker Room?" *Esquire,* October 1934, 14.
Saag, Leon Der. "Curtain Call for the Old Lady." *Esquire,* February 1935, 10.
Liberman, Jules. "Deep-Sea Low-Down." *Esquire,* May 1935, 12.
Farrington, S. K. "Comes the Counter-Revolution." *Esquire,* September 1935, 6.

Sauer, J. M. "Little Essay on Hem and Haw." *Esquire,* September 1935, 6.
Bailey, Warren Worth. "The Monthly Class in Hemstitching." *Esquire,* October 1935, 6.
Lansby, Ira. "A Farewell to Stench." *Esquire,* October 1935, 6.
Zuro, Arthur. "Argument for Hem." *Esquire,* November 1935, 6.
Chapin, C. L. "The Sideshows Have Tricky Mirrors Too." *Esquire,* November 1935, 8.
Powell, E. Alexander. "Carpetcall for Johannes Steel." *Esquire,* December 1935, 6.
Taylor, Lalah. "Fun Is Fun, But. . . ." *Esquire,* December 1935, 6.
Cook, C. N. "Miami, Where Fish Are Fish." *Esquire,* December 1935, 10.
H., E. D. "Handshake from the Fleet." *Esquire,* December 1935, 10.
Williamson, O. A. "Broad-Minded, Esq." *Esquire.* December 1935, 10.
Foster, Bob. "Hem Ain't for Hire." *Esquire,* January 1936, 6.
Serwer, H. "S. & F. in Three Ruts." *Esquire,* January 1936, 6.
Pinson, Roberta W. "Odd SHRDLU McIntyre." *Esquire,* February 1936, 8.
Baxter, Wm. F. "Cultivated Taste." *Esquire,* July 1936, 6.
Bresnahan, B. A. "A Crack a Day . . . Page Hemingway." August 1936, 6.
Caverhill, Ernest A. H. "*Esq*'s Advocate." August 1936, 6.
Newmeyer, Fred, Jr. "Flatterer!" *Esquire,* August 1936, 6.
Hindley, Howard. "Relax, You're In." *Esquire,* October 1936, 6.
Spaulding, W. L. "Redemption of Hem." *Esquire,* October 1936, 8.
Buckler, Ernest Redmond. "Promoting Mr. Ernest Redmond Buckler." *Esquire,* January 1939, 5, 10.
James, Polly. "Donne Exegesis." *Esquire,* February 1941, 8.
Clark, Don. "Chacun Sa Vérité." *Esquire,* April 1941, 8.
Condo, Susan. "Off-Day in a Normal Life." *Esquire,* April 1941, 8.
Savage, Richard. "Good Gripe Gone Wrong." *Esquire,* April 1941, 8.
Buckler, Ernest Redmond. "A Note on 'Life' and the Old Esquire." *Esquire,* December 1952, 10.
Brenesen, Lillian. "[Untitled letter regarding "The Snows of Kilimanjaro."] *Esquire,* July 1957, 16.

• • •

Hemingway was written about in *Esquire* after his death (1961) until editor-publisher Arnold Gingrich retired (1973):

**Publisher's Page**

Gingrich, Arnold. "E.H.: A Coda from the Maestro." *Esquire,* October 1961, 8.
——. "The Seventh *Esquire* Symposium This Month at Chapel Hill." April 1965, 6.

———. “On the Mixed Pleasures of Uncovering New Talent.” *Esquire,* February 1966, 6.
———. “Naming Day at *Esquire.*” *Esquire,* December 1966, 8, 321.
———. “The Truth as Private Property.” *Esquire,* March 1967, 6, 12.
———. “Censorship by Boredom.” *Esquire,* June 1967, 6.
———. “The Proclamation of a Small Masterpiece.” *Esquire,* June 1970, 6.
———. “Notes on *Bimini.*” *Esquire,* October 1970, 6, 12.
———. “Financing Fitzgerald: Two Saints in One Scene.” *Esquire,* June 1971, 6.
———. “The Sweet Common Sense of Thurman W. Arnold.” *Esquire,* February 1972, 6.
———. “That Slovenly Servant, Memory.” *Esquire,* September 1972, 6.
———. “Memory Can Be a Damnable Liar.” *Esquire,* October 1972, 6.
———. “Buckler vs. Lish, or What Is Fiction?” *Esquire,* February 1973, 6.
———. “Some Amplification of This Issue’s Headnotes.” *Esquire,* October 1973, 8–10, 40.

**Editor’s Notes**

Hayes, Harold. “The Matter of Page Size.” *Esquire,* March 1971, 6.
———. *Esquire,* July 1971, 8, 18.
———. *Esquire,* May 1972, 13, 32.
Plimpton, George. *Esquire,* May 1972, 13.

**Articles**

Ginna, Robert Emmett. “Life in the Afternoon.” *Esquire,* February 1962, 104–6, 136.
Turnbull, Andrew. “Scott Fitzgerald and Ernest Hemingway.” *Esquire,* March 1962, 110–13, 115–24.
Mailer, Norman. “The Big Bite.” *Esquire,* November 1962, 134.
Belfrage, Sally. “The Haunted House of Ernest Hemingway.” *Esquire,* February 1963, 66–67.
Talese, Gay. “Looking for Hemingway.” *Esquire,* July 1963, 44–45, 106, 108, 110.
Muggeridge, Malcolm. “Books.” *Esquire,* June 1966, 34, 36.
Newman, David, and Robert Bonton. “Remember the Sixties?” *Esquire,* August 1966, 114.
Gingrich, Arnold. “Scott, Ernest, and Whoever.” *Esquire,* December 1966, 186–89, 322–25.
Beatty, Jerome, Jr. “Hanging Up on Hemingway.” *Esquire,* February 1967, 116.
Cowley, Malcolm. “Papa and the Parricides.” *Esquire,* June 1967, 100–103, 160–62.

Fitzgerald, F. Scott. "My Generation." Reprint. *Esquire,* October 1968, 119–23.
Styron, William. "My Generation." *Esquire,* October 1968, 123–24.
Russell, Robert. "Gawd, These Jokes Were Painful." *Esquire,* December 1968, 164–69.
Bruccoli, Matthew J. "Ernest Hemingway as Cub Reporter." *Esquire,* December 1968, 207, 265.
Gingrich, Arnold. "Backstage with *Esquire.*" *Esquire,* October 1970, 30–32.
Hayes, Harold T. P. "Bimini." *Esquire,* October 1970, 121.
———. "The Fitzgerald-Perkins Papers." *Esquire,* June 1971, 107–11, 171–83.
Brian, Dennis. "The Importance of Knowing Ernest." *Esquire,* February 1972, 98–101, 164–70.
Arthur, Robert. "Hanging Out." *Esquire,* October 1973, 104–10.
Fitzgerald, F. Scott. "My Generation." Reprint. *Esquire,* October 1973, 132–34.
Styron, William. "My Generation." *Esquire,* October 1973, 132–34.
Gingrich, Arnold. "The Fitzgerald Hemingway Epoch." *Esquire,* October 1973, 139.
———. "Scott, Ernest, and Whoever." *Esquire,* October 1973, 151–54, 374–80.
———. "Great Stories." *Esquire,* October 1973, 291.

**"The Sound and the Fury"**

Lanahan, Scottie Fitzgerald. "Scott, Ernest, Arnold and Whoever." *Esquire,* March 1967, 159.
Schoettler, Jim. "Ex Pluribus, Quantum." *Esquire,* May 1967, 18.
Goldfaden, Bruce M. "Exit Cathedra." *Esquire,* May 1967, 176.
Bosley, John. "Dear Mr. Gingrich, Buddy." *Esquire,* September 1967, 10.
Rogers, William C. "Clarifications of Dottie." *Esquire,* October 1968, 64–66.
Fritz, Nat. "Papa in Kansas." *Esquire,* February 1969, 8, 12.
Foor, Mel. "Re: *Hemingway as Cub Reporter.*" *Esquire,* February 1969, 12.
Hemingway, Mary. "'Pistol-packin' Mama." *Esquire,* December 1970, 108.
Reese, Roy N. "Praise for Papa." *Esquire,* December 1970, 108.
Mink, Charles. "More Praise for Papa." *Esquire,* January 1971, 30.
Rutherford, M. "Pollution in the Stream." *Esquire,* January 1971, 30.
Limandri, Bob. "untitled: re 'Bimini.'" *Esquire,* January 1971, 30.
Lansford, William D. "Mucho Macho." *Esquire,* September 1973, 213.
Long, Barbara. "The Delicate and the Adequate." *Esquire,* December 1973, 14.
Forshaw, William S. "Unidentified Standing Object." *Esquire,* December 1973, 14.

### Hemingway Reprinted Pieces

Hemingway, Ernest. "On the Blue Water: A Gulf Stream Letter." *Esquire,* October 1973, 141–42, 380, 382.

———. "The Snows of Kilimanjaro: A Long Story." *Esquire,* October 1973, 143–47, 366, 370, 372.

### Miscellaneous

Hemingway, Ernest. "Bimini." *Esquire,* October 1970, 122–37, 190–202. (Excerpt from newly published *Islands in the Stream.*)

# OTHER WORKS CITED

Baker, Carlos. *Ernest Hemingway: A Life Story*. New York: Scribner, 1969.
——. *Ernest Hemingway: Selected Letters*. New York: Scribner, 1981.
——. "A Working Check-List of Hemingway's Prose, Poetry, and Journalism—with Notes." *Hemingway: The Writer as Artist*, 409–26. 4th ed. Princeton: Princeton University Press, 1972.
Baron, Herman. *Author Index to Esquire, 1933–1973*. Metuchen, NJ: Scarecrow Press, 1976.
Beatty, Jerome, Jr. "Hemingway vs. *Esquire*." *Saturday Review*, August 23, 1958, 9–11, 36. (See also *New York Times*, August 6, 1958, 1; August 7, 1958, 27; *Newsweek*, August 18, 1958, 27–28; *Publishers' Weekly*, August 18, 1958, 28–29. Hemingway sues to prohibit *Esquire* from reprinting his three Spanish Civil War stories from 1938 to 1939.)
Beegel, Susan F. "Conclusion: The Critical Reputation of Ernest Hemingway." In *The Cambridge Companion to Ernest Hemingway*, edited by Scott Donaldson, 269–99. Cambridge: Cambridge University Press, 1996.
Berg, A. Scott. *Max Perkins: Editor of Genius*. New York: New American Library, 2016.
Bina, Clarence Adolph. "The Literary Achievement of *Esquire Magazine* during the Great Depression." PhD diss., University of North Dakota, 1975.
Brian, Denis. *The True Gen: An Intimate Portrait of Ernest Hemingway by Those Who Knew Him*. New York: Grove Press, 1988.
Broun, Heywood. "It Seems to Me" column. *New York World-Telegram*, August 18, 1934, 34.
Bruccoli, Matthew J., ed. *Conversations with Ernest Hemingway*. Jackson: University Press of Mississippi, 1986.
——. *Fitzgerald and Hemingway: A Dangerous Friendship*. New York: Carroll and Graf, 1994.
Bruccoli, Matthew J., with Judith Baughman, eds. *Hemingway and*

*the Mechanism of Fame: Statements, Public Letters, Introductions, Forewords, Prefaces, Blurbs, Reviews, and Endorsements.* Columbia: University of South Carolina Press, 2006.

Bruccoli, Matthew J., with Robert W. Trogdon. *The Only Thing That Counts: The Ernest Hemingway / Maxwell Perkins Correspondence, 1925–1947.* New York: Scribner, 1996.

Burrill, William. *Hemingway: The Toronto Years.* Toronto: Doubleday Canada, 1994.

Cappel, Constance. *Hemingway in Michigan.* Petoskey, MI: Little Traverse Historical Society, 1999.

Chamberlin, Brewster. *The Hemingway Log: A Chronology of His Life and Times.* Lawrence: University Press of Kansas, 2015.

Cohen, Gordon L. "Esquire-Coronet's *Ken:* Magazine Everyone Hated." *Media History Digest* (Spring–Summer 1987).

Cohen, Milton A. *Hemingway's Laboratory: The Paris in our time.* Tuscaloosa: University of Alabama Press, 2005.

Cowley, Malcolm. "A Portrait of Mister Papa." *Life* 25, January 10, 1949, 86–101.

Curnutt, Kirk. *Reading Hemingway's "To Have and Have Not": Glossary and Commentary.* Kent, OH: Kent State University Press, 2016.

Curnutt, Kirk, and Gail D. Sinclair, eds. *Key West Hemingway: A Reassessment.* Gainesville: University Press of Florida, 2009.

Dearborn, Mary V. *Ernest Hemingway: A Biography.* New York: Knopf, 2017.

Dewberry, Elizabeth. "Hemingway's Journalism and the Realist Dilemma." In *The Cambridge Companion to Ernest Hemingway,* edited by Scott Donaldson, 16–35. Cambridge: Cambridge University Press, 1996.

———. "'Truer than Anything True': *In Our Time* and Journalism." *Hemingway Review* 11, no. 2 (Spring 1992): 11–18.

Donaldson, Scott. *By Force of Will: The Life and Art of Ernest Hemingway.* New York: Viking, 1977.

———. "Hemingway of the *Star.*" In *Ernest Hemingway: The Papers of a Writer,* edited by Bernard Oldsey, 89–107. New York: Garland, 1981.

———. *Hemingway vs. Fitzgerald: The Rise and Fall of a Literary Friendship.* Woodstock, NY: Overlook Press, 1999.

Donaldson, Scott, ed. *The Cambridge Companion to Ernest Hemingway.* Cambridge: Cambridge University Press, 1996.

Earle, David M. *All Man! Hemingway, 1950s Men's Magazines, and the Masculine Persona.* Kent, OH: Kent State University Press, 2009.

Eastman, Max. "Bull in the Afternoon." *New Republic* 75, June 7, 1933, 94–97.

———. "Red Blood and Hemingway." *New Republic* 75, June 28, 1933, 184. (Also in *New York Times,* August 14, 1937, 15; August 16, 1937, 21; and August 17, 1937, 18.)

Fenstermaker, John J. "Agnes and Ernest: A Decade before Catherine." *NDQ: North Dakota Quarterly* 70, no. 4 (Fall 2003): 19–39.

———. "'Ave Atque Vale': F. Scott Fitzgerald, Ernest Hemingway, Thomas Wolfe—and Charles Scribner's Sons." *Thomas Wolfe Review* 37 (2013): 131–41.

———. "Ernest Hemingway in *Esquire:* Contextualizing Arnold Gingrich's Posthumous Portrait(s) of Man and Artist, 1961–73." In *Literature and Journalism: Inspirations, Intersections, and Inventions from Ben Franklin to Stephen Colbert,* edited by Mark Canada, 187–207. New York: Palgrave Macmillan, 2013.

———. "Hemingway and the Gulf Stream: The *Esquire* Letters as Informal *Apologia.*" *Studies in American Culture* 20, no. 2 (October 1997): 41–57.

———. "Why *Esquire*? The Multiple Voices of Hemingway's Complex Public Persona." In *Key West Hemingway: A Reassessment.* Edited by Kirk Curnutt and Gail Sinclair, 206–19. Gainesville: University Press of Florida, 2009.

Fenstermaker, John J., with Michael S. Reynolds and Keneth Kinnamon. "Hemingway in the 1930s: A Conversation." *Arkansas Review* 30, no. 2 (1999): 143–62.

Fenton, Charles A. *The Apprenticeship of Ernest Hemingway.* New York: Farrar, Straus and Young, 1954.

Fitzgerald, F. Scott. "The Crack-Up." *Esquire,* February 1936, 41, 164.

Fleming, Robert E., ed. *Hemingway and the Natural World.* Moscow: University of Idaho Press, 1999.

Ford, Hugh. *Published in Paris: American and British Writers, Printers, and Publishers in Paris, 1920–1939.* New York: Macmillan, 1975.

Fowler, Henry. "Description of a New Scorpaenoid (*Neomerinthe* Hemingway) from Off New Jersey." *Proceedings of the Natural Academy of Philadelphia* 87 (1935): 41–43.

Franklin, Sidney. *Bullfighter from Brooklyn: An Autobiography of Sidney Franklin.* New York: Prentice-Hall, 1952.

Gellhorn, Martha. *Travels with Myself and Another.* New York: Dodd, Mead 1979.

Gingrich, Arnold. "Arnold Gingrich Writes to F. Scott Fitzgerald." *Fitzgerald/Hemingway Annual* (1979): 233.

———. "Carlos Baker, *Ernest Hemingway: A Life Story.*" Review. *Chicago Sun-Times Book Week,* April 20, 1969, 1, 10.

———. "Horsing Them in with Hemingway." *Playboy* 12, September 1965, 123, 256–58.

———.*Nothing But People: The Early Days at Esquire.* New York: Crown, 1971.

———. *The Well-Tempered Angler.* New York: Knopf, 1965.

——, ed. "Introduction." *The Bedside Esquire*, 5–8. New York: Grosset and Dunlap, 1940.
——. "Introduction." *The Esquire Treasury*, xi–xv. New York: Simon and Schuster, 1953.
——. "Preface." *The Armchair Esquire*, 17–21. New York: G. P. Putnam's Sons, 1958.
Griffin, Peter. *Along with Youth: Hemingway, The Early Years*. New York: Oxford University Press, 1985.
——. *Less Than a Treason: Hemingway in Paris*. New York: Oxford University Press, 1990.
Grimes, Carroll [Sister Richard Mary, OP]. "Addition to Hemingway Bibliography." *Papers of the Bibliographical Society of America* 59 (July–September 1965): 327. (Hemingway letter in *Outdoor Life*, June 1936.)
——. "Hemingway: 'Old Newsman Writes.'" *Fitzgerald/Hemingway Annual* (1972): 215–23.
——. "Hemingway: The Years with *Esquire*." PhD diss., Ohio State University, 1965.
——. "Hemingway's 'Defense of Dirty Words': A Reconsideration." *Fitzgerald/Hemingway Annual* (1975): 217–27.
Grissom, C. Edgar. *Ernest Hemingway: A Descriptive Bibliography*. New Castle, DE: Oak Knoll Press, 2011.
Hanneman, Audre. *Ernest Hemingway: A Comprehensive Bibliography*. Princeton: Princeton University Press, 1967; and Supplement, 1975.
Hawkins, Ruth A. *Unbelievable Happiness and Final Sorrow: The Hemingway-Pfeiffer Marriage*. Fayetteville: University of Arkansas Press, 2012.
Hayes, Harold. "Arnold Gingrich: *Esquire*." *New Republic*, September 4, 1976.
Hemingway, Ernest. Ernest Hemingway Collection. John F. Kennedy Presidential Library and Museum, Boston.
——. *The Letters of Ernest Hemingway, vol. 1: 1907–1922*. Edited by Sandra Spanier and Robert W. Trogdon. Cambridge: Cambridge University Press, 2011.
——. *The Letters of Ernest Hemingway, vol. 2: 1923–1925*. Edited by Rena Sanderson, Sandra Spanier, and Robert W. Trogdon. Cambridge: Cambridge University Press, 2013.
——. *The Letters of Ernest Hemingway, vol. 3: 1926–1929*. Edited by Sandra Spanier, Albert DeFazio III, and Robert W. Trogdon. Cambridge: Cambridge University Press, 2015.
——. *The Letters of Ernest Hemingway, vol. 4: 1929–1931*. Edited by Sandra Spanier and Miriam Mandel. Cambridge: Cambridge University Press, 2018.
——. *The Letters of Ernest Hemingway, vol. 5: 1932–1934*. Edited by San-

dra Spanier and Miriam Mandel. Cambridge: Cambridge University Press, 2020.
Hemingway, Mary Welsh. *How It Was*. New York: Knopf, 1976.
Hemmingson, Michael. "*Esquire*'s Failure with Hemingway's 'Bimini.'" *Hemingway Review* 29, no. 1 (Fall 2009): 140–44.
Hendrickson, Paul. *Hemingway's Boat: Everything He Loved in Life, and Lost, 1934–1961*. New York: Knopf, 2011.
Hoffman, Frederick J. *The 20s: American Writing in the Postwar Decade*. Rev. ed. New York: Free Press, 1965.
Hutchisson, James M. *Ernest Hemingway: A New Life*. University Park: Pennsylvania State University Press, 2016.
Joost, Nicholas. *Ernest Hemingway and the Little Magazines: The Paris Years*. Barre, MA: Barre Publishers, 1968.
juliawick. "Ernest Hemingway's WWII Spy Network." *Longreads*, February 27, 2015. https://longreads.com/2015/02/27/ernest-hemingways-private-wwii-era-spy-network.
Justice, Hilary K. *The Bones of the Others*. Kent, OH: Kent State University Press, 2006.
Kale, Verna, ed. *Teaching Hemingway and Gender*. Kent, OH: Kent State University Press, 2016.
Kaul, A. J. "Arnold Gingrich." In *American Magazine Journalists, 1900–1960: Dictionary of Literary Biography*, edited by Sam G. Riley, 137:104–11. 2nd series. Detroit: Gale, 1994.
Kert, Bernice. *The Hemingway Women*. New York: Norton, 1983.
Knott, Toni D., ed. *One Man Alone: Hemingway and* To Have and Have Not. Lanham, MD: University Press of America, 1999.
Koven, Joseph. "The Liberal Literary Legion." *Monthly Review* 1 (June 1934): 44–45.
Kuehl, John, and Jackson Bryer, eds. *Dear Scott / Dear Max: The Fitzgerald-Perkins Correspondence*. London: Cassell, 1971.
Lewis, Wyndham. "The Dumb Ox: A Study of Ernest Hemingway." *Life & Letters*, April 10, 1934, 33–45.
Lynn, Kenneth S. *Hemingway*. Cambridge: Harvard University Press, 1987.
Madden, David, ed. *Proletarian Writers of the Thirties*. Carbondale: University of Southern Illinois Press, 1968.
Maier, Kevin. "'A Trick Men Learn in Paris': Hemingway, *Esquire*, and Mass Tourism." *Hemingway Review* 31, no. 2 (Spring 2012): 65–83.
Main, Georgianna. *Pip-Pip to Hemingway in Something from Marge*. Bloomington, IN: iUniverse, 2010.
Mandel, Miriam B. *A Companion to Hemingway's "Death in the Afternoon."* Rochester, NY: Camden House, 2004.
——, ed. *Reading Hemingway: The Facts in the Fictions*. Metuchen, NJ: Scarecrow Press, 1995.

Mason, Alane Salierno. "To Love and Love Not." *Vanity Fair*, July 1999, 108–18, 146–52.
Maziarka, Cynthia, and Donald Vogel Jr., eds. *Hemingway at Oak Park High: The High School Writings of Ernest Hemingway, 1916–1917*. Oak Park, IL: Oak Park and River Forest High School, 1993.
Mazzeno, Laurence W. *The Critics and Hemingway, 1924–2014: Shaping an American Literary Icon*. Rochester, NY: Camden House, 2015.
McIver, Stuart B. *Hemingway's Key West*. Sarasota, FL: Pineapple Press, 1993.
McLendon, James. *Papa: Hemingway in Key West*. Key West, FL: Langley Press, 1972.
Mellow, James. *Hemingway: A Life without Consequences*. Boston: Houghton Mifflin, 1992.
Merrill, Hugh. *ESKY: The Early Years at Esquire*. New Brunswick, NJ: Rutgers University Press, 1995.
Meyers, Jeffrey. *Hemingway: The Critical Heritage*. London: Routledge & Kegan Paul, 1982.
Moore, Jack B. *Joe DiMaggio: Baseball's Yankee Clipper*. New York: Praeger, 1987.
Moorhead, Caroline. *Gellhorn: A Twentieth-Century Life*. New York: Henry Holt, 2003.
Nagel, James, ed. *Ernest Hemingway: The Oak Park Legacy*. Tuscaloosa: University of Alabama Press, 1996.
——, ed. *Ernest Hemingway: The Writer in Context*. Madison: University of Wisconsin Press, 1984.
North, Michael. "Ernest Hemingway's Media Relations." In *Camera Works: Photography and the Twentieth-Century Word*, edited by Michael North, 186–207. Oxford: Oxford University Press, 2005.
Oliver, Charles M. *Ernest Hemingway A to Z: The Essential Reference to the Life and Work*. New York: Checkmark Books, Facts on File, 1999.
Paul, Steve. "'Drive,' He Said": How Ted Brumback Helped Steer Ernest Hemingway into War and Writing." *Hemingway Review* 27, no. 1 (Fall 2007): 21–38.
Plimpton, George. "The Art of Fiction, XXI: Ernest Hemingway." *Paris Review* 5 (Spring 1958): 60–89.
Pottle, Russ. "Travel." In *Ernest Hemingway in Context*, edited by Debra Moddlemog and Suzanne Del Gizzo, 367–77. Cambridge: Cambridge University Press, 2013.
Pringle, Henry F. "Sex, Esq." *Scribner's Magazine*, March 1938, 33.
Raeburn, John. *Fame Became of Him: Hemingway as Public Writer*. Bloomington: Indiana University Press, 1984.
Reynolds, Michael. *Hemingway: The American Homecoming*. Cambridge, MA: Blackwell, 1992.
——. *Hemingway: The Final Years*. New York: Norton, 1999.

———. *Hemingway: The 1930s.* New York: Norton, 1997.
———. *Hemingway: The Paris Years.* New York: Norton, 1989.
———. "Portrait of the Artist as a Very Young Man." In *Hemingway at Oak Park High: The High School Writings of Ernest Hemingway, 1916–1917,* edited by Cynthia Maziarka and Donald Vogel Jr. 13–17. Oak Park, IL: Oak Park and River Forest High School, 1993.
———. *The Young Hemingway.* Oxford, UK: Blackwell, 1986.
Reynolds, Nicholas. *Writer, Sailor, Soldier, Spy: Ernest Hemingway's Secret Adventures, 1935–1961.* New York: William Morrow, 2017.
Rosenblatt, Roger. "Hemingway at 100." *PBS NewsHour,* July 21, 1999.
Rosengren, John. "The Last Days of Hemingway at Mayo Clinic." *St. Paul Magazine* (March 2019).
Ross, Lillian. "How Do You Like It Now, Gentlemen?" *New Yorker,* May 13, 1950, 36–62.
Salierno, Jane Mason. "An Introduction to Jane Mason's *Safari.*" *Hemingway Review* 21, no. 2 (Spring 2002): 13–21.
Samuelson, Arnold. *With Hemingway: A Year in Key West and Cuba.* New York: Random House, 1984. (See also *Esquire,* October 1935, October 1961, and May 1981.)
Sanford, Marcelline Hemingway. *At the Hemingways: With Fifty Years of Correspondence between Ernest and Marcelline Hemingway.* Moscow: University of Idaho Press, 1998.
Sarason, Bertram D., comp. *Hemingway and The Sun Set.* Washington, DC: National Cash Register Co., 1972.
Schleden, Ina Mae, and Marion Rawls Herzog, eds. *Ernest Hemingway as Recalled by His High School Contemporaries.* Oak Park, IL: Historical Society of Oak Park and River Forest, 1973.
"*Scribner's* to the Smoking Room." *Time,* September 4, 1939, 34.
Seldes, Gilbert. "The Prize-fighter and the Bull: Evaluating Hemingway and Lardner in Light of the Former's Now-Famous Phrase." *Esquire* II, November 1934, 52, 173–74. (Response to Hemingway's essay on Ring Lardner in "Defense of Dirty Words," *Esquire* II, September 1934, 19, 158B, and 158D.)
Shiflet, E. Stone, and Kirk Curnutt. "Letters and Literary Tourism: Hemingway as Your Key West Correspondent in 'The Sights of Whitehead Street.'" In *Key West Hemingway: A Reassessment,* edited by Kirk Curnutt and Gail Sinclair, 220–40. Gainesville: University Press of Florida, 2009.
Smith, Paul. *A Reader's Guide to the Short Stories of Ernest Hemingway.* Boston: G. K. Hall, 1989.
Stein, Gertrude. *The Autobiography of Alice B. Toklas.* New York: Harcourt, Brace, 1933.
Stephens, Robert O., ed. *Ernest Hemingway: The Critical Reception.* New York: B. Franklin, 1977.

———. *Hemingway's Nonfiction: The Public Voice.* Chapel Hill: University of North Carolina Press, 1968.

Stoneback, H. R. "'Nothing Was Ever Lost': Another Look at 'That Marge Business.'" In *Hemingway: Up in Michigan Perspectives,* edited by Frederic J. Svoboda and Joseph J. Waldmeir, 59–76. East Lansing: Michigan State University Press, 1995.

"Success without Editorial Policy." *Literary Digest,* February 6, 1937, 20.

Susman, Warren I. *Culture as History: The Transformation of American Society in the Twentieth Century.* New York: Pantheon, 1984.

Svoboda, Frederic J., and Joseph J. Waldmeir, eds. *Hemingway: Up in Michigan Perspectives.* East Lansing: Michigan State University Press, 1995.

Trogdon, Robert W., ed. *Ernest Hemingway: A Documentary Volume. Dictionary of Literary Biography.* Vol. 210. Detroit: Gale, 1999.

———. *The Lousy Racket: Hemingway, Scribners, and the Business of Literature.* Kent, OH: Kent State University Press, 2007.

Unrue, John. *On Books and Writers: Selected Essays of Matthew J. Bruccoli.* Columbia: University of South Carolina Press, 2010.

Vaill, Amanda. *Hotel Florida: Truth, Love, and Death in the Spanish Civil War.* New York: Farrar, Straus and Giroux, 2014.

Vargas, Alberto. *Varga, the Esquire Years.* New York: Alfred Van Der Marck Editions, 1987.

Villard, Henry S., and James Nagel. *Hemingway in Love and War: The Lost Diary of Agnes Von Kurowsky.* New York: Hyperion, 1989.

White, William, ed. *By-Line: Ernest Hemingway. Selected Articles and Dispatches of Four Decades.* New York: Scribner, 1967.

———. *Ernest Hemingway, Dateline Toronto: The Complete Toronto Star Dispatches, 1920–1924.* New York: Scribner, 1985.

Wilson, Edmund. "Ernest Hemingway: Bourdon Gauge of Morale." *Atlantic,* July 1939, 36–46.

"Within the Editorial Ken." *Ken,* August 25, 1938, 4.

# INDEX